PENGUIN BOOKS

THE CURSE OF THE BAMBINO

Dan Shaughnessy is a sports columnist for *The Boston Globe*. He is the author of *One Strike Away*, the story of the 1986 Red Sox; *Ever Green: The Story of the Boston Celtics*; *Seeing Red: The Red Auerbach Story*; *At Fenway*; and *Fenway: A Biography in Words and Pictures*. He lives in Newton, Massachusetts, with his wife, Marilou, and children, Sarah, Kate, and Sam.

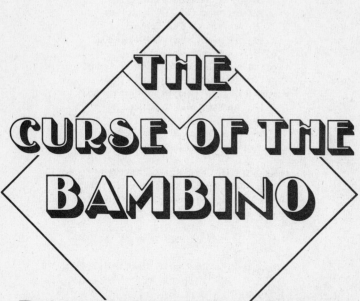

THE CURSE OF THE BAMBINO

DAN SHAUGHNESSY

PENGUIN BOOKS

PENGUIN BOOKS

Published by the Penguin Group

Penguin Putnam Inc., 375 Hudson Street,
New York, New York 10014, U.S.A.
Penguin Books Ltd, 27 Wrights Lane,
London W8 5TZ, England
Penguin Books Australia Ltd, Ringwood,
Victoria, Australia
Penguin Books Canada Ltd, 10 Alcorn Avenue,
Toronto, Ontario, Canada M4V 3B2
Penguin Books (N.Z.) Ltd, 182–190 Wairau Road,
Auckland 10, New Zealand

Penguin Books Ltd, Registered Offices:
Harmondsworth, Middlesex, England

First published in the United States of America by Dutton,
an imprint of Penguin Books USA Inc., 1990
Published with a new epilogue in Penguin Books 1991 (fifteen printings)
This edition with a new afterword published in Penguin Books 2000

1   3   5   7   9   10   8   6   4   2

THE LIBRARY OF CONGRESS HAS CATALOGED THE HARDCOVER EDITION AS FOLLOWS:
Shaughnessy, Dan.
The curse of the bambino/Dan Shaughnessy.—1st ed.
p.   cm.
Included bibliographical references.
ISBN 0-525-24887-0 (hc.)
ISBN 0 14 02.9633 6 (pbk.)
1. Boston Red Sox (Baseball team)—History. I. Title.
GV875.B62S52   1990
796.357'64'0974461—dc20   89–78450

Printed in the United States of America
Set in Times Roman

To Marilou, for loving the bambinos and me

Mike: *"Archie, you can't use a double negative."*
Archie: *"Tell that to the guy who wrote* No, No, Nanette.*"*
—From "All in the Family"

ACKNOWLEDGMENTS

This book involved a lifetime (thirty-six years so far) of research; that's the way it is when you grow up watching the Red Sox. A lifetime of thank yous is difficult to list and tedious to read, but there are many people who've been directly involved with the words between these covers.

Thanks to Peter Gammons for helping me every step of the way in this business and to Bill Tanton, Dave Smith, Vince Doria, and Don Skwar, those who've dared hire me in Baltimore, Washington, and Boston. Thanks to everyone in the Baltimore Orioles organization for showing me how a baseball club should be run. Ken Nigro was the model reporter for a young journalist, and Peter Pascarelli, Peter May, and Steve Fainaru have been trusty traveling companions through the years. I owe a great deal to the good fathers of Holy Cross and to Dave O'Hara and the late Jerry Nason for getting me into the business. Best friends Kevin Dupont and Lesley Visser walk with me always. Tim Kurkjian in Baltimore, John Lowe in Detroit, Laurel Prieb in Minneapolis, and Phyllis Merhige in New York are always a phone call away.

Colleagues Bob Ryan, Leigh Montville, Mike Madden, Jackie MacMullan, Will McDonough, Larry Whiteside, John Powers, Jack Craig, Mike Barnicle, Marty Nolan, Tom Mulvoy, Bud Collins, Bill Griffith, Larry Johnson, and Ian Thomsen made life easier, and a special thanks to Charlie Liftman and Sean Mullin in systems. The great Ray Fitzgerald is always missed. Nick Cafardo, Steve Krasner, Charlie Scoggins, Mike Shalin, Dave Cataneo, Charlie Pierce, Joe Giuliotti, Win Bates, Jon Miller, Sean McAdam, Steve Buckley, Bill Ballou,

Art Davidson, and Phil O'Neill make a great corps of reporters, and we get plenty of help from those combative and ever-capable Red Sox publicists, Dick Bresciani, Josh Spofford, and Jim Samia. Thanks also to Lou Gorman, John Donovan, Mary Jane Ryan, Frank MacKay, Arthur Morris, and Jim Gately at the ballpark.

Clark Booth remains the best of role models, and there's been help and support from Ed Kleven, George Sullivan, Ken Picking, Jon Yardley, Bob Duffy, Tom Callahan, Dick Johnson, Eddie Andelman, Stan Grossfeld, Steve Sheppard, and David Halberstam. Deanna McGovern introduced me to the microfilm machines in the *Globe* library. Batboy-turned-reporter Jack Burke emptied his notebook. Max Frazee could not have been more helpful. Friends John Iannacci and John Horn are loyal Sox fans and good sounding boards.

There would be no book without the ideas and patience of Meg Blackstone. The book was also supported by late commissioner A. Bartlett Giamatti, perhaps the greatest Red Sox fan of them all. The 1989 Red Sox players deserve special thanks for perpetuating the storyline so nicely. Dick McGrath at E. P. Dutton was also instrumental in making the book a reality.

Thanks to my new editor, Al Silverman, who did a great job after inheriting the project.

Thanks to my mother, who encouraged a son's immersion in sports, and to my late father, who explained baseball to me and repaired the broken windows of youth. The author gets unending support from Bill and Joy in Arizona, Mary and Don in New Hampshire, Joan and Paul in Colorado, and Ann and Peter in Massachusetts. I have the best in-laws on the planet, and there's always a place to work and sleep at the Wits' homes in Michigan, Indiana, and Kentucky.

Sarah, Kate, and Sam are beginning to understand why Dad loves his work. Everybody thinks I'm lucky because I get to write about sports, but I know that I'm lucky because I'm married to Marilou.

Dan Shaughnessy
October 1989
Newton, Massachusetts

On Monday January 5, 1920, the Harvard University football team, still celebrating its New Year's Day, 7–6, Rose Bowl victory over Oregon, rolled eastward into Chicago on the California Limited. In Washington, in a five to four decision rendered by Justice L. D. Brandeis, the Supreme Court upheld the right of Congress to define intoxicating liquors, sustaining the constitutionality of provisions in the Volstead Act. Elsewhere, the last of the U.S. troops in France made their way home across the Atlantic, and a New York state supreme court justice ruled that it was not immoral for women to smoke cigarettes.

There was one more bit of news on this day. Late in the afternoon, Red Sox owner Harry Frazee held a press conference and announced that slugger/pitcher Babe Ruth had been sold for cash only to the New York Yankees.

"The price was something enormous, but I do not care to name the figures," said Frazee. "It was an amount the club could not afford to refuse. I should have preferred to have taken players in exchange for Ruth, but no club could have given me the equivalent in men without wrecking itself, and so the deal had to be made on a cash basis. No other club could afford to give the amount the Yankees have paid for him, and I do not mind saying I think they are taking a gamble."

Prohibition was eleven days away when Frazee made this move, which would drive Sox fans to drink. Ruth had been instrumental in bringing three World Championships to Boston, in 1919 had hit an unthinkable twenty-nine homers (tops in major league history), and yet Frazee traded him for cash. Frazee pocketed $100,000 plus a $300,000 loan for a mortgage on Fenway Park. The Sox owner compounded the calamity by saying that the Yankees were taking a gamble and that he planned to use the cash to replenish his team.

"With this money the Boston club can now go into the market and buy other players and have a stronger and better team in all respects than we would have had if Ruth had remained with us," said Frazee. "I do not wish to detract one iota from Ruth's ability as a ball player nor from his value as an attraction, but there is no getting away from the fact that despite his twenty-nine home runs, the Red Sox finished sixth in the race last year. What the Boston fans want, I take it, and what I want because they want it is a winning team, rather than a one-man team that finishes in sixth place." Frazee went on to explain:

It would have been impossible for us to have started next season with Ruth, and have had a smooth-working machine, or one that would have had any chance of being in the running. We have had other stars on the Boston team besides Ruth and have them now. McInnis, Scott, Shang, and Vitt are all great players and hard, conscientious workers, but last season they were totally eclipsed by Ruth, which made the Red Sox a one-man team that finished near the bottom of the second division. Now the investment of the stockholders cannot be protected by a one-man team, which is not in the race. You will notice that the one-man team is almost invariably in the second division, Washington with Johnson, St. Louis with Sisler, Detroit in recent years with Cobb, may be mentioned. The other players have little incentive or encouragement for great effort when the spectators can see only one man in the game and so the one man has an upsetting influence on the others. It rarely does and never should win a championship. With the money received in exchange for Ruth, the Boston club can afford to pay $10,000 or $20,000, even more for another player than I think he is really worth, and be ahead, both financially and in playing strength. Then again, Ruth has shown neither the Boston club, nor myself—nor the Boston fans for that matter—much consideration. He has been rather selfish. A year ago, he dictated the terms of his contract, which was for three years at $10,000 a year. It was quite a risk for the club to assume. Last season, Ruth became the idol of the fans and appears to have lost his head. He has been telling everybody, it appears, except myself, what he contemplated

doing if his salary for next year was not increased to $20,000. All
that I have had directly from him was his three-year contract, which
he enclosed in an envelope without a word of explanation and
mailed to me November 2.

The rambling diatribe continued.

Ruth has been insubordinate on occasions and has insisted upon
having his own way to such an extent that he endangered the
discipline of the whole squad. Hardworking men like McInnis,
Scott, Shang, and Vitt, and all the others do not like to see one
of their own clubmates doing as he pleases while they feel that
they are bound to obey the rules and regulations laid down by the
management. We lost the last game of the season in Washington,
which would have landed us in fifth place in the standing, because
Ruth wanted to and did return north to appear in an exhibition
game in Connecticut. If he had remained with us we probably
would have won. After the season was over his business manager
began dictating terms for next season through the press when he
was already under contract for the next two years.

Those Yankees were taking on quite a gamble, yes they were.

Led by Babe Ruth, the greatest player in the history of baseball, the
Yankees won their first American League pennant in 1921 and their
first World Championship in 1923. Ruth became the foundation for the
greatest dynasty in the history of professional sports. The Pinstripers
won six pennants and three World Series in the twenties. Since Frazee's
shrewd transaction, the Yankees have won thirty-three pennants and
twenty-two World Championships, while the Red Sox have won four
pennants and zero championships.

How and why did this happen?

◇

This is a story about excessive, irrational passion for a baseball team
that has come close to but hasn't won a World Series since our grandfathers and great-grandfathers were on the threshold of victory in World
War I. It is a story about baseball's original sin—the selling of Babe

Ruth—and the subsequent seventy years of sorrow for New England's baseball fans.

Red Sox fans *care.* That's what makes the Boston baseball saga irresistible and eternal. Other professional ball clubs fail to win championships, although none has teased like Boston's Olde Towne Team. There's nothing special about the annual flops of the Seattle Mariners and the San Diego Padres, because there is no baseball tradition in those towns and because nobody really cares. It's different with Boston and the Red Sox.

The Red Sox home opener at Fenway Park is a pardonable excuse in some Massachusetts towns to leave school early. Cars stop at the entrance to the Callahan, Sumner, and South Station tunnels if the Radio Free Sox are rallying in the ninth. Commercial pilots flying between Boston and Nova Scotia notice more lights lit in houses during the midnight hours when the Sox are playing on the West Coast. Loaves of Big Yaz Bread sit in freezers, souvenirs from the summer of 1967.

The Boston ball club has inspired a glut of books, song lyrics, and poems, including the never-published "A Week on the Concord and Merrimack Rivers with Ned Martin," submitted to the *Boston Globe* by a weepy fan after the 1975 World Series loss. In Rome in 1978 the late Archbishop Humberto Medeiros took time during a recess of the College of Cardinals to ask Boston television journalist Clark Booth how the Red Sox were doing back home. After Pope John Paul I died in 1978, WBCN's Charles Laquidara teased the upcoming newscast with "Pope Dies, Sox Still Alive." Oil Can Boyd made the front page of the *Boston Herald* eight times in thirteen days during a midsummer walkout/suspension in 1986. When the Red Sox played a Fenway day game in the 1986 American League Championship Series, a plane flew over the park, trailing a banner that read, "Stop Nuclear Tests Before First Strike. Go Sox." After Game 6 of the 1986 World Series, a South Shore man trekked into the wet Back Bay, walked down empty Lansdowne Street, and touched the outside of Fenway's left-field Wall for good luck. When the Red Sox lost their opening game in 1988, the back page of the *Herald* screamed, "Wait 'Til Next Year."

"Everything hinges on the Red Sox," said Joe Morgan, a Walpole, Massachusetts, native who in 1988 became the first local Red Sox manager since Shano Collins in 1932.

In New England, the Red Sox are a way of life, no less cyclical and predictable than the four seasons, which define the routines of every person in Massachusetts, New Hampshire, Vermont, Maine, Rhode Island, and Connecticut. Elsewhere in the Americas, baseball is perceived as a summer game, but in Red Sox Country, baseball, like politics, is a year-round sport. There is never a true "off-season," and interwoven threads connect the Sox' annual campaign with the dramatically different climates of spring, summer, winter, and fall.

A baseball year starts in the spring, and Red Sox spring is like New England's: short, cold, wet, and hopeful. Since 1920, the Red Sox have held spring training in Hot Springs, Tampa, San Antonio, New Orleans, Bradenton, Pensacola, Savannah, Sarasota, Medford, Baltimore, Pleasantville, Scottsdale, and Winter Haven. The precise setting is incidental to the baseball-starved masses in the frozen north. While the east wind is cutting a chill to the bone, a photograph in the local paper reveals that the Red Sox equipment truck is heading south—and it is spring. There might be an oil delivery truck outside your house and you might have a space heater working to unfreeze a basement pipe, but at that moment, the Sox truck tells you that winter is over. Look for your shadow. Six weeks till Opening Day.

No spring baseball story is too trivial when the local ball team goes to "work" in the Sunshine State. Red Sox fans want to know it all. Which player from south of the equator will have visa problems? Which unknown will emerge as the official camp phenom? Which pitcher will come to camp too heavy? Who will be the first to say that "the games down here don't mean anything"? Who'll hold out for more money? Who'll say "play me or trade me"? Which Boston writer will be the first to predict that the flag will fly over Fenway this fall? It's nonstop anticipation, and every forty-five-name box score means you are another day closer to Opening Day.

The Sox come north, and players lose their tans during the first frosty batting practice. Northeastern spring baseball weather is rotten, and the Red Sox usually play to the level of the conditions. They don't hit many home runs, and it's too cold to throw, catch, or run. Each April on Patriot's Day, the Sox and some lucky opponent play the only morning game in the major leagues. Outside the ballpark, a few blocks toward the Charles River, hundreds of spare-time athletes do something the Red Sox rarely do: they sprint to the finish line. This is the time of year that the Red Sox share the sports pages with the Boston Marathon and the annually playoff-bound Bruins and Celtics. In the sixties, seventies, and eighties, a string of Celtic championships served to deflect attention from some of the Sox' abysmal starts.

"We always liked to lie in the weeds until the Celtics got through with their playoffs," noted former Sox ace lefty Bruce Hurst.

The Red Sox and New England summers are usually hot. If there is any wind, it is blowing toward the Wall, and the ball flies out of Fenway toward the eastbound lane of the Massachusetts Turnpike. Life is easier. The college kids are out of town and there's a slight reprieve from the traditional traffic and parking horrors. People tote transistor radios to the beach, the company cookout, and across the Arthur Fiedler footbridge to the Esplanade. Voices of Joe Castiglione and Ken Coleman crackle from screened-in porches where respectful neighbors keep an ear to the radio while bugs are zapped by neon deathtraps. July is kind. The Red Sox usually lead the majors in hitting and send four or five guys to the All-Star game. This is when the Sox are hot, and suburban home owners let the grass grow long so it won't burn. The gonfalon is ours. "Pennant Fever Grips Hub." Elsewhere in the American League, rivals are singing "See You in September."

The Red Sox truly are the boys of summer; it's always been the fall that's given them trouble.

Autumn is Boston baseball's season of the witch. Such irony. Crisp, color-splashed New England in September/October is the best place on the planet, but Red Sox fans dread the ninth and tenth months because they've learned that the local ball team never peaks when the foliage does. Autumn means harvest in the apple orchards, but it's been seventy years since the last bumper crop for Red Sox fans. When it's time to get out the storm windows, rake leaves, and smell the horse chestnuts, Red Sox players are usually back at their Florida and California homes, waiting for the mailman to bring a check for third-place money. New Englanders know winter is coming and expect the worst. They don't call this season *fall* for nothing. Reggie Jackson did tours of duty in Oakland, Baltimore, New York, and Anaheim, but Mr. October never gave any thought to playing in Boston. The Red Sox haven't had a Mr. October since Babe Ruth patrolled the Fenway grounds in 1918.

Southpaw/philosopher Bill Lee said, "What does 'em in is they have never evolved into a modern ball club of speed and defense. Their whole attitude here is predicated on offense, and that only works in the middle part of the season. I always say they're horse shit in the beginning of the season and they're horse shit at the end of the season, when the winds change. They're a fucking monster ball club in the middle."

New England's baseball winter is long and cold. It starts at the end of October when the furnace kicks on, and local legions dissect what went wrong—as they watch some *other* team win a World Series. November, December, and January are set aside for discussions of what the Sox will do in the upcoming season.

Red Sox crises, past, present, and future, fuel hot stoves from Providence to Bangor. When it gets a little nippy outside you can just toss a Don Zimmer log on the fire and talk about why the Gerbil let Butch Hobson stay at third when the Sox collapsed in 1978. If the new cordwood is too damp, blow the dust off a Joe McCarthy log and debate the decision to start journeyman Denny Galehouse in the first playoff game in American League history in 1948. In many ways, the winter is the best time for Red Sox baseball. The cold months are full of hope and hype, and "Wait 'til next year" too often is better than next year.

◊

Who are these faceless fans? Why are they so devout and why are there so many of them?

Eddie Andelman has been a sports talk show host in Boston for more than twenty years. His grandfather Jacob Andelman took Eddie's father, Maxwell Andelman, to his first major league game in 1918, and they watched Babe Ruth beat the Athletics. Eddie Andelman understands the soul of the Red Sox fan. "I am not blowing smoke, but they are without question the most knowledgeable people and they really care about the Red Sox," he said. "It's an integral part of their life. The whole attitude of the spring, summer, and fall is a reflection of how the Red Sox are doing. When the Red Sox are in it and things are going well, the movie business falls off, restaurants fall off, vacations fall off, European travel falls off. People really get into the Red Sox because it's a parochial thing. We're New Englanders, and the rest of the country is screwballs. Nobody test-markets a new product here because New Englanders are very strange and don't represent the rest of the country."

Baseball best suits the pace and thoughtfulness of America's six-state northeastern corner. New England was the first area of America that was truly "finished," so it follows that the oldest game should have the most appeal in this region. In Texas it's established that the only two sports are football and spring football. Meanwhile, college towns in the south and the far west are immersed in the self-important frenzy of NCAA basketball or football, and folks in California simply gravitate toward whichever team is currently winning. Wayne Gretzky makes the Los Angeles Kings hot even though none of the fans has ever worn double-runners.

There is little that is trendy about the Red Sox fandom. Of course, there are front-runners in every town, and the white-wine-and-red-glasses crowd will attach itself to anything that represents upward mobility, but there remain legions of loud and loyal followers who're emotionally tied to the Olde Towne Team no matter how bleak the prospects.

"I truly loved the New England fans," Ted Williams told Bob Costas in 1988. "I thought they were the greatest. It took me quite a long, long time to realize that."

◇

Baseball has no clock and needs little equipment and was the perfect day-long exercise for young boys in small towns with nothing but time and energy to burn. Organized Little League has taken away much of this, but when our fathers and grandfathers were growing up, youngsters didn't join anything; they just played. The organized ball was left to the hundreds of town teams that provided early evening entertainment for agricultural communities and mill towns.

Edward McNulty was born in Billerica, Massachusetts, in 1915, five years before Babe Ruth was sold to the Yankees. The Red Sox won the World Series three times in the first four years of McNulty's life, but he, of course, was too young to remember. Soon, baseball became his passion. He gave up smoking at the age of twelve when his Uncle Charlie refused to take him to Fenway because he'd caught him smoking. By day, McNulty worked in the local mills and the Boston and Maine railroad car shops. By night, he was a pitcher, a lean, right-handed knuckleballer. Baseball was *the* form of recreation and socialization.

"Those were the good old days as far as baseball was concerned," McNulty said in the winter of 1988/1989.

As kids, we just played. We'd play all morning, then have lunch, then go back and play all afternoon. It was second nature. You played ball and you followed the home team and never gave up. I was never good enough to play in the Middlesex County League. This was in the early thirties and they would get crowds of three or four thousand people in North Billerica. Everybody had jobs during the day, so the games were played evenings and on Saturdays and Sundays. Most of the players weren't paid, but if a guy was really good they'd give him thirty-five or forty dollars under the table. There was a lot of betting going on in those days, you know. A lot of the guys worked in the mills, and this was where you had your fun. When the town team was playing, that was it. Everybody went. You had to get down there a half hour ahead of time to get a place on the bank. They weren't supposed to charge anything on a Sunday so you donated some money and they'd give you a stick of gum. They had some great baseball. You would make no plans to go anywhere when the town team was playing in Billerica. They had barnstorming teams come up. Sometimes you'd have two or three players who'd played double-A ball. When the game was out of Billerica, there'd be practically nobody in town. People didn't have the dough to be going down to see the Red Sox. These were seven-inning games, and in the last inning you were playing in half dark. Outfielders would store an extra baseball by the outfield fence in case it got dark and they had to find a ball out there.

Older Americans love baseball more than any group (crowds today at spring sites in Florida retirement communities are as polite and appreciative as you'll find), and New England's old-timers have passed the torch of Sox passion to sons and daughters, grandsons and granddaughters. Adolescents resist parents' preferences regarding everything from sweaters to sweethearts, but the Red Sox can be a singular point of agreement in a household split by a generation gap. Bloodlines have much to do with all of this. A man whose father and grandfather were

Catholic and Democrat may reject the church and the party, but with few exceptions, one's baseball persuasion is genetic. You can't change the color of your Sox any more than you can change the color of your eyes. If your father and grandfather were Red Sox fans, you are a Red Sox fan. When grandparents and parents pass away, loyalty to their team seems a trivial-yet-true way to carry their spirit.

Media coverage of the Red Sox is enormous and would certainly border on excessive were it not for the thousands of thirsty fans who want more. New York, Chicago, Detroit, and Philadelphia are the only towns close to Boston in terms of saturation baseball coverage, but no major league team is followed by more writers than the Red Sox of Boston. In addition to the usual television and radio flagship stations, plus the representatives of major metropolitan daily newspapers, the Red Sox media entourage includes dozens of reporters from suburban dailies and weeklies from the six-state region. Many representatives of these publications travel with the team to Winter Haven and on the road during the season. Obviously, marketing research shows that it pays to cover the Red Sox. You can let the Metro section slip a little and use wire services for national and international news, but you can't leave the Red Sox alone for a minute. Baseball is right up there with the comics, the crossword puzzles, and the obituaries among the most-read items in a newspaper. You never know when a pitcher named Gene Conley is going to take a hike for Israel (this happened in 1962), or when Roger Clemens is going to storm out of camp over a contract dispute (1987). The glut of microphone-waving, notebook-wielding reporters creates intense competition among members of the press, which results in inevitable friction between the team and the press. There are simply too many reporters with too many questions, and it's a point of unending distraction and annoyance for the Red Sox ball players. It is, however, great for the Boston fans, who are more knowledgeable than those anywhere in the land. Peter Gammons, renowned as the best baseball writer in the country when he covered baseball for the *Globe* in the seventies and early eighties, was described by *The New Yorker*'s Roger Angell as, "as important to New England baseball as a Yastrzemski or a Fisk."

In 1986 this typist, in the midst of a 3,000-word Sunday baseball notes column for the *Boston Globe,* incorrectly identified Duane Josephson as the man Sox right-fielder Jose Tartabull threw out at home plate in a game-ending play during the stretch drive of the 1967 pennant race. In fact, it was Josephson who hit the ball and Chicago's Ken Berry who was thrown out at home by Tartabull. No less than a dozen letters poured into the *Globe* to correct this grievous error concerning one play from one of 162 regular season games nineteen years earlier.

The unwashed masses who move here from other regions have two choices: convert to the cult of Red Sox watchers or endure a lifetime of exclusion from conversations at drugstore counters and checkout lines throughout New England.

Bill Franklin is a stockbroker at Merrill Lynch in downtown Boston. Born and raised in New Jersey, he was a devout Yankee fan for twenty-two years, including four spent at Holy Cross College in Worcester, Massachusetts. In his second year in Boston, he switched his allegiance to the Red Sox.

> All my life I've been a very strong baseball fan, I just love the game. I remember going to bed at night with earphones stuck in my ears listening to Yankee games from the coast. Those were the days of Mickey Mantle. I moved here and made a commitment to living here, and remember going to a Red Sox game and being divided on the issue. That was in 1976. It was like a dividing point. I was real stubborn. Basically it was a matter of being here versus being there. I got very familiar with the team and players and adopted Boston as my home. I have a lot of friends who didn't do it. For me it was psychological. If I stuck with the Yanks, I would always be harboring thoughts of returning to New York. I guess I felt kind of out of it, not being a Red Sox fan. In a work environment the day after a game, people over coffee are talking about a game. You can't go around talking about the Yankees around here, nobody is interested in it, or you might start a fight. Remember, this was before cable was prevalent. . . . The only difference between being a Yankee fan and a Red Sox fan is the curse. The Red Sox have that tradition of folding and Yankees have that tradition of pennants. But there's a little more drama in the Red Sox. Part of being American is rooting for the underdog, and the Red Sox are the true underdogs of all time.

◊

Boston's timeless home park contributes to the mystique of the local nine. Fenway Park, the Sox home field, is a civic jewel. Built in 1912, refurbished in 1934, the evergreen Boston ballyard is a charming, priceless antique, steeped in history and beloved by the millions who pour through its portals from April to October, year after hopeful year. A Harvard professor once compared it with the bullring of Knossos on the island of Crete. Fenway is *only* a ballpark the way the Sistine Chapel is only a church. And it was left-handed philosopher Lee (Red Sox 1969–1978) who observed, "Fenway Park is a shrine where people come for religious rites."

The Fenway lawn has been used for football (Boston Patriots, Boston Yanks, Boston Redskins, Boston College, and Boston University) and after World War I was the site of a military Mass in memory of the war dead, but it is inappropriate for anything other than baseball. The Beatles played Shea Stadium and Candlestick Park, but they never played Fenway. An electric guitar has never sent good vibrations off the left-field Wall. John Fitzgerald Kennedy was welcome to speak at the Boston Garden and the State House, but in Fenway he was confined to the lower box seats.

The walls and menus at Durgin Park, Boston's Quincy Market dining institution, claim, "Your grandfather and perhaps your great-grandfather dined with us, too." This is the feeling one gets when one walks into Fenway Park for the first time. It is very old with odd, classic, asymmetrical lines, like a rambling Victorian house. You can almost hear the small children playing and smell the pies baking—even when it's empty. Antiques frame and retain the past, and our selective memories remind us that the past was very good. An old ballpark is very good.

Former House Speaker Tip O'Neill, who attended his first game at Fenway in 1920, later characterized the park this way: "There's nothing like it. It's intimate, it's homey, it's chummy. You feel as though you're in your own living room. The Red Sox become part of your life, part of your family."

Most American youths first play baseball in a backyard or playground that has odd shapes and asymmetrical boundaries. You have to be

careful not to smash the windows of the neighbor's garage, an edifice
that serves nicely as a left-field foul pole. A crooked driveway can be
a perfect baseline, and the sidewalk is a natural warning track. Your
mother's clothesline low-bridges more than a few unsuspecting outfielders. The curious characteristics of Fenway Park remind us of the
backyard/backlot ballparks of our youth.

There are eight different wall angles in Fenway's fair territory. The
left-field Wall is almost as fabled as the great walls in China or Jeru-
salem. There's a ladder on the left-field Wall and a garage door on the
foul-territory wall in the left-field corner. Dads tell their sons of the time
Ted Williams or Don Buford or Luis Polonia got caught in the nook,
watching a baseball rattle like a pinball around the door frame. Foul
territory is scarce, and fans sitting near the on-deck circle are close
enough to inhale resin dust and pine tar fumes. The bullpens in right
were originally dubbed Williamsburg because they were built (in 1940)
to make a more inviting target for Teddy Ballgame. Cleveland's Al
Luplow leaped into the pen to take a home run away from Dick Williams
in the hard-times sixties. The fence in left reads 315 feet, but everybody
knows it's a lie. A man who flew reconnaissance in World War II
reviewed aerial photos of the yard in 1975 and determined that it's 304
to the Wall in left. Mr. and Mrs. Yawkey's initials are etched in Morse
code on the left-field Wall, and a giant big-screen, multicolor scoreboard
looms over the bleachers in center. Driving eastbound on the Massachusetts Turnpike, a fan no longer needs a car radio to know who's
batting; you can see the man's image on the new, monstrous, multicolor
screen. There are luxury boxes and a few rows of seats on the roof
down the lines, but capacity is limited to the mid-30,000s. When Cardinal ace Bob Gibson first walked into Fenway, in 1967, he expressed
the surprise felt by many when he asked, "Where's the upper deck?"

The Boston ballpark is different, and New Englanders like this. It's
hip to be slightly out of step with mainstream America.

Boston was a city of 500,000 when the Boston Americans played at
the Huntington Avenue Grounds, a onetime carnival site. In 1911
owner John I. Taylor ordered a new park be built between Lansdowne
and Jersey streets in the heart of the Fens, a centerpiece park in Frederick Law Olmsted's Emerald Necklace. Taylor said, "It's in the Fenway section, isn't it? Then call it Fenway Park." The ballpark was

dedicated April 16, 1912, two days after the *Titanic* struck an iceberg in the North Atlantic. A superstitious sort might have interpreted this juxtaposition of events as a bad omen.

After a pair of rain outs, Fenway Park opened on April 20. Mayor John "Honey Fitz" Fitzgerald (grandfather of John Fitzgerald Kennedy) threw out the ceremonial first ball, and Tris Speaker drove in the winning run as the Red Sox beat the New York Highlanders, 7–6, in the first Fenway game. There was a ten-foot embankment in left field that became known as Duffy's Cliff, named after left-fielder Duffy Lewis, who was particularly skilled at playing the hill. Backed by Smokey Joe Wood's 34–5 pitching, the Red Sox won a World Series in that first season.

Ironically, Fenway later played a crucial role in the single most destructive transaction in the history of the franchise. When financially strapped owner Harry Frazee sold Babe Ruth to the Yankees for $100,000, he also got a $300,000 loan from Yankee owner Jake Ruppert—in the form of a mortgage on Fenway Park. The hated Yankees in the early twenties thus held the title to the Red Sox's greatest star *and* the beloved Boston ballpark.

In 1978, the ballpark again played a role in perhaps the most tragic on-field event in franchise history: with the Red Sox leading the Yankees, 2–0, in the second playoff game in American League history, Bucky Dent hit a cheap, pop-fly homer that would have been an out in every other major league park. The Red Sox lost the game, 5–4. Sox legend Carl Yastrzemski, who got the last look at Dent's ball as it plopped into the net, later said, "We talk about loving Fenway Park so much; that's probably the one time I hated Fenway Park."

The Fenway bleachers burned down in 1926, but attendance was sparse and nobody bothered to fix the charred section for seven years. Thomas A. Yawkey bought the Sox and the ballpark in 1933 and had Fenway renovated. Duffy's Cliff was leveled and the left-field Wall was built. The Wall is there because they couldn't push the fence back. They couldn't push the fence back because behind left field in Fenway is Lansdowne Street, and behind Lansdowne were tracks for the Boston & Albany Railroad. Later, the Mass. Pike was built alongside the tracks.

In the early years, Fenway had billboard advertising on its huge Wall, where there was often a Lifebuoy soap sign. The ad claimed that the

Red Sox ballplayers used Lifebuoy soap. A popular joke of the times was, "the Red Sox use Lifebuoy, but they still stink." The ballpark got its first lights in 1947. The first electronic scoreboard was erected in 1976.

Fenway Park is a nice fit for the contest-living of twentieth-century Boston. From breakfast coffee to postdinner nightcap, Bostonians compete for parking spaces, clients, lunch tables, exact-change lanes, and good sightlines at Fenway. Locals are trained to believe that nothing good comes easily. You have to be a competitor to attend a ball game at Fenway. When relief pitcher Joe Sambito joined the Sox, in 1986, he talked of his first drive to the park and the frustration of seeing the light towers, yet not being able to find a street that led to the park. It was like the tale of "Charlie on the MTA"—above ground.

You've got to *really want* to see a game in Fenway Park. Sox fans are faced with pregame and postgame gridlock, $10 parking fees (for the privilege of having your car blocked in), long bathroom lines, longer lines and high prices for hot dogs and beer, small hard seats, and occasional obstructed views. Good seats are hard to get without help from season-ticket holders, ticket brokerage houses, scalpers, or players' wives. Too often, it rains. All this hassle means that the experience must be worthwhile.

The inconvenience does little to deter the Sox fandom. They file through the rusty turnstiles in record numbers for the privilege of seeing the hometown team in its historic ballpark. Red Sox fans are like people who pay $25 for a two-mile ride in Central Park in a horse-drawn carriage: they don't mind the chill of the open air, the smell of the horse dung, or the exorbitant fee for a ride to nowhere; they're blinded by charm and thoughts of yesteryear. Fenway offers the same accoutrements.

The sophistication of Sox fans is something else. Fenway is the only ballpark on the planet where you can keep score without actually watching the game. If you've been to enough Fenway productions, you can form a composite of what is happening on the field just by listening to the reactions of the Fenway crowd. Standing over a porcelain trough in the men's room, a veteran fan's ears can tell when there's been a walk, a strikeout, a foul back to the screen, a double off the Wall, and a shot into the bullpen.

Certainly the Sox wouldn't claim to have the only unique ballpark or the only loyal following in all of professional sports. Wrigley Field in Chicago is no less a civic shrine than Fenway in Boston, and Yankee Stadium has been the home office for more great players and historic sports moments than any outdoor arena in North America. Obviously, most regions embrace their big-league teams, and everybody loves a winner. Rational people in the Twin Cities stood in line for hours to purchase silly Homer Hankies when the underdog Minnesota Twins were winning their first World Series. A ticket to the Inaugural Ball is easier to get than a fifty-yardline seat to a Redskins game, and the faceless Portland Trailblazers haven't played in front of an empty seat since 1977.

◇

The Red Sox are different because of history. They have a longer history than almost any professional sports team, and it is a bizarre lineage, stocked with great stars but cluttered with tarnished silver medals and chronic underachievement. The Red Sox won the World Series five times between 1903 (the first year it was played) and 1918. George Herman Ruth played on two of those championship teams, but he was sold to the New York Yankees after the 1919 season, and the Red Sox are still waiting for their next championship. Since Ruth was shipped to Gotham, New York City (including the Dodgers, Giants and Mets as well as the Yankees) has boasted twenty-nine World Series winners, Boston none.

It would be pitiful, but perhaps more tolerable, if the Red Sox were merely a bad team, bereft of talent. This was, in fact, the case after owner Frazee sold Ruth and a host of other stars to the Yankees in the early twenties. But since Tom Yawkey took over the team in 1933, the Red Sox have almost always been competitive, and they have perfected the Big Tease/Near-Miss seasons that have become as much a part of Boston as the Old North Church and the Union Oyster House. This is why Red Sox fans are different from Cubs fans. Both teams date back to the beginning of baseball time, both play in wonderful old ballparks, and both have legions of sophisticated followers starving for a World Championship. The difference is that the Cubs are usually bad while the Red Sox are usually good enough to tease their fans into thinking that this is the year. It's easy to sit in the Wrigley bleachers and drink beer and laugh at the Cubbies. It's tough to watch the Red

Sox bring you to the point of satisfaction, then let you down. It's like *almost* sneezing.

The Red Sox have been in four World Series since 1918, and lost all four in the seventh game. The 1986 Red Sox came closer to winning, without actually winning, than any team in the history of the Fall Classic. Only twice in American League history has there been a one-game playoff, and the Red Sox lost both of them (in 1948 and 1978). In 1949 Boston finished the season with two games in New York and needed only one victory to win the American League pennant; Boston lost both games. From 1972 to 1988 the Sox nine times led the American League East after the All-Star break, yet won the division in only three of those seasons.

A. Bartlett Giamatti, a native New Englander who became commissioner of baseball in 1989, made this observation during the pennant race of 1986: "There's an almost Calvinistic sense of guilt at success, that we must reenact the Garden of Eden again and again. There's a sense that things will turn out poorly no matter how hard we work. Somehow the Sox fulfill the notion that we live in a fallen world. It's as though we assume they're here to provide us with more pain."

The Red Sox certainly fall in line with New England's Puritan ethic. John Calvin was a sixteenth-century French Protestant theologian who emphasized the sovereignty of God and preached the doctrine of predestination and limited atonement. Without doubt, this has been the Red Sox modus operandi since 1920. Calvin wrote that "some are chosen to be among the elect and some are not." Can it be totally accidental that a man named *Calvin* Schiraldi was on the mound when the Red Sox were within one pitch of clinching their first World Series victory in sixty-eight years? When *Calvin* Schiraldi lost the sixth and seventh games of the 1986 World Series for the Red Sox, some of those who'd scoffed at the presence of larger forces began to wonder.

It is the same every summer. Boston baseball fans are like survivors of the great stock crash of 1929: they keep their dollars in mattresses, under sofa seats, and inside book flaps. You can't trust a bank. There is no true security. The fandom is usually more comfortable if the Sox are trailing the pack because there is nothing to be lost. The responsibility of leading the league is unsettling for New England fans. Put the Red Sox in first place and oft-burned legions wait for the fall.

Andelman, the talk show czar, explained it this way: "The one common bond that native-born New Englanders have to carry them through the end of the World Series until the opening of spring training is, 'What's the matter with the Red Sox?' We all play it, and if you couldn't spend your winter worrying about what they did wrong and how they blew it and the fact that they had no balls and were stupid, you wouldn't be as emotional about the Red Sox as you are now. It's like trying to catch the beautiful blonde, and when you get her, what do you do with her? It's not the winning of it, it's the anticipation of winning it. I think once the Red Sox win it, nobody will be that much interested in them anymore, maybe for a season or so, but interest would fall off."

Preposterous as this sounds, it may be true. Examine the long, inglorious history of the Philadelphia Phillies. The Phils have been around for 107 years and have been largely unsuccessful most of the time. They were formed in 1883 and appeared doomed never to win a World Championship, yet they play in a wonderful baseball town with hungry, sophisticated fans. From 1883 to 1980, the Phillies frustrated their loyal/critical legions. In 1964 the Phils had a juggernaut, but the team blew a six-and-a-half-game lead with twelve to play, and manager Gene Mauch stewed while the St. Louis Cardinals upset the Yankees in the World Series. The Phillies had playoff games in the late seventies, but they couldn't win the Big Ones and the players were reminded of 97 years of failure. In 1980, the Phillies finally won the World Series, beating the Kansas City Royals in six unspectacular games. The celebration wasn't what many predicted it would be. In an effort to subdue their fans, the Phillies' front office had attack dogs and police horses on the field when the final out was made. And so the Phillies finally won and the reaction seemed to be, "Is that all there is?" The Phils made it back to the World Series in 1983 and lost to the Orioles in five games, but the thrill was gone. The love/hate relationship between the Phillies and their fans just hasn't been there since the team threw the monkey off its back by winning the World Series. The Phils aren't special anymore. They are just another ball team.

The Red Sox are still special.

In *What Are You Worth?* Dr. Edward Hallowell of Cambridge wrote, "The real reason the Red Sox will never win the World Series is that the Red Sox fans do not want them to. . . . The fans so fill the team with their own gloom that the team can never win. And the fans' worldview remains intact."

Andelman's tombstone has already been chiseled to read, HE NEVER LIVED LONG ENOUGH TO SEE THE RED SOX WIN IT ALL.

"It does exist," he says. "It has been bought and prepaid for in a family plot in Sharon Memorial Park. It's bronzed."

On February 2, 1989, House representative Silvio Conte (R, Mass.) read this into the *Congressional Record:* ". . . those of us in New England have experienced something perhaps more profound than victory, something that has toyed with our emotions, teasing us into a frustrated state of hope and tension that has only become bearable through years of numbing and the company of generations of fellow Red Sox fans. Yes, it is 'near victory' that truly tries men's souls. Red Sox fans have felt the ecstasy of victory in their grasps so many times, have had their fists clenched, waiting for that final out in heady anticipation, only to be put through the agony of another lost victory. It is a ritual that has been repeated many more times than a kinder and gentler God would ever allow. . . ."

After the 1986 World Series, John McKeon of Amesbury, Massachusetts, went to work creating the Baseball Hall of Pain. A high school teacher in his mid-thirties, McKeon said, "I came up with an idea, born of restless nights. My wife seemed relieved I stopped talking about the Red Sox and started doing something about them." With help from friends, McKeon printed one thousand sixteen-page booklets (detailing lowlights from sixty-eight years of anguish), packaged them with hats and pins, and sold them outside Fenway on Opening Day, 1987. McKeon said, "We'll never win, we'll never be free of this warped, evil cycle. This is the Curse of the Bambino. Once a fan accepts this fate and understands the cycle, he can make peace with himself and accept any loss, any disappointment, because *he. knows* it is coming. The joy of being a Red Sox fan now becomes the thrill of marveling, not at the great plays and dramatic moments, but at the creative ways the Red Sox bring about disappointment."

Most Red Sox players have never understood the doomsday customers who patronize this team. An athletic young man who grows up in Tampa, Florida, or El Segundo, California, can't possibly understand the peculiar thought processes of those who've followed the Red Sox since 1918. The only pro sports team in Wade Boggs's childhood was the Tampa Bay Buccaneers. Roger Clemens is from Katy, Texas, a half hour from the Astrodome. These young men can't possibly comprehend the mind-set of the long-suffering Fenway legions. When the Red Sox were one strike away from winning the 1986 World Series in Shea Stadium, Sox wives stood and cheered wildly in anticipation of the final out. Why not? These were young women from Texas and California who'd watched championships won at every other level. The only wife who remained seated was Sherry Gedman, wife of Sox catcher Rich Gedman. Mrs. Gedman grew up in central Massachusetts and knew the celebration was premature.

Todd Benzinger, an infielder/outfielder on the 1988 Red Sox division champs, observed, "It's something to be watching TV and hear fans interviewed saying, 'This is great and everything, but I'm just waiting for them to blow it.' It's like they're waiting for something to happen so they can say, 'I told you so.' Well, we're a different team. When all that stuff happened, I wasn't born or I was playing for my elementary school. We have nothing to do with that. It's not like we're a big family and all related and have got the genes from all the other teams. If we don't do the job, then blame us. But don't say, 'Here we go again. How are we *not* gonna do it this time?' "

Rene Lachemann was a Red Sox coach when the Sox came within one strike of winning the World Series in 1986. Three years later he talked about the depressing dynamic that engulfs the town and its team:

There's a continuous flow of the negative talk. You come to the park and instead of looking at the games that Clemens pitched or how we came back in another ballgame, everything seems to be brought out of why we lost or if somebody off the field is having problems. The focus is not on the good things. Everything is focused and seems to be pushed toward things that are failures or things that are negative. Guys that are constantly put in that for years and years and years, it's got to be wearing on 'em mentally.

I didn't realize how big the skeletons were until that [not winning in 1986] happened. The skeletons here go back to grandmothers and grandfathers and everything else. It's mentally draining. The fact that it's put in the backs of their minds. The questions are asked and the thing is on television and they read it in the paper.

It's constantly brought up so they become aware of it. It puts some wear and tear on you. For some of those guys to go through what they've been through for the years they have, it had to be mentally draining.

The tragic theme of Boston's Olde Towne Team has always appealed to men of letters. When the Red Sox made it to the 1986 playoffs, *Boston Globe* sports editor Vince Doria had no trouble rounding up a fine lineup of literary giants who were only too happy to wax poetic on the Red Sox. John Updike, author of the timeless "Hub Fans Bid Kid Adieu," batted cleanup for a murderers' row that included Stephen King, Ward Just, Geoffrey Wolff, Robert Parker, Doris Kearns Goodwin, George Will, and David Halberstam. Roger Angell concluded, "One begins to see at last that the true function of the Red Sox may not be to win but to provide New England authors with a theme, now that guilt and whaling have gone out of style."

Seeing the Red Sox win a World Championship is an obsession of millions of Sox fans. Peter Gammons remembers, "The last time my brother, Ned, and I spoke to our father before he died in 1981, he said to us, 'The Red Sox will win in your lifetime.' "

In this spirit, more than a few infants were jostled awake and snatched from cribs in the midnight hour when the Sox were one strike away in 1986. Sox fans actually held these children in front of television sets as if they were to be absolved of original sin. The babies instead were baptized into the fold of the long-suffering and cried themselves back to sleep, along with their parents, after the hideous, unthinkable Game 6 defeat.

When the Red Sox were swept from the playoffs in 1988, seventy-three-year-old Edward McNulty of Billerica said, "I thought this was the year. But that's the trouble. I've thought it for a lot of times. I figured if I didn't see it this year, I never will because I'm not gonna live to be a hundred."

Ernest Lawrence Thayer wrote the most famous piece in all of baseball literature, "Casey at the Bat." Thayer was a Worcester, Massachusetts, native and a Harvard man. There were more than 2,000 New England baseball teams when he wrote his famous poem in 1888, but Thayer must have been a time traveler. He was writing about the Red

Sox' future. In a 1936 publication, *The Best Loved Poems of the American People,* Thayer's classic poem starts with, "It looked extremely rocky for the Boston nine that day," and ends with, "But there is no joy in Boston: Mighty Casey has struck out."

Boston *is* Mudville, and there has been no joy in Mudville since a Red Sox owner sold the greatest player who ever lived to the hated New York Yankees.

Lee, a southpaw who won five more games for the Red Sox than a left-handed pitcher named Ruth, said, "My theory is that it happened because of a curse by an orphan child from Baltimore. I remember the day I first said that. I gave a speech and said, 'Until they exhume the body of Babe Ruth and publicly apologize for selling him to New York, where he became an alcoholic, the city of Boston will never win a major baseball championship.' "

TWO

From 1901 through 1918, the Red Sox were the dominant team in baseball, winners of five World Series. Known as the Boston Pilgrims in their early years, they beat the Pittsburgh Pirates in the first World Series, in 1903. Pitcher Bill Dineen fanned Honus Wagner for the final out of the Series, and Boston of the upstart American League was on top of the baseball world. A year later, Boston won its second American League flag, but the National League champion New York Giants refused to play a World Series. *The Sporting News* declared the Pilgrims "World Champions by default."

In 1907, owner John I. Taylor changed the team's name to the Red Sox. The Red Sox christened Fenway Park in 1912 and enjoyed what was probably their finest season. Led by the 34–5 pitching of Smokey Joe Wood, and the sensational outfield trio of Duffy Lewis, Tris Speaker, and Harry Hooper, the Sox went 105–47, winning the American League by fourteen games. On Friday, September 6, Wood extended his personal winning streak to fourteen games with a 1–0 victory, beating Washington's Walter Johnson in front of 30,000 fans. The Red Sox took the World Series from John McGraw's New York Giants, with Wood beating Christy Mathewson in the finale at Fenway. The only stain on the season came when the ubiquitous, rowdy, and loud (these men could sing "Tessie" until the cows came home) Royal Roosters had their regular seats sold to other customers and were removed by police when they attempted to protest the unseating. As a consequence of this altercation, only 17,034 showed up for the final game of the World Series.

◊

The Sox slumped to fourth in 1913, but in 1914 got a look at a beefy, nineteen-year-old left-handed rookie pitcher named George Herman Ruth. In early June of 1914, the Sox bought Ruth from the International League Baltimore Orioles for $2,900. He was still on probation from the St. Mary's Industrial School in Baltimore. Sox owner Joe Lannin gave the kid a contract for $2,500. The Babe took a room at Mrs. Lindbergh's rooming house on Batavia Street (now Symphony Road).

Ruth recalled, "When I went to the Red Sox I got the same kind of rough treatment I had experienced in the training camp with the Orioles. Someone must have told them I was a fresh kid who didn't have much respect for big baseball reputations, and I guess some of the old guys let me have it. I suppose I did talk back, but not because I was fresh. I just wanted to show them I was as good as any of the other pitchers Bill Carrigan had. But the thing the older Boston players most resented about me was that I insisted on taking batting practice. One day I came to the park and found that all my bats had been neatly sawed in two."

After Ruth left the Red Sox, Boston's failure to win another World Series is generally explained by the Sox' annual lack of pitching depth. Is it possible the baseball gods are punishing the Sox for employing the best hitter of all time as a pitcher?

Ruth pitched and won the first major league game he ever saw, beating Cleveland, 4–3, on July 11, 1914. The first batter he faced was Jack Graney, and Graney singled. Ruth left the game when Duffy Lewis pinch-hit for him in the seventh, and the subheadline in the *Globe* account read, "Southpaw Displays High Class in Game Against Cleveland." Ruth pitched in five games in 1914, went 2–1, and got two hits in ten at-bats. He also met Helen Woodford, a shy, sixteen-year-old waitress, in a Copley Square coffee shop the first day he arrived in Boston. Helen's family had moved to South Boston from Manchester, New Hampshire. The Babe was quite taken with this young girl and hated to leave her when the Sox sent him to Providence to finish the season. He hit .300 for Providence, came back to Boston after the season and proposed to Helen in the coffee shop. They took the train to Baltimore and were married in St. Paul's Church in Ellicott City on October 13, 1914.

Lannin paid Ruth $3,500 for 1915 and the Babe later recalled, "That made me feel like a plutocrat."

In 1915 Ruth went 18–6 with a 2.44 ERA and hit .315 with four homers in forty-five games. Manager Bill Carrigan opted not to use Ruth in the 1915 World Series, which was won by Boston in five games against the Phillies. But Ruth was established as a Boston star. He returned to Baltimore for the 1915/1916 off-season but was starting to think of Boston as his hometown, and later wrote, "I began looking around for a home near Boston, for it had become my hometown and I fully expected to spend the next twenty years there, pitching for the Red Sox."

In 1916 Ruth went 23–12 with a league-leading 1.75 ERA, beat Walter Johnson five times, pitched nine shutouts, and allowed only 6.4 hits per nine innings. The Red Sox won the pennant again, and this time Ruth got to pitch in the World Series, shutting out Brooklyn in the final thirteen innings of an epic, 2–1, fourteen-inning clash that has often been called the best World Series game ever played. Ruth's post-game blurtation to Carrigan was, "I told you a year ago I could take care of those National League bums and you never gave me a chance." The Babe's World Series check weighed in at $4,000, and he bought an eighty-acre farm at 558 Dutton Road in Sudbury, twenty miles west of Boston, paying approximately $12,000. The twelve-room farmhouse, located a mile and a half from the Sudbury train station, was built in 1737 and stocked with what Ruth figured was "junky old furniture." The Babe hired somebody to haul away the valuable antiques.

Frazee bought the team before the start of the 1917 season. He was sixth in a line of early owners, following Charles W. Somers, Henry J. Killilea, John I. Taylor, James R. McAleer, and Joseph J. Lannin. Since Frazee, the only owners have been John A. Quinn and the Yawkey family.

◊

Harry H. Frazee was born in Peoria, Illinois, June 29, 1880, the son of William Byron and Margaret A. Frazee. He went to public schools in Peoria and first worked as a bellhop, then as an usher and box office man at the Peoria Theatre. At the age of sixteen he went on the road as an advance man for a production titled *Uncle Josh Perkins*. He worked briefly as general manager of Peoria's club in the Western

League, but the theater was his first love, and from 1904 through 1907 he launched several successful musical comedies. He was heavyset with dark hair and a thirst for the saloon life. His friends called him Frazz. While traveling with his productions in the West, Frazee met and befriended John Cort, who controlled most of the theatrical enterprises west of the Missouri River. Cort gave Frazee plenty of help in those early years, and when Frazee financed and built a theater in Chicago in 1907, he named it the Cort Theatre. In 1913, Frazee completed his second theater project, the Longacre Theatre in New York City. He also controlled the Arlington Theatre in Boston. He married Elsie Clisbee and they had a son, Harry H., Jr. Frazee was a well-known Broadway figure, producer of such frivolous stuff as *The Kissing Girl, Ready Money, A Pair of Sixes, Nothing but the Truth, Leave It to Jane,* and *Madame Sherry.* He promoted the Jess Willard–Jack Johnson heavyweight championship fight in Havana in 1915. Willard beat Johnson in twenty-six rounds as Frazee lost thousands. He took boxer James J. Jeffries on a fourteen-week tour of California and netted $60,000. He made attempts to buy the Boston Braves and the New York Giants before finding an eager seller in Lannin.

Songwriter Irving Caesar said this of Frazee: "He made more sense drunk than most people do sober."

At 6:00 P.M. on Wednesday, November 1, 1916, in the law offices of Fowler, Bauer & Kenney on 60 Congress Street in downtown Boston, Harry H. Frazee, Philadelphia's Hugh Ward, and G. M. Anderson bought the Boston Red Sox from Joseph Lannin for $675,000. The new group paid less than half cash, and Frazee made up the rest in notes to Lannin.

Lannin said, "I am pleased to find the new owners good sportsmen, great lovers of the game, and I am sure the Boston public will be pleased to receive them in the same manner they received me. I think I have turned over to the new owners the best team in the world, and it is now up to them to keep the champions at the top."

And so there they sat—Lannin, Frazee, Ward, attorney Thomas J. Henry, and several newspapermen. It was a moderate 55 degrees on the dark Boston streets as the great-grandfathers of today's Red Sox fans made their way home. None of them could have known that inside the walls of the building on 60 Congress Street, well-heeled gentlemen sat around a mahogany table, smoking cigars and toasting a transaction that would prove to be the first snag in the unraveling of the Boston Red Sox. They listened to Frazee tell stories from his days in Peoria. Frazee claimed his minor league team developed the famous Iron Joe McGinnity. He said his own hope was that someday he would own a championship baseball team. "I have always enjoyed the game and now I think that I shall have a chance to show what I know about handling a baseball club," he said. "I think that by giving the public a first-class article, I am bound to hold their support. And this goes double for Boston, by all odds the greatest ball town on earth."

He said he would file papers to become a citizen of Massachusetts, as long as he had a permit to celebrate New Year's Eve in New York. And then he left town on the midnight train for New York, a gesture of infinite symbolism for millions of Sox fans not yet born.

The *Boston Globe* gave Frazee this endorsement: "Harry Frazee, at least, combines experience in the game and a genuine love for it. Like Joe Lannin, he is a fan 'from way back,' and that is reassuring to the fans of Boston and New England."

Frazee was doing pretty well at the time; he had a smash hit called *Nothing but the Truth* playing at the Longacre. Willie Collier was the star of the play and was originally listed as one of Frazee's partners in the Red Sox ownership transfer.

Frazee spent money in his first years in Boston. He made it known that he bid $60,000 to get Walter Johnson from the Senators (although skeptics later charged this was a self-promotion scam by Frazee). He raised Ruth's salary from $3,500 to $5,000. The Babe had an apartment at 20 St. Stephen Street, near Symphony Hall. Ruth won twenty-three again and hit .325 with two homers in 1917, but the Sox finished second, nine games out. Frazee kept spending. He paid Connie Mack for Stuffy McInnis, Amos Strunk, Wallie Schang, and Joe Bush. He hired combative Edward Grant Barrow as manager.

The relationship between the owner and the star player started out as a good one. Ruth was Frazee's kind of guy and vice versa. Ruth was somewhat of a loose cannon, but the Broadway showman didn't mind. When Ruth ran his car into a trolley one night, it didn't bother Frazee to learn that the woman passenger injured in Ruth's car was not Helen Ruth. Ruth sold tickets, and Harry Frazee was in the business of putting fannies in seats. On the advice of outfielder Harry Hooper, Barrow made a decision to play Ruth every day. He called the Big Fella into his hotel room early in the 1918 season and said, "Babe, everybody knows you're a big fellow, healthy and strong. Why can't you take your turn in the box and still play the outfield on days when you're not pitching?" Ruth agreed. His salary was up to $7,000 and was guaranteed to go to $10,000 in 1919 if he had a good year. Playing every day would increase his chances of getting the ten grand in 1919.

Ruth won thirteen games in 1918 while hitting .300 with eleven homers (tops in the league) and 64 RBI in ninety-five games. He also got into a shouting match with Barrow and walked out on the team in July. He was fined $500 by the manager and in a fit of frustration and foolishness, signed to play with the Chester (Pennsylvania) Shipyards in the Delaware River Shipbuilding League. He was back with the Red Sox two days later, but Barrow and Frazee were not pleased with the stunt.

The Red Sox made it to the World Series again and beat the Cubs in six games. Ruth pitched a shutout in the opener and set a World Series record by extending his scoreless-inning string to a record twenty-nine innings. On September 11, 1918, Boston's Carl Mays beat Chicago, 2–1, before a crowd of 15,238 fans to clinch Boston's fifth (and last?) World Series championship.

Burt Whitman of the *Boston Herald* wrote, "People who think Harry is a boob can have their little fun, but he'll be there with bells on when a lot of them will be eating hay."

By this time, Ruth was among those who thought Frazee was a boob and later wrote, "After helping the Red Sox win another pennant and the World Series in the last war year I wanted more money from Frazee. I put my price at $10,000 and felt I had it coming. But Frazee yelled as if I were trying to rob the cash drawer at the old Frazee Theatre in New York. For $10,000 he said he'd expect at least John Barrymore. I asked him what good Barrymore's profile would be with the bases filled in a tight ball game."

What Ruth wanted from Frazee was $30,000 spread over two years, a salary which would have put him in a league with Ty Cobb. Frazee said "no," as in *No, No, Nanette*. Red Sox attendance had plummeted 35 percent in 1918, and World Series gate receipts were unusually low. There was a war on. Frazee's theater revenues were also sagging. Frazee sent Duffy Lewis, Ernie Shore, and Dutch Leonard to the Yankees for four bit players and a $50,000 check from Colonel

Jacob Ruppert and Colonel Tillinghast L'Hommedieu Huston. It was a harbinger.

Ruth changed his demands and asked for either $15,000 in 1919 or $30,000 spread over three years. His World Series share had been just over $1,000 and he felt underpaid. The Babe told Frazee he could retire to his Sudbury farm with his cattle, pigs, and hens. Ruth had invested in the cigar business (Connecticut tobacco factory cigars for five cents each) and was offered $5,000 to go into the ring against boxer Gunboat Smith. In the spring of 1919 the Red Sox went south without Ruth, but on Friday, March 21, Ruth took the train to New York (Frazee's office was at 44 West 45th Street) and shook hands with Frazee on a contract that would pay him $30,000 for three years.

The Red Sox trained in Tampa in 1919, and Ruth hit a homer at the Tampa racetrack diamond that was estimated to have traveled well over 500 feet. Meanwhile, the loss of Lewis left a hole in left field and allowed Ruth to start playing every day. The American League homer record was sixteen, held by "Socks" Seybold of the 1902 Athletics. Ed Williamson held the major league record with twenty-seven for Chicago's White Stockings in 1884. Ruth made a charge at the record and revived some interest in the summer game. He also got into a curfew bout with Barrow. The Babe almost came to blows with his manager, then was suspended. Star pitcher Mays was suspended for walking out on the team and was sold to New York at midseason. It was Frazee's second lopsided deal with his friends in New York, but no one suspected the heinous exchange that was in the works.

While the defending champion Red Sox struggled, Ruth became a one-man show. Late in the season, Boston fans gave the Babe a "day" at Fenway. The Boston ballyard was packed, and a writer asked Ruth what Frazee had given him for filling Fenway. Ruth, the cigar manufacturer, said, "a cigar," and pointed out that Mrs. Ruth had to pay her way into the park. Frazee was livid. Ruth finished with a record-smashing twenty-nine homers and a slugging percentage of .657. He knocked in 114 of Boston's 565 runs and scored 103, but the Sox slipped to sixth place. They had a chance to vault into fifth on the final day, but Ruth left for his Baltimore home after hitting his record-setting twenty-ninth homer on the next to last day of the season, September 27, in Washington. Frazee claimed the Babe left to play an exhibition in Connecticut. The Sox lost their finale, 8–7.

After visiting Baltimore and playing in additional lucrative exhibitions, the new home run king went to California to play golf and more sideshow baseball games. Meanwhile, a series of events that would forever curse the Boston Red Sox was unfolding back east.

The Yankees were still playing in the Polo Grounds in 1919, but their offices were on Forty-second Street, two blocks from the Frazee Theatre where the Broadway/Boston owner hung his hat. Yankee co-owner Colonel Huston knew Frazee was strapped for cash and started to grease the skids for Ruth's departure from Boston.

In his autobiography, Ruth wrote, "It was Ruppert's wealth which enabled him to make the big loan to Frazee which made the deal possible, but I have always believed the idea originally was Huston's. . . . Huston was downright impatient over the failure of the Yankee clubs and I believe it was he who first got the inside on Frazee's financial condition. . . . Frazee was one of his favorite drinking companions, and I believe that it was over a few glasses of beer that Huston first learned of Frazee's need and that if the amount was right he could obtain me for the Yankees."

◇

Huston grew up in Ohio and had made a fortune in the construction business in Cuba after the Spanish-American War. He was a captain of engineers in that war and became a colonel after serving overseas in World War I. Ruppert was a second-generation millionaire brewer, the son of a New York aristocrat, grandson of a Bavarian brewer. He was made an honorary colonel at the age of twenty-two by New York Governor David B. Hill and served in Congress from 1899 through 1907. He lived in a twelfth-floor Fifth Avenue apartment and never married. He had a butler, maid, valet, cook, and a laundress. Huston and Ruppert bought the Yankees for $460,000 in 1915. Huston was the idea man and Ruppert was the money man. When Huston learned from drinking buddy Frazee that Ruth was for sale, he went to partner Ruppert to see if he'd come up with the cash. On the threshold of prohibition (Ruppert's brewery was turning out 1.3 million barrels of beer per year), Ruppert was afraid to dole out too much cash, so the $300,000 loan was arranged to go along with the $100,000 cash payment.

Ruth was enjoying himself out west. In addition to the golf and the exhibitions-for-cash, he had contracted to appear in a series of movie shorts. The Babe was making plenty of extra money and beginning to regret the three-year $30,000 deal he'd struck with Frazee. He didn't confront the owner face-to-face, but let the word out that he wanted $20,000 for 1920.

After the deal was done but before it was announced, Ruppert sent Yankee manager Miller Huggins west to settle things with the slugger. Huggins took the train to Los Angeles, visited a friend at a local sporting goods store, and learned that Ruth was playing golf at a Griffith Park course. Huggins rented a car, drove the course, and waited on the clubhouse porch next to the eighteenth hole. Ruth was surprised to find the manager of the Yankees waiting for him on the porch of a Los Angeles golf course, but he was not totally surprised to learn what had brought Huggins three thousand miles west. Ruth knew Frazee was financially strapped and the Babe also knew his contract demands were testing the patience of the Red Sox owner. Huggins was in LA to get some assurance that Ruth could be signed by the Yankees. The Sox slugger and the Yankee manager got into Huggins's car and drove downtown, discussing details of Ruth's pending move to New York. Ruth promised to behave himself and signed a contract for $20,000, a raise of $10,000 over what Frazee had been scheduled to pay him.

The sale contract was signed on Friday, December 26, 1919. Frazee received $25,000 in cash, plus three promissory notes for $25,000 each. Frazee also received a letter from Ruppert that stated, "I hereby offer to loan or cause to be loaned to you $300,000 . . . to be secured by a first mortgage on land now used as a baseball playing field by the Boston American League Baseball Club."

"The Ruth deal was the only way I could retain the Red Sox," Frazee later told author Frederick G. Lieb.

Red Sox manager Ed Barrow was living in New York at 644 Riverside Drive when he got a Sunday morning telephone call from Frazee. It was December 28, two days after the deal had been signed. Barrow was in the shower when the call came and wrapped a towel around himself to talk to the owner. Frazee wanted to see his manager at six o'clock that night at the Knickerbocker Hotel. Frazee was sitting in the cafe with actor Frank McIntyre when Barrow walked into the Knickerbocker. Frazee always called Barrow "Simon."

"Simon," said the owner. "I am going to sell Ruth to the Yankees."

"I thought as much," said Barrow. "I could feel it in my bones. But you ought to know that you're making a mistake."

Frazee explained. Former owner Lannin was calling in his notes. Frazee's shows weren't doing well. This was a chance for a lot of cash and maybe a couple of ball players. Barrow pleaded with the owner to forget about getting players in exchange; the Yankees had nobody he wanted and it would only make it tougher for the manager.

It was fitting that the shameless sale of Ruth took place during baseball's darkest hours. There was a stench left over from the 1919 World Series, and eventually eight members of the American League Champion Chicago White Sox were accused of having fixed the Series and were barred for life by Commissioner Kenesaw Mountain Landis. Landis's appointment as the first-ever commissioner came too late to save Sox fans from the Frazee fire sale, but he was instrumental in cleaning up baseball.

Ironically, it is doubtful the game could have rebounded as quickly without the heroics of Ruth in New York in the twenties. There are those in Chicago who believe the Black Sox scandal is responsible for decades of baseball letdowns in the Windy City, just as Boston fans feel cursed since the sale of the Bambino. Perhaps *Sox* is the connection. Since the sale of Ruth, which came on the very heels of the Black Sox scandal, no team from Chicago or Boston and no team with a surname Sox has ever won a World Series. And remember that it was the Cubs who the Red Sox defeated in the 1918 World Series.

There was some outrage when the Ruth transaction was announced, but none of the hysteria that would accompany such a transaction in today's age of media overkill. The sale of Babe Ruth to Gotham was front-page news in all the Boston papers. John J. Hallahan of the *Evening Globe* led his story with: "Boston's greatest baseball player has been cast adrift. George H. Ruth, the middle initial apparently standing for 'Hercules,' maker of home runs and the most colorful star in the game today, became the property of the New York Yankees yesterday afternoon."

The *Boston Post* described the transaction as "a tremendous blow to the army of loyal fans," and predicted the Sox would be "crowding the Athletics for eighth place in 1920." Johnny Keenan, leader of the Royal Rooters, said, "Ruth was 90 percent of our club last summer. It will be impossible to replace the strength Ruth gave the Sox." A newspaper cartoon showed Faneuil Hall and the Boston Public Library wearing For Sale signs. Frazee had a show running in Boston entitled *My Lady Friends,* and the local joke was that the lady friends were the only ones Frazee had left. *My Lady Friends* was a farce. Perfect.

Edward E. Babb, president of the Boston Athletic Association, said, "If such a deal has been made, it's a big mistake. However, as baseball is handled today, it is not surprising to learn of startling things happening."

The South Boston Père Marquette K of C adopted a resolution that declared, "It is in the consensus of opinion in K of C circles that Boston fans were dealt with very unfairly in the sale of Brother Ruth, and it is felt that commercialism is fast gaining control over baseball . . . terming the sale of Ruth an unfair proposition to him, to Boston fandom and to the sport-loving city of Boston."

Francis J. Hurney of the K of C added, "Baseball is severely hurt by such deals as the one which takes Babe Ruth from the Red Sox. The management of the Red Sox will have to travel some to get a player that will draw like Ruth and I am sure that the gate receipts this year will show a decided decrease now that the true sportsmanship in the game is banished and financial interests take its place."

A subheadline in the *Globe* stated, " 'Babe' Says He Will Play in Boston or Nowhere," and Ruth's agent, Johnny Igoe, claimed to have received a telegraph from Ruth in Los Angeles that read, "Will not play anywhere but Boston. Will leave for the East Monday." It was an interesting message considering the fact that Ruth had already agreed to terms with Huggins, but it no doubt made the Boston fans feel better.

A day later, Ruth sent this telegram message to Igoe: "Tell the newspapermen that I am sorry to be traded to New York and hate to get away from Boston fans. Am leaving here in a few days for Boston and upon my arrival will answer Frazee's statements." He spoke of his intention to pocket $15,000 of Frazee's sales profit, but he had no leverage to squeeze any more from the sorry Sox owner.

In mid-January Ruth came to Boston and said Frazee was blaming him "to alibi himself with the fans." He demanded to see Frazee to get his $15,000 cut of the proceeds, but the owner refused to see Ruth. The Babe said, "I like Boston and the Boston fans. They have treated me splendidly. The time of a ball player is short, and he must get his money in a few years or lose out. Any fair-minded fan knows that my efforts on the Boston club last season warranted a larger salary and I asked for it. I have always hustled as much as any man on the diamond."

In his autobiography, Ruth admitted, "As for my reaction over coming to the big town, at first I was pleased, largely because it meant more money. Then I got the bad feeling we all have when we pull up our roots. My home, all my connections, affiliations and friends were in Boston. The town had been good to me."

Yankee owner Colonel Jacob Ruppert certainly wasn't worried about any intervention from league authorities. Ruppert said American League President Ban Johnson would be advised of the deal, but added, "We don't care what he thinks of it and do not even consider the idea of him trying to block it. All I can say is that whether Mr. Johnson likes it or not, Ruth will be in our opening lineup." The Yanks took out a $150,000 life insurance policy on Ruth.

January 5 was a day of mixed emotions for Colonel Ruppert. The millionaire brewer was delighted to have Ruth, but sad to learn that the Supreme Court would not allow the sale of 2.75 percent beer.

Frazee promised to use some of his proceeds from the sale to acquire ball players, and two days after Ruth was sold, James C. O'Leary of the *Globe* wrote, "He (Frazee) declared that he had made the deal after a great deal of deliberation and was satisfied that it was a good move. One of the first things he wishes to do now is to get a hitting, right-handed outfielder of experience and known ability. There is no question but what [Happy] Felsch of the Chicago White Sox would come up to that description in Frazee's opinion. He will get Felsch if he can."

Felsch had batted only .192 in Chicago's odious World Series loss to the Reds three months earlier. Small wonder. Happy Felsch was one of the players who had agreed to throw the World Series in exchange for $100,000, which was paid by a syndicate headed by New York gambler Arnold Rothstein. Harry Frazee never replaced Ruth with Chicago's outfielder, and Happy Felsch was banned for life from playing professional baseball by Judge Landis after the 1920 season.

Frazee got his $300,000 loan in the spring of 1920 and began to settle some debts and produce some new shows. Meanwhile, with Ruppert holding the mortgage on Fenway Park, Frazee was only too happy to keep sending quality players to New York for money. Wally Schang,

Waite Hoyt, Deacon Everett Scott, Bullet Joe Bush, Sad Sam Jones, Jumpin' Joe Dugan, and Herb Pennock were sold or traded to New York after Ruth. The *Herald*'s Burt Whitman correctly called it "the Rape of the Red Sox."

Frazee used the blood money to keep himself on his feet and started to cash in when *Madame Sherry* netted more than a half million dollars. There was no limit to what Frazee would do for Ruppert. When the Yankees and the St. Louis Browns were locked in a tight pennant race, Red Sox manager Hugh Duffy wanted to start tough lefty Pennock against the Yanks on the next-to-last day of the season. Frazee ordered Duffy to pitch Alex "Cousin" Ferguson instead. Ferguson lost, and the Yankees won the flag by one game. Three months later, Frazee traded Pennock to the Yankees, and the young lefty became a 240-game-winning Hall of Famer. Hoyt became the big winner for the 1927 Yankees, acknowledged as the greatest baseball team of all time. Dugan, a Holy Cross man and another Red Sox castoff, was the third baseman on that fabled Yankee team.

When Ruth made his first appearance for the Yankees in Boston (the Yanks stayed at the old Sheraton hotel, which is now Boston University's Miles Standish Hall), a scorecard ad urged fans to smoke a Babe Ruth cigar, the best in Boston and his true greatest hit. Mel Webb of the *Globe* wrote, "The Sudbury farmer is a great favorite in Boston, and twice today holiday crowds are likely to show him how much they regret his sale to New York." The afternoon game drew a regular-season record 28,000, and the Sox swept both games, holding the Babe to two singles and a double.

Joseph G. Foy was born in Quincy in 1910 and started going to games just after Ruth was sold to New York. Foy and his uncle would hop in the train at the Quincy Adams station, ride to South Station, take the subway from South Station to Park Street, then change again and ride a street car to Fenway Park. "It was when Frazee got rid of everybody," Foy remembered. "The Red Sox weren't very good, but we'd go in to see the Babe and say, 'Gee, he used to play for the Red Sox.' Everybody still loved him, even though he was with the Yankees. He had that farm out near the Wayside Inn, you know, and I remember one day some fans brought him two boxes of little chicks for his farm. He took them right over the rail and then he dropped one and there were little chicks running around the field. Oh, he was a character."

Babe and Helen were living in the Ansonia Hotel in New York City during the 1920 season when Ruth hit a record-smashing fifty-four homers and led the Yankees to a second-place finish and a league record attendance of 1,289,422. It was the first time in history a team had drawn a million fans. The Red Sox went 72–81, finished twenty-five and a half games out, and drew 402,445. Seeing that the Red Sox were going up in smoke like one of the Bambino's stogies, manager Barrow left after the 1920 season and, naturally, went to work for the Yankees as business manager. Boston finished last nine times in the first twelve Ruthless seasons.

During the 1920 season former owner Joe Lannin, still waiting for some of his money, tied up Frazee with an injunction. Meanwhile, Sox ticket prices were higher than those of the crosstown Braves because Frazee was not absorbing the war tax. Frazee promised to spend freely to make the Sox "wonders of 1923" and forked over $17,500 for three no-name ballplayers (the 1923 Sox finished last, thirty-three games out).

On April 18, 1923, New York's baseball club dedicated Yankee Stadium—the House that Ruth Built. Twenty-five thousand people were turned away because the place was already filled with seventy thousand a half hour before game time. Bandleader John Philip Sousa led the pregame procession, and Frazee was there alongside Ruppert marching in a pregame parade in center field. One can only wonder if Frazee felt any trace of guilt when the 1922 American League pennant was raised as the sellout crowd howled. New York's starting lineup had four of Frazee's gifts—Ruth in right, Schang catching, Dugan at third, and Scott at short. On Opening Day, 1923, the Red Sox once again were gracious guests, losing 4–1. Governor Al Smith threw out the first ball, and Babe Ruth hit the first homer, a two-run shot to right in the third off Howard Ehmke. As it is now, it was then, and forever will be.

◊

Frazee's name was mud in Boston then, just as it is now. One night he was out in Boston with character actor Walter Catlett. In an attempt to impress a pair of young ladies, Frazee had a cab driver take the group to Fenway Park. He got out of the cab and proudly displayed his baseball empire. The cabdriver overheard the boasts and asked if this passenger was in fact Harry H. Frazee, owner of the Red Sox.

Frazee said he was, and the driver decked him with one punch.

At this time, according to the publication *Current Opinion,* Babe Ruth was "the most talked-of American."

"Everything would have been different if he stayed in Boston," House Speaker Tip O'Neill remembered.

I was born in 1912 and I never did see Babe Ruth pitch, but Harry Frazee was an enemy of everybody. I was only eight years old when he sold the Babe, but everybody had a broken heart. And then we had our dismal years.

I remember a few years later there was a fire in Everett. There had been a gasoline explosion and about twenty guys got killed. They had a fund-raiser for those who had been killed. The Roach Town team, which was the Mayor Roach team, played the Boston Red Sox in a game in which Babe Ruth pitched for the Roach team and Gehrig played first base. This was at Wheeler Park in 1927. Carrigan was the manager and he's standing behind the bench and his pitcher struck out the Babe and when he came off the mound—it was the biggest crowd I had ever seen—Carrigan said, "You silly sonovabitch, do you think these thousands came to see you strike out the Babe? Throw it down the pipe." Anyway, the next time up he threw it down the pipe and Babe hit it out of the goddamn park so far. Many times I have gone over to take a look at the spot to see if it was my imagination, but it wasn't my imagination. About the fourth inning, the crowd surged on the field. They ripped the Babe's shirt off him. They stole his hat. Christ, they had to get the cops in to stop 'em.

I remember as a kid, he came down to St. John's school in North Cambridge for what we used to call in those days a sports night. He never got into the hall. The crowd was so huge. Christ, they practically attacked him he was such an idol. Finally the police had to get him out to get an escort to get back to the automobiles. He never got into the hall. I can remember that night as though it were yesterday. They came from miles around. That's the kind of a hero he was. That was an era in which there were idols, but nobody, nobody ever in the history of this country was the idol that Babe Ruth was.

On July 11, 1923, Frazee sold the Red Sox to J. A. Robert Quinn for $1,250,000. After the transaction was announced, Frazee broke bread with American League President Ban Johnson at the Copley Plaza then left town on the midnight train to New York, just as he had done the day he bought the Red Sox. The deal was temporarily held up because Frazee's books were a mess. There was a small matter of hot dogs that hadn't been paid for, so the club couldn't be sold until frankfurter czar Harry M. Stevens got his money.

The day the sale was announced the 1923 Red Sox did not have a single player left from the championship season of 1918. The Sox were, according to Mel Webb, Jr., of the *Globe,* "the most-buffeted outfit in the American League." On that same day, in the same newspaper, Babe Ruth was referred to as "the Sudbury agriculturalist," in a story that recounted his four hits for the surging New York Yankees. Those Yankees had taken quite a gamble, yes they had.

The Sox were stooges. In an episode that best demonstrates the buffoonery of the 1923 Sox, pitcher Clarence "Climax" Blethen bit himself in the buttocks while sliding into second base. Blethen, it seemed, carried his false teeth in his back pocket while on the ball field and nipped himself in the butt going into second. Bring on the new owners.

Webb wrote, "The fans surely welcome a change of ownership, for the club has been slipping steadily for years and the patrons of the game have seen their favorites sent to other fields and without any real benefit to the sport in this city."

The Golden Age of American Sport was sweeping the land. Ruth broke fences and won championships for the Yankees, but this was also the time of Red Grange, Jack Dempsey, Gene Tunney, Walter Hagen, Gertrude Ederle, the Four Horsemen, Big Bill Tilden, Helen Wills, and Bobby Jones. Meanwhile, the Red Sox whimpered through the roaring twenties, finishing last almost every year and drawing fewer than 300,000 fans five times during the decade. When Ruth set a major league record with sixty homers in 1927, Red Sox pitchers served eleven of the Bambino's meatballs.

The man who did the dirty deed didn't care anymore. While the Sox stumbled through the roaring twenties, Frazee finally hit the mother lode in 1925 with *No, No, Nanette.* The musical was written by Vincent Youmans, with lyrics by Otto Harbach, and opened in Detroit in 1924.

The farce flopped in its early days, which resulted in the replacement of the director and a revision of the script by Frank Mandel and Harbach. Several songs were dumped and Irving Caesar and Youmans wrote four new numbers, including a ditty entitled "Tea for Two." "I Want to Be Happy" was another smash from the show. It was easier to rebuild a theater production than a ball club, and Frazee recast several of the leads then booked the play in Chicago, where it had a successful run of almost a year. Touring companies began playing across America, and the show landed in New York in September 1925. It had a New York run of 321 performances and was one of the most successful shows of the twenties. Four companies went on the road, and the play ran for three seasons in the USA, then had a long, profitable run in London. From there, it went to Australia, Paris, Berlin, Switzerland, and Italy. The play came to symbolize the spirit of the Jazz Age, and Frazee made more than $2.5 million. Meanwhile, the former owner of the Red Sox and his second wife, Margaret Boyd, ran in the fastest New York circles, leaving $100 tips in their wake. In 1927, when Colonel Charles A. Lindbergh came to New York for a ticker-tape parade down Broadway, Lucky Lindy and his mother stayed at the Frazees' Park Avenue apartment.

Frazee didn't have much time to enjoy his money. The shows after *No, No, Nanette* didn't do as well, and four weeks shy of his forty-ninth birthday, Harry H. Frazee died of Bright's disease at 5:30 P.M. on June 4, 1929, at his home on 270 Park Avenue. New York City Mayor James J. Walker (godfather to Frazee's grandson, Harry III) was dedicating a new Bronx Terminal Market when he heard his friend was near death. He rushed to the Frazee home and was at Frazee's bedside when Frazee passed away.

The mayor of New York issued this statement: "Harry Frazee was one of the most popular figures in the theatrical and baseball worlds. I have known him for a great many years . . . he was immensely popular with everyone who knew him. He was a man of great energy, great mental ability and was greatly respected in the business and baseball world."

Frazee was buried in a sarcophagus in the Frazee family burial plot in Kensico Cemetery. The cemetery is in Valhalla, New York, in Westchester County, and the train leaving Grand Central Station goes right by it. Frazee's second wife, Mrs. Margaret Frazee, and Harry H., Jr., were listed as his only heirs. Despite the smash success of *No, No, Nanette,* and his theater holdings, Frazee's estate did not exceed $50,000. Family members believe that he spent most of his fortune once he knew he was dying. According to Frazee's obituary in *The New York Times,* "It was reported among his associates that his fortune had dwindled. His more recent ventures were less fortunate and he always was a generous spender."

Apparently, Frazee's heirs did not carefully guard the family fortune. In 1972, an elderly New Rochelle couple decided to sell their house and move to Florida. They'd been in the home for forty years and had never touched some of the junk that was left in the attic by the previous owners—stuff that was bound for the dump one week later. Vivian Cord, an antiques dealer taking a Sunday drive, inspected the junk and bought the contents of the attic for $850. She had purchased the business files of Harry Frazee. Cord had the papers catalogued and inventoried, then sent the list to sixty-five universities. Only two schools bid on the papers, and the University of Texas purchased the sheet music and scripts from sixty plays, including the original parts from the 1925 production of *No, No, Nanette.* The Frazee family is still trying to get the papers back. In 1971, a Broadway revival of *No, No, Nanette* started a run of 861 performances, longer than the original production, but the Frazees had been frozen out.

Harry, Jr., was a broker, then worked in the broadcast industry in New York City. Harry III left New York as a teenager and became automotive editor and an advertising executive for the *San Diego Union.* He operates his own business in Washington state. Great-grandson Mark Frazee (Max) is a construction foreman and artist in New York City.

An attempt to speak with Harry H. Frazee III proved futile and intriguing. Answering his phone in the spring of 1989, Harry III would not discuss his grandfather, who died sixty years earlier. He sounded extremely bitter and hurt. It can't be easy being a descendant of the disgraced. Frazee's family members believe that "Big Harry" did no wrong, just as great-grandchildren of Richard Nixon will someday insist that their famous forefather was framed. Most of us no doubt would chuckle at retelling tales of a grandfather who did a little bootlegging on the side during Prohibition, but this is different. The Frazee name has been mocked in Boston for seventy years. Can it be coincidence that Harry Frazee III settled in the Pacific Northwest—

the farthest point from Boston in the continental United States?

Great-grandson Max said, "In many ways it is too bad that my father won't talk about him. He has been that way ever since all those articles trashing Big Harry."

In 1986, Harry Frazee's other great-grandson, Jim Frazee, wrote an article for the *Tacoma News-Tribune* and stated, "Despite what has been often called the worst deal in the history of baseball, Harry never lost his ambition. He made his fortune on his own skills just as Ruth was able to do."

Jim Frazee defended his great-grandfather's transaction with this explanation. "More often than not, Harry and Barrow had to lock Ruth in his room so he wouldn't go out on all-night drinking, fighting, and womanizing sessions right up until the next game time. . . . I know and my family knows that Harry didn't bail out on the team, that he wouldn't let someone take them out of town, and that he wouldn't let them die in the dust. He found an answer in Ruth, who went where he would have gone had Harry not bothered to juggle finances to keep the team alive. And Harry found an answer for himself—in spite of all the emotional, tunnel-vision criticism—in theatrical production, what certainly he wanted to do after making the most misunderstood deal of the century."

Harry H. Frazee left his mark on the game of major league baseball in more ways than one. It turns out that Frazee was the first owner to have "The Star-Spangled Banner" played before a baseball game. He started the tradition September 9, 1918, prior to the fourth game of the World Series, a game won by Ruth, 3–2. Red Sox fans need not be reminded of this, but every time they stand for the anthem before a game, they are following a tradition set forth by the man who sold Babe Ruth to the Yankees for 100,000 pieces of silver.

The day Frazee died, the last-place Red Sox were beaten by Cleveland, 4–0, and dropped to 12–29. The American flag in front of the Red Sox offices on Jersey Street was flown at half-mast—a gesture that would have been more appropriate the day Frazee sold Ruth to the Yankees.

◊

There has been no shortage of indulgent hyperbole (much of it between the flaps of this book) regarding the seventy years of fallout from the Ruth transaction. In 1979 Boston writer Dan Valenti wrote, "The betrayal by Frazee had moral implications, for it cast the team into the role of martyr. . . . So 'disappointments' . . . are like stations of the cross to Red Sox fans, renditions hanging invisibly on the green walls of Fenway Park as the Catholic stations of Jesus' suffering and death hang affixed to church walls. . . . Ted Williams and Carl Yastrzemski died for the sins of Harry Frazee. The deaths were well publicized and well-paid-for deaths that became objects of love. They died for us, for Red Sox fans, so we could be reborn each spring."

Darrell Berger, minister at the First Parish Unitarian Church in Scituate, Massachusetts, says, "I think there's a real similarity between the House of the Seven Gables and Fenway Park."

In both cases you have a cursed family because of evil that had been done and it's passed down several generations later. I think of the selling of Ruth as the sin that cannot be atoned for. There hasn't been a savior that can come along and make that atonement. The Sox over and over again keep paying for that sin. Frazee sins against Sox fans by selling Ruth. This severs trust between fans and ownership that has never healed. A curse is also merely a folkwise way of explaining the unexplainable, but who wants to leave it at that? So is the Old Testament.

The key for the curse to be lifted is acknowledgment that both sin and curse exist and why, in the same way an alcoholic or any dysfunctional relationship must be named before it can heal. The great danger of a curse is that the closer it gets to being overcome, the greater the anxiety becomes. Anxiety causes bad things to happen and the curse continues.

Bad things happen. The curse continues.

THREE

The Sox won five of baseball's first fifteen World Series, but after selling the game's god, they became God-awful. From 1920 through 1966, Boston's American League entry won one pennant.

Prohibition came and went; Harvard graduated forty-seven classes; Franklin Delano Roosevelt four times was elected president; the Olympic games moved from Antwerp to Paris to Amsterdam to Los Angeles to Berlin to London to Helsinki to Melbourne to Rome and to Tokyo. And in all this time, Boston finished first in the American League exactly once. King Farouk, Flannery O'Connor, Malcolm X, Marilyn Monroe, James Dean, and Lenny Bruce were born, lived, and died. Social Security was enacted, air-conditioning was invented, and New York had two World's Fairs, and in this half century, one pennant flew over Fenway.

The immediate impact of Ruth's loss was obvious, and things only got worse when Frazee traded or sold the rest of his high-priced stars, most of them to New York where they were taken care of by Frazee's landlord, Jake Ruppert. Barrow's move from Red Sox field manager to Yankee business manager expedited the process and assured that the Yankees would acquire only Boston's best. Barrow knew the Red Sox talent like no one else and later wrote, "It was more than generous that he [Frazee] should direct me to the part owner of the Yankees. At the time Frazee was in terrible shape financially. He was heavily in debt and about to step up his player-selling spree to a point unequalled in baseball history . . ."

The Red Sox became like an L. L. Bean catalogue for the Yankees. Every time the Yankees needed to fill a hole, Barrow called Boston, ordered the player he wanted, and had Ruppert write out a check. Recalling the purchase of pitchers Sam Jones and Joe Bush, Barrow wrote, "Of course, the hard-pressed Harry Frazee also got a check. It was a fine deal for the Yankees, but once more a terrific howl went up and not alone in Boston, but throughout the rest of the league." Eleven of the twenty-four players on the Yankees' first championship team came from the Red Sox. And you wonder why so many Yankee-haters fill Fenway?

Sox outfielder Harry Hooper held out for $15,000 after the dismal 1920 season and was sold to the White Sox. "All Frazee wanted was the money," Hooper said later. "He was short of cash and he sold the whole team down the river to keep his dirty nose above water. . . . Frazee did me a favor. . . . I was glad to get away from that graveyard."

Commissioner Landis finally stepped in and recommended a rule that would prohibit all player transactions, except those done for the standard waiver price. For Red Sox fans, it was too late; they could have used some of the latter-day wisdom of much-maligned Commissioner Bowie Kuhn who nixed the sales of Joe Rudi and Rollie Fingers to the Red Sox and Vida Blue to the Yankees when Charles Oscar Finley was strip-mining his championship A's in 1976.

The post-Ruth Sox suffered a nonstop series of indignities and tragedies. Walter Johnson pitched his only no-hitter, against Boston in 1920. The Cleveland Indians humiliated the Red Sox by a score of 27–3 in 1923. Fenway's third-base bleachers burned down in 1926, and there was no need to repair them. A string of last-place finishes did little to help the finances of new owner Bob Quinn. Quinn's partner, Palmer Winslow, the moneyman in the operation, died in 1926. In 1929, Sox club secretary Jim Price committed suicide by slashing his wrists. The Great Depression struck the nation, and in 1930 a tapped-out Quinn had to follow Frazee's footsteps and sell pitcher Red Ruffing, another future Hall of Famer, to the powerful Pinstripes. In 1931, Quinn sold Somerville's Danny MacFayden, another promising pitcher, to the Yankees. Still in debt, Quinn felt cursed, even by the weather. It seemed that every time the Sox were ready to draw some fans for a big weekend series or holiday, it rained. Bad weather in Beantown became known as "Quinn weather."

There was no end to the Sox' woes. A few days before the start of spring training in 1932, Sox pitcher Big Ed Morris (a nineteen-game winner for the last-place Sox in 1928) got into a fight with a gasoline station operator in Brewton, Alabama. The fight started during a going-away party for Morris, and the pitcher wound up with a knife in his chest. Morris died two days later in a Florida hospital.

From 1925 through 1932 the closest the Red Sox came to a pennant winner was forty-three and a half games. The Sox lost over a hundred games in 1925, 1926, 1927, 1930, and 1932. In 1927, Ruth outhomered the entire Red Sox team, 60–28. In 1932, the Sox finished a whopping sixty-four games behind the Yankees, compiling a hideous won-loss percentage of .279 (43–111). Quinn hired a specialist to attend to his players' feet, and a headline aptly proclaimed, "Expert Hired by Quinn to Care for All Aching Dogs." Manager Shano Collins quit the cause in mid-June, and the Sox went 11–47 (.190) in the second half. By this time, amateur Twilight League games in Cambridge outdrew Red Sox games at Fenway. Quinn had to borrow on his life insurance to meet the payroll before spring training in 1933.

Thomas Francis Mulvoy went to the games in the twenties. His mother had moved the family from Galway, Ireland, to Roxbury, Massachusetts, in 1921, and he started going to games in 1923. "I would hop a truck to go over," Mulvoy said in 1989, one week after his eightieth birthday. "The team wasn't very good. Bob Quinn was the poobah and he didn't have any money. But nobody cared. It was ball games. We hated the Yankees. They stole Ruth from us."

Mulvoy raised his sons to be Red Sox fans, and Mark Mulvoy today serves as managing editor of *Sports Illustrated* while Thomas Jr. is managing editor of the *Boston Globe*. Tom Jr. woke his infant son, Stephen, to watch the Sox win the World Series in 1986. Stephen Mulvoy is still waiting for the Sox to win, as are his father and grandfather.

J. A. Quinn had it tougher than anybody who ever owned the Red Sox, and he is the single link connecting the Yawkey regime with Harry Frazee. Quinn is also a progenitor of another Yankee man. Quinn's son John became general manager of the Boston Braves for twenty-three years, and John's son Robert became a baseball executive, rising to the position of general manager of the New York Yankees in 1988.

Bob Quinn's recollection of his grandfather's tenure as Red Sox owner:

Grampa Quinn was a troubleshooter for Judge Landis. His obituary said he was known as "honest Bob Quinn." Grampa Quinn and Landis were quite close and were almost inseparable as far as discussing league matters. Baseball often called upon him as a troubleshooter to help right troubled franchises, and I think Landis asked him to go into Boston. Poor Grampa. He came into a situation that was a mess. He inherited a mess and at the time was in debt. He did not have his own money. He represented the Winslow family, and I know Dad was disappointed because he felt if Grampa could have held on, the Quinns would have owned the ball club. Grampa and my dad had a good relationship with Yawkey and Eddie Collins. The team I think was sold for a million dollars, of which Grampa had to use four to six hundred thousand to pay off his debts. My dad I know was very disappointed at the time Grampa sold the team because it would have been Dad's dream to own the Red Sox. Now, a couple of generations removed, I end up sitting here in New York. You have to wonder about what might have been, but I got a chance to talk to Mrs. Yawkey in 1986 and we got a few moments to reminisce. She remembered my grandfather. There always seems to be a connection between the Yankees and the Red Sox.

Two men emerged from the rubble of Frazee's ruins: Tom Yawkey and Ted Williams. Yawkey purchased the ball club from Quinn on February 25, 1933, and Williams came along six years later to lead the Red Sox into a new era: an era of high payrolls, home runs, and underachievement. With Yawkey writing the checks and Williams bashing the baseball, the Red Sox took on a new identity. No longer a laughingstock, they struck fear into the opposition, yet still failed to get back to the holy land where Ruth had taken them.

After Boston's pitiable 1932 season, a discouraged Quinn went to the Yankees-Cubs World Series looking for a buyer for his ball club. In New York, Philadelphia coach Eddie Collins, a clean member of the 1919 White Sox, arranged a meeting between Quinn and a twenty-nine-year-old millionaire baseball fan named Tom Yawkey. Yawkey was a Yale grad, the adopted son of William Hoover Yawkey. Bill Yawkey was Tom's maternal uncle, and he became the child's foster father when Tom's mother died. Yawkey was a former part owner of the Detroit Tigers and a man whose fortune was made in mining and lumber. These were the glory days of the Tigers (three pennants in three years), and players would sometimes come to the Yawkey home for dinner. As a ten-year-old boy in Sandwich, Ontario, Tom Yawkey fielded ground balls hit by Ty Cobb.

He played second base at Irving prep school in Tarrytown, New York, probably because that was where Eddie Collins played. Collins was an Irving alumnus and the greatest second baseman of his time. Yawkey's proudest moment came when he was runner-up for the annual Edward T. Collins Trophy (best scholar-athlete) at Irving. Bill Yawkey believed that a young man should learn business from the bottom up, so Tom Yawkey spent one summer 3,000 feet underground in a copper mine near Phoenix, and another subterranean summer wielding a shovel in West Virginia. He also did some logging in Wisconsin between Yale semesters. He played freshman baseball at Yale and also participated in intramural baseball his last three years. He was a member of Phi Gamma Delta, graduated in 1924, and some of his Yale friends called him "Tim."

When T. A. Yawkey was a young businessman in New York, Cobb introduced him to his idol, Collins, and the two Irving grads occasionally dined together. It was during one of these dinners that Collins told Yawkey that Quinn was ready to sell the Red Sox. Tom Yawkey was due to come into his inheritance when he turned thirty, and he wanted to buy a baseball team.

The sale of the Sox to Tom Yawkey was announced on February 25, 1933, four days after Yawkey's thirtieth birthday, four days after Yawkey inherited his millions. Like Quinn, Yawkey had to pay off concessionaire Harry M. Stevens, and the Sox also owed the American League $150,000. The deal was closed April 20. Yawkey said, "I don't intend to mess around with a loser." Collins was named general manager.

There was plenty of Yawkey money for other projects. Tom Yawkey poured money into charities, gave people jobs in his native South Carolina, and in the thirties he even financed a bordello in Georgetown, South Carolina. Sunset Lodge, run by madam Hazel Weiss, became internationally famous and wasn't closed until 1969. This business interest is not acknowledged on Yawkey's plaque in Cooperstown, New York.

Yawkey's business affairs were handled at T. A. Yawkey Enterprises in New York. He had residences at the Pierre Hotel in Gotham and at the Ritz in Boston, but he preferred to be in a ballpark or at his island home off the coast of South Carolina. In the spring of 1933, Yawkey's Red Sox got off to a fitting start when, en route from spring training in Sarasota, the team was involved in a train wreck in New Jersey. Pitcher Bob Kline wrenched his back and several nonplayer passengers were badly injured when half the cars on the train were derailed. There have been a lot of trainwreck seasons in the ensuing years.

The young owner would not be discouraged and started pouring thousands into his new ball club. Boston fans, still staggering from Frazee's treason and Quinn's powerless caretaker reign, delighted in the prospect of once again competing with the billionaire bullies in New York.

Yawkey's rebuilding was costly in every way. Quinn had never been able to settle all of Frazee's ball club debts, and when Yawkey bought the team, he had to assume the mortgage on Fenway. Despite all the friendly favors Frazee had sent to New York, Colonel Ruppert still held the mortgage note on Fenway Park. When Yawkey bought the Red Sox he asked Ruppert if the Yankee owner would mind carrying the mortgage into the following year. Ruppert was happy to have Yawkey in the league and agreed—until his team went into Fenway in 1933 and lost five straight games to the new Yawkey Red Sox. Ruppert's lawyer was on the phone to Yawkey's lawyer after the sweep and it was made clear that Ruppert wanted his money immediately. In 1975, Yawkey told Henry Berry, "Jake didn't like to lose five straight. So I sent the SOB a check the next day."

The 1933 Red Sox won twenty more games than the 1932 edition and vaulted out of the cellar for only the second time since 1924. It was a small, but symbolic move. The Sox were out of the cellar for good. There would be varying degrees of success and failure in future decades, but the Boston Red Sox never again finished in last place after Thomas A. Yawkey purchased the club in 1933.

On December 12, 1933, in the teeth of the Depression, Yawkey sent $125,000 to the Philadelphia A's along with Rabbit Warstler and Bob Kline for Max Bishop, Rube Walberg, and the man who may have been at that moment the best pitcher in baseball—Lefty Grove. The

Sox had entered a new age. From this point forward, Boston would be the team writing checks for superstar ball players. The Red Sox played .500 ball in each of the next two seasons, something they hadn't done since Ruth left. Attendance swelled from 182,150 of 1932 to 610,640 in 1934.

The Grove deal was only the start for Yawkey. In his first two years he dealt players and cash to obtain Rick Ferrell ($75,000), George Pipgras ($50,000), Dusty Cooke ($35,000), Fritz Ostermueller ($25,000), and Moose Solters ($25,000). Fred Muller, Bucky Walters, Mel Almada, Carl Reynolds, and Gordie Hinkle each came in deals that required a $10,000 check. And these were Depression dollars, coins the size of manhole covers. These deals were made in the weeks and months after President Roosevelt ordered all banks closed for six days after he was inaugurated for the first time, in March of 1933. These baseball players were bought for huge sums during a time of 13.4 percent unemployment, when 3.5 million American families were on the nation's relief rolls.

Yawkey didn't confine his spending to the uniformed personnel. He spent $750,000 on the renovation of Fenway Park. The Osborn Engineering Company, a Cleveland-based outfit that originally built Fenway, came back to rebuild the ballyard in the fall of 1933. The Coleman Brothers Corporation, a Boston-based contractor, worked with the men from Osborn.

Bostonians love their ballpark, and the face-lift Yawkey financed was desperately needed, but there are those who believe that the owner would have been better off relocating his team. The Fenway area is all landfill, and there's a far-fetched theory that strange things happen there because it is on the site of ancient Indian burial grounds. This has been used to explain why windows inexplicably kept popping out of the John Hancock building in the seventies. Most businesses located in the Fenway area have had problems, and the site was the home of one of the only Sears Roebuck outlets that's failed. Restaurants, hotels, and theaters have gone out of business, and there have been an inordinate number of fires in the area.

Yawkey experienced some of this bad luck right after his construction effort started when a five-hour, four-alarm blaze destroyed all the work the Coleman Brothers and the Osborn Engineering Company had started. Reconstruction began again after the fire, and the wooden center-field stands were replaced by concrete bleachers. Duffy's Cliff, in left, was reduced and a tall wood fence was replaced by a taller one (thirty-seven feet high) made of sheet metal and steel. Fenway's left-field Wall would become the most famous façade in sport. American League pitchers came to know it as the wailing wall. It cost Yawkey $45,556.10 to add 15,708 new seats, which increased capacity to 38,000. The "new" Fenway Park opened April 17, 1934, and Joe Cronin's Washington Senators defeated the Red Sox, 6–5, in eleven innings.

On August 12, 1934, 41,766 poured into Fenway to see Babe Ruth say good-bye in a Yankee–Red Sox doubleheader. It was the largest crowd in the history of Fenway, one that will never be equaled because of rigid fire laws and league regulations that were implemented after World War II. The Sox and Yankees split the doubleheader, and Ruth played left field in both games, going 2–6, without a homer or RBI. The Red Sox won the first game, 6–4, helped by Ruth's misplay on a Billy Werber liner. New York won Game 2, 7–1, and Ruth was given several lengthy standing ovations. He told the *Globe*'s Hy Hurwitz, "Boston has always been kind to me, and I was a bit disappointed that I couldn't have hit a homer for that big mob."

Hurwitz wrote, "The man who made baseball a double-decker proposition yesterday appeared in his valedictory game on the field where he made his major league debut. . . . What was more fitting for the Ruthian farewell than a record turnout of New England fans? If those who were not able to get into the park were added to those who were there, the crowd would surpass all previous marks by a good 10,000. New England in general and Boston in particular loves its baseball, and methinks it loves its Ruth, too."

Indeed, the Babe's popularity hadn't waned a bit. In 1934 the Associated Press photo service set out to find "the most photographed person in the world," and the winner was Babe Ruth. The runners-up were Franklin Roosevelt, the Prince of Wales, Jimmie Walker, Douglas Fairbanks, Jack Dempsey, Eleanor Roosevelt, Mary Pickford, Al Smith, Adolf Hitler, Benito Mussolini, and Herbert Hoover.

Yawkey was considering Ruth as manager of the Red Sox but was discouraged by Collins, who claimed Ruth would interfere with the front office. Instead of making a bid for Ruth, Yawkey paid $250,000 for Washington's hard-hitting twenty-eight-year-old shortstop/manager Joe Cronin. Yawkey's dollars were pretty persuasive; Cronin was the son-in-law of Washington owner Clark Griffith, but money was thicker than blood, and Cronin was dealt from the capital club. Meanwhile, Massachusetts governor James Michael Curley, a Babe Ruth kind of guy, persuaded Emil Fuchs to bring Ruth back to Boston. Fuchs was Curley's campaign manager and owner of the Boston Braves, and it was Fuchs, not Yawkey, who brought Ruth back home. Yawkey's chance to lift the curse was erased when he hired Cronin instead of the Bambino.

Cronin was delighted to leave. With his arm around his wife, Mildred, the shortstop said, "Well, Mil, it looks like good-bye Washington and hello Boston, and here's hoping we bring the pennant to Boston, their first since 1918."

Mildred smiled and said, "Well, Joe, if you bring home that old bacon, I'll cook it for you."

The fourth-place .500 Sox didn't improve in their first year under Cronin, and Yawkey promptly spent $150,000 to buy Jimmy Foxx from the financially weakened Philadelphia Athletics. Foxx had hit fifty-eight homers in 1932 and was a right-handed power hitter designed for Fenway. Folks started calling Yawkey's team, "The Gold Sox."

These were the days when young Yawkey took great delight in putting on a Red Sox uniform and working out with his high-priced talent. When the Sox were on the road, Yawkey would sit in the outfield grass with his wife and enjoy a picnic on the Fenway lawn, listening to the game on the radio. He made no attempt to disguise his hero worship, and it was easy to see why none of his players ever had to worry about a pay cut. T. A. Yawkey loved his ballpark and his ball players, worked out with them all season, and invited them hunting in South Carolina in the off-season.

The 1936 and 1937 seasons saw the Red Sox finish sixth, then fifth. Second baseman Bobby Doerr came up from San Diego in 1937, giving the Red Sox an infield with three .300 hitters. The Red Sox had the hitting but didn't have enough pitching. Grove was too old and Wes Ferrell too inconsistent. Cronin struggled at the plate and the fans hooted him. Yawkey was discouraged. The Yankees had been able to buy pennants by raiding the Red Sox, but Yawkey had less success with his purchases of Connie Mack's erstwhile champions.

Foxx hit fifty homers and drove in 175 runs in 1938 as the Red Sox finished second with an 86–61 record. It was Boston's best showing since the selling of Ruth, and it was instrumental in establishing the identity of the Red Sox that exists today—plenty of power (four regulars batted over .320 and the team batting average was .299), not enough pitching, and just good enough to finish second. The Red Sox would go on to finish second five more times in the next eleven years, while winning only one pennant. The 1937 and 1938 seasons were significant also because these were the years when Yawkey committed to his own farm system. The Boston owner would no longer have to depend solely on other organizations when he went searching for talent. It was during this time that the greatest player in Red Sox history was discovered and signed.

◊

Ted Williams was born in San Diego exactly twelve days before the Red Sox won their last World Series. His mother was a Salvation Army worker, part French, part Mexican. His father joined the army when he was sixteen and fought in the Philippines during the Spanish-American War. Williams had a frail younger brother, Danny, who once broke his arm merely by throwing an orange. Later it was discovered that he had leukemia. Williams went to Hoover High School and hit .583 and .406 in his last two years of high school. The Yankees could have signed him out of high school for $1,000, but refused to pay the steep sum. Mrs. Williams held out, and her son signed in 1936 with the San Diego Padres of the Pacific Coast league. He was the terror of the PCL when Boston's Eddie Collins bought him for $35,000 in 1937. In 1938 he reported to Sarasota with the Red Sox regulars and alternately infuriated and entertained everyone with his arrogance and ability. Regular outfielders Doc Cramer, Joe Vosmik, and Ben Chapman rode the Kid mercilessly. Williams was nineteen years old, six foot three, 175 pounds, when the Sox farmed him out to Minneapolis that spring, but he vowed to come back and make more money than Cramer, Vosmik, and Chapman combined.

Williams's announced ambition was simple enough; he wanted to become the greatest hitter who ever lived.

After the 1938 season, Cronin sent Chapman and some Yawkey cash to Cleveland for pitcher Denny Galehouse and utility infielder Tom Irwin. The move opened a spot in the outfield for Williams, but it also delivered to Fenway a man who ten years later would be the subject of one of the most controversial and doomed decisions in club history. Williams was bound for baseball's Hall of Fame, but Galehouse was destined for the Hall of Shame wing built by the inimitable Harry Frazee.

Teddy Ballgame was in the majors in the spring of 1939 and played his first big-league game in Yankee Stadium. Red Ruffing struck out Williams in his first two at-bats, and veteran pitcher Jack Wilson needled the brash Kid. Williams pledged to take Ruffing over the wall in his next at-bat and almost did—he doubled off the wall in right center, missing a homer by one foot.

The Sox came to Boston and Williams moved into the Shelton Hotel, where he would live until it closed in 1954. In his first Fenway game, he hit a double, a triple, and a homer. The Red Sox were on their way to another second-place finish (they finished second to the Yankees four times between 1938 and 1942) and won eighty-nine games, tops since 1917. Williams hit .327 with thirty-one homers and a league-high 145 RBI. The highlight of the summer was a five-game sweep of the Yankees in Yankee Stadium in July. The Sox beat the Yanks eleven of nineteen in 1939. The New York–Boston rivalry was intensifying because the Sox finally had an owner who could compete with his bankbook and a star who could carry a team in the manner of a Ruth or a Gehrig.

But while the Sox found a rookie phenom in Williams, they let another one get away. Pee Wee Reese was the best shortstop in the American Association and he played for Louisville, the farm club that was one-third owned by Yawkey. Yawkey made the erroneous assumption that he would get first crack at the flossy infielder, but the Dodgers beat him to the wallet and bought Reese from Yawkey's Louisville partners, Frank McKinney and Donie Bush. Yawkey bought out McKinney and Bush almost immediately, but the damage was done. Cronin was conspicuously passive in this episode, and it has long been suspected that the highly paid player/manager was threatened by Reese's talent.

"Reese was a lot better ball player than I was," Sox shortstop John Pesky admitted thirty years after both stopped playing.

Boston's pitching fell apart in 1940, and the Red Sox dropped to fourth place. The Sox led the league in hitting and scored a whopping 872 runs, but Grove was forty years old and there was nobody to replace him. Meanwhile, a rookie outfielder named Dominic DiMaggio took over in right field, moving Williams to left.

Williams was the foundation of Red Sox teams for the next two decades, and it was during this era that the Sox carved out their silver medal status. When Williams hit .406, in 1941, the Sox finished second. Grove won his three hundredth game in 90 degree heat on July 25, 1941, but there wasn't much else to grip the fandom, and America was on the threshold of war.

The Kid hit .356 and won the Triple Crown in 1942, and the Red Sox won ninety-three games, finishing with a .612 winning percentage, best since 1915. The Sox had the perfect table setters in Dom DiMaggio and Pesky. The Sox trailed the Yankees by only four games at the All-Star break and had a reliable starter named Tex Hughson. But in the end, the Townies were bridesmaids for the fourth time in five seasons, finishing a full nine games behind the hated New Yorkers.

Stocked with talent and primed to make a charge at the Yankees, the Red Sox in 1943 again were thwarted by outside forces. This time global conflict intervened, and the Red Sox dropped to seventh when Williams, Bobby Doerr and shortstop Johnny Pesky went off to fight in World War II. The 1943, 1944, and 1945 seasons were lean for all of baseball, but typically, the Boston Red Sox were hit hardest. There are those who believe the Sox would have won the American League flag in all three war years, and based on what happened when the boys came home, a case can be made for a midforties Sox dynasty. But it's always something with the Red Sox, and this time it was something bigger than any baseball game.

It was a sorry lot that suited up while Williams and Company joined the dogfaces. If you were 4-F, you might be good enough to play in the depleted big leagues. People who previously couldn't get into Fenway without a ticket were suddenly batting cleanup for the local nine. Baseball might have been better off closing down, but FDR wanted the game to go on to give the soldiers abroad something to follow. Baseball, even these games played by minor league rejects, could be a morale booster for Americans in Europe or the South Pacific.

It was hard for anyone to focus on grown men in flannels, even harder to imagine the St. Louis Browns as league champions. Red Sox spring training was in Pleasantville, New Jersey, and on the road as many as six players shared a single room. Tom Yawkey was not without conscience or vision. The Sox owner shifted his emphasis and steered his ore and lumber interests toward the war effort. The Sox owner was also in the midst of a marital crisis. His first wife, Elise, filed for divorce after the 1944 season, claiming they had not lived together for three years. Yawkey married Jean Hollander Hiller on Christmas Eve, 1944. Jean Yawkey had worked as a model and a salesperson at Jay Thorpe, an exclusive woman's clothing store in New York City, and legend has it that the Sox owner met his second wife while he was on a shopping junket with his first bride.

◇

The final war year was 1945, and Red Sox fortunes were forever changed when a former UCLA football star named Jackie Robinson went through a charade of a tryout with the Red Sox. One day after the death of FDR, Boston scout Hugh Duffy and pitching coach Larry Woodall auditioned Robinson, Sam Jethroe, and Marvin Williamson at Fenway Park. All three were black and playing in the Negro Leagues. Boston City Councilor Isadore Muchnick (a representative of Roxbury, which had been a Jewish stronghold, but was becoming predominantly black) arranged the tryout, through sponsor Wendell Smith, sports editor of the *Pittsburgh Courier*.

The day after the tryout, an Associated Press report stated, "Cronin exhibited interest in the work of Robinson . . . coach Hugh Duffy commented that Williamson seemed to be a good ballplayer, that he was fast and had possibilities. All three were given the customary forms in which to enter their athletic history and background. . . . Muchnick argued that the American game should conform with the tradition of democracy and that Negro baseball players should have equality of opportunity. His comment drew a response from the Red Sox that no Negroes had ever sought a place on the team."

The *Globe*'s Jerry Nelson wrote, "Without doubt there are Negro ball players with enough ability and brains to play major league baseball. . . . But I don't think, or ever will, that their ability can be judged in one morning or one afternoon, or one 'tryout' by even the smartest talent picker in the game. . . . After all, ball clubs spend thousands of dollars carrying young ball players for a month to six weeks each spring before they make a decision to cut them loose or place them in lesser leagues."

"I was there," Clif Keane said. "Jack Barry covered it and he said, 'Come on over, we'll go and watch it.'"

So we went over for about an hour. Somebody up in the back of the building yelled, "Get those niggers off the field." And they left shoftly after it and we never heard from them again. It wasn't Yawkey. Yawkey wouldn't do that. I would guess they heard it, I didn't ask them. When it was said, I looked back. It was somebody in the back of the ballpark. I looked back. It was up in the back and there were a few people walking around. Nobody ran away and nobody said, "Yeah, I said it." I just couldn't identify who said it. He said it good and loud. It happened. That absolutely happened. I was there. I talked to Yawkey several times about black athletes after that and he said, "Get me a good one and I'll sign him. I don't want to get a black guy simply because he's black." This was in the fifties when [Mike] Higgins was the manager. Higgins was bad. That's why I often wonder about Tom. I never thought Yawkey was that smart. He did nothing to earn the money. His foster father handed him fifty million and he went from there.

The Robinson tryout wasn't a huge story at the time and there were certainly more newsworthy events transpiring. Smith took the three players to New York, contacted Dodger president Branch Rickey, and the rest is hardball history. Robinson signed with the Dodgers four months after he tried out for the Red Sox. In his 1972 autobiography *I Never Had It Made*, Robinson wrote, "Black players were familiar with this kind of hypocrisy . . . not for one minute did we believe the tryout was sincere. The Boston club officials praised our performance, let us fill out application cards, and said 'so long.' We were fairly certain they wouldn't call us and we had no intention of calling them."

His instincts were probably correct. The Sox had been playing Sunday baseball since the midthirties but needed an annual unanimous vote from the city council in order to sustain the practice. The Sox needed Muchnick's vote, and he used it as leverage to make the ball team give black players a chance. The Sox had little choice but to accommodate the city councilor.

Duffy later said that Robinson showed as much promise as any player he'd seen, but the aging scout had no clout and the Sox maintained that the three players were not ready for the majors and that the players would have gotten especially bad treatment at the Sox triple-A affiliate in Louisville. So instead of bringing the first black player to the major leagues, the Red Sox would become the last—Pumpsie Green broke Boston's color line in 1959.

In his book *What's the Matter with the Red Sox?* Al Hirshberg claimed that two-time Red Sox manager and general manager Higgins told him, "There'll be no niggers on this ball club as long as I have anything to say about it." Higgins was not fired until 1965 and later did time in a Louisiana State prison after he was convicted of negligent homicide in a drunk-driving incident. He died of a heart attack in 1969, two days after his release from prison.

Twenty years later, Earl Wilson remembered Higgins's death and said, "Good things happen to some people."

Wilson, a pitcher, was the Red Sox' second black player. He was called up six days after Green, in 1959, and they, of course, roomed together. Wilson was still with the Red Sox when the team moved its spring headquarters to Winter Haven, Florida, and Wilson was turned away from two nightspots because he was black. He told writers about the situation and he was traded that spring. He won eighteen games in 1966, then won twenty-two more for the Tigers in 1967. Higgins was Wilson's manager for parts of four seasons in Boston.

"It's not very hard to tell if a guy likes you or dislikes you," remembered Wilson. "It's like if a dog comes into a room, he can tell if a person likes him or dislikes him, just by the vibes. It was real, man."

How could Tom Yawkey hire a man like Mike Higgins to manage his baseball team for more than seven seasons?

"Tom Yawkey had his farmers on his farm," answered Wilson. "They were black. What other people call great is bad for other people. Some people probably thought Hitler was a great person. And they truly thought that he was, but they wasn't Jewish and didn't have to deal with it. But once you're in that little guy's empire—everybody's got their cronies and junk. I don't know. I might have been a public pressure. You never know. And now they always have a pain, don't they? Shame on them if they passed on a Willie Mays or a Jackie Robinson. The Red Sox, yes, they always have a pain."

Willie Mays? Yes, Willie Mays. In 1949, Mays was playing for the Birmingham Black Barons. The white Birmingham Barons were a Red Sox farm club, and Eddie Glennon, the affiliate's general manager, called Cronin after watching Mays play. Cronin failed to act, but Sox scout George Digby (who later signed Wade Boggs) heard about Mays and went to Birmingham to watch the kid. Digby and Glennon called Cronin and raved about Mays. They could buy the rights to the young outfielder for $5,000. Cronin backed off and said he'd send someone down. Pitching coach Larry Woodall (the same man who worked the Robinson tryout) was sent for a look and reported that Mays was not the Red Sox type. Instead, the Sox signed a thirty-three-year-old black player/manager named Piper Davis for $7,500.

In 1985, fired Sox coach Tommy Harper filed a racial discrimination suit against the Red Sox and was pacified with an out-of-court settlement. The Sox had certainly come a long way since the Robinson tryout.

Darrell Berger, Unitarian minister from Scituate, Massachusetts, firmly believes that the rejection of Robinson was the second great sin of Sox management.

> The Sox lost three pennants in the next five years by a total of six games. Easily, Robinson could have brought those pennants to Boston instead of Brooklyn. This was a sin of omission, rather than a sin of commission, but my feeling is that the only way they can atone for these sins is to have a black manager. In a way, this goes back to the Ruth sale. Think of the taunts to Ruth—they accused him of being black because he had black features, thick lips, and a flat nose [the kids at St. Mary's in Baltimore had called young Ruth "Nigger Lips"]. Can a rational man believe the Sox are paying for these sins? Absolutely. The ritualistic aspects of baseball are very real. When you get into the racial aspect of this incident, it's no longer frivolous, and I think there's a real connection.

Television and newspaper personality Bud Collins says, "Why have they never won a World Series since 1918? It's a double curse of Ruth and Robinson. The Red Sox were punished for dealing Ruth and then for having had the opportunity to sign Robinson and not doing it."

Jackie Robinson was born in 1919—Ruth's last year in Boston and the year Frazee sold the Babe to New York.

Three days after the Robinson tryout, Cronin shattered his right leg rounding second base in Yankee Stadium and ended his playing career at the age of thirty-eight. The only sunshine in 1945 came in the person of rookie pitcher Boo Ferriss who was 16–1 by the end of July. He was a twenty-three-year-old righty with an asthma condition that kept him out of the army. Ferriss won twenty-one of the Sox's seventy-one victories in this saddest of sad seasons.

Cronin was starting to catch a lot of grief along with the grounders and liners he handled at short. Fans and newspapermen decided that the manager's decisions and defense were dragging the Sox down. He was blamed for a quick hook with his starters, then for waiting too long to make pitching changes. He was blamed for sore arms and for Boston's inability to win away from Fenway Park. Cronin was from San Francisco and was accused of favoring California players. He was also charged with overmanaging, showboating, and paranoia. Did the Sox get rid of Jimmy Foxx because Cronin thought Foxx was managerial timber? Did the Sox let Reese slip away because Cronin was jealous? Cronin's assessment of Reese was that the youngster was too small and would never be a hitter, but Reese led Brooklyn to a pennant in 1941 while the Red Sox were finishing their usual second.

Bad second halves became a trademark of the Red Sox. In nine of Cronin's first ten seasons with Boston, the Sox were better in the first half than they were in the second half. Red Flops had a nice ring to it.

The annual disappointment about Boston's baseball team was becoming a national cliché. Washington was first in war, first in peace, and last in the American League, but Boston was forever second, the underachieving rich kid of the junior circuit. In March 1946, esteemed *Boston Globe* sportswriter Harold Kaese penned a lengthy article for the *Saturday Evening Post* titled "What's the Matter with the Red Sox?"

What's the matter with the Red Sox? Every New England Boy Scout, lobsterman, mailman, priest, and hod carrier goes through life asking himself this question. You can talk about it at a family gathering on any holiday. When chestnuts roast on an open fire, cozy New Englanders talk about what's wrong with the Red Sox. They know that they'll have their answer by Columbus Day, and the upcoming season will supply more fodder for next winter's analysis.

◊

It was during this time that the multiheaded monster that is the Boston media began to become part of the Red Sox story. Due to the year-round interest in the local ball team, and the numerous major metropolitan and suburban newspapers that are within driving distance of Fenway, the Red Sox are the subject of twelve months of saturation coverage. It's great publicity for the ball club and in part accounts for the ease with which Fenway is filled in these times, but the Sox have paid a price for all this free publicity. The local media is competitive and cynical, representative of the region's fans. As a result, there is a harder edge to much of the Red Sox reportage, and the sheer volume of coverage assures that players and front office personnel will sometimes be annoyed and/or offended.

The best example of this dynamic was furnished by Theodore Samuel Williams and the men who wrote about him from 1939 to 1960. The relationship was acrimonious, sometimes vile, and there was a good portion of unfairness and stubbornness on both sides. Boston had four morning papers (Globe, Herald, Post and Record) and three afternoon journals (Globe, American, Traveler) when Williams broke in, and circulation wars contributed to Williams's rough treatment.

Who could blame Williams for hating writers when a sportswriter named Mel Webb (the same man who covered Ruth's first game in Boston as a Yankee) carried out a personal vendetta by not putting Williams in his top ten among MVP candidates in a season in which Williams hit .343 with thirty-two homers and 114 RBI compared with Joe DiMaggio's .315, twenty, and 97? Williams finished second to DiMaggio, but would have won if Webb had listed him anywhere on his ballot.

"I don't like the sonofabitch and I'll never vote for him," was Webb's response.

Clif Keane, a colleague of Webb's, recalled the roots of the dispute.

"Ted gave him a hard time in spring training that year and said, 'You old goat, why don't you go and die.' Webb said he'd get even."

Dave Egan, columnist for the Boston Record, a Hearst tabloid, was the most vindictive and unfair writer in town, and he would stop at nothing to goad Williams.

Keane remembered Williams's stormy relationship with the members of the fourth estate.

> He was a perfect gentleman when he was a kid ball player. His mother insisted on him behaving. She was a Salvation Army worker. And his history was bad. His father was a bad guy and his brother was in jail. He told me once he sent six thousand dollars worth of furniture home to his mother. The old man hocked every goddamn bit of it. I used to say to him "Why don't you like to meet good people?" And he'd say, "Clif, you know what smart people are like. They ask a million questions. I don't want to sit around with people and have them say to me, 'Was your father a ballplayer, Ted? Was your brother a good athlete?' What am I gonna say about my parents?" He could be an awful prick and he could be a good guy. I remember being on a train to St. Louis. Twenty-six hours. I'm sitting in the goddamn seat across the way from Ted and a guy from *Life* magazine is sitting with him and Ted is a nut on cameras. So he starts taking the guy's camera apart. He's got the whole fuckin' camera all over the table. The guy's watching him. So he's there for about an hour. Everything's fine. So Ted says to the guy, "I'll be right back, I'm going down to take a leak." He goes down to the front of the train, comes back, and the guy is sitting there. Williams looks at him and says, "Are you still here, for Christ's sake? What are you doing here? I've been with you for two hours and I'm going to have you for the whole goddamn day."

In his autobiography, Williams wrote, "I think without question that Boston had the worst bunch of writers who ever came down the pike in baseball. I think certainly any professional sport has to have press coverage, has to have color written about the teams, but you can do all that without being unfair, without picking on somebody, without making a damn mountain out of a molehill, without putting somebody on the spot. In Boston they weren't content to do it that way. After a while, I didn't cooperate because I didn't want to."

In 1989, Williams said, "I look back and I don't even think it's important, but it had an effect on me that it shouldn't have had and I reacted probably a little strongly about it. In fact I would say today that Steve Carlton, it got away from him a little bit. . . . If somebody asked me fifteen years ago about him being in a cocoon, I'd say, 'Well, ease up on 'em a little bit.' "

Yawkey failed to intervene in the war between Williams and the press, and the writers resented it when Yawkey took Williams's side in the feud. The petulant scribes thereafter were less patient with Sox management and ownership.

However, for all their cynicism and criticism, the Red Sox press corps could also be faulted for setting up the fans with faulty expectations. There has always been a tendency for Boston scribes to inflate the talents of the local nine, and picking the Red Sox to win the American League flag has been described as an occupational hazard among Boston baseball writers.

There was, therefore, no great surprise when several Sox beat reporters picked Boston to win the AL pennant before the 1946 season. Among knowledgeable baseball people, only Cleveland player/manager Lou Boudreau shared the sentiments of the Boston writers. The Yankees and Tigers were preseason favorites. But the Red Sox were going to win. They were going to put a new twist on the Curse of the Bambino. They were going to have the best team in baseball and still manage to lose the World Series.

Even to this day,
some people look at me like I'm a piece of shit.

—*Johnny Pesky*

John M. Paveskovich was born in Portland, Oregon, on September 27, 1919, the same day Babe Ruth played his last game in a Red Sox uniform. He married Ruth Hickey on January 10, 1945. *Ruth Pesky.* Is it any surprise that John Paveskovich was the first vivid victim of the Curse of the Bambino?

The 1946 Red Sox were unstoppable. For once, the April optimists in the press box were right. Williams, Pesky, Bobby Doerr, Dominic DiMaggio, Tex Hughson, Mickey Harris, Joe Dobson, and Hal Waner came back from the war, and first baseman Rudy York was acquired in a winter trade with the Tigers. Cronin had four top starters in Harris, Boo Ferriss (twenty-five-game winner), Dobson, and Hughson . . . and the Red Sox won their first pennant since 1918, and their last until 1967.

This was a wire-to-wire job. The 1946 Sox were in first place for all but two days of the season, ripped off fifteen straight (still a franchise best) in April and May, broke to a 21–4 start, won forty of their first fifty, and went 60–17 at Fenway. They shredded the competition. President Harry Truman threw out the first ball when Boston opened at Washington in April, and Williams's homer led the Sox to a 6–3 victory. The All-Star game was at Fenway, and Williams hit two homers (in-

cluding one off Rip Sewell's famous eephus pitch) and two singles in
a 12–0 rout of the National League. The mighty Red Sox had eight
players on the American League All-Star team. York hit eighteen home
runs in August, while Williams was on his way to the MVP (.342, 38,
123) despite the introduction of a daring defensive alignment by Cleveland player/manager Lou Boudreau. Pesky slapped 208 hits, Dominic
DiMaggio hit .316, and Williams and Doerr combined to drive home
239 runs. Yawkey's millions were finally paying off (it's estimated that
he poured $4 million into the team between 1933 and 1946), and there
was little doubt that Boston had the best baseball team on the planet.
It had been twenty-eight years since Boston's AL entry won its last
pennant, and Sox fans already were answering to the surname "long-
suffering." The Red Sox won the flag by twelve games, clinching in
Cleveland September 13, a few hours after Hughson beat the Indians,
1–0, on an inside-the-park homer by Williams. The Yankees defeated
Detroit later in the day and the Sox were champions of the American
League for the first time since Frazee sold Ruth to the Yankees. New
York finished third, seventeen games behind Boston.

Thomas A. Yawkey was with his boys at the Statler Hotel in Cleveland when the Sox learned of their official pennant-clinching. Yawkey
heaped all the credit on Cronin's shoulders. Cronin got into a swearing
contest with Huck Finnegan of the *Boston American,* and Yawkey
almost came to blows with Duke Lake of the same paper. Everything
was in place.

Sox fans, revived by the end of the drought, pushed the turnstile
count to a record 1,416,944, and the Townies drew 1,250,000 on the
road. World Series tickets were almost impossible to get.

How could any of these people have known that this would be it?
With Williams and DiMaggio and Doerr and Pesky and young Boo
Ferriss and Tex Hughson, all bankrolled by Yawkey's millions, Sox
fans figured this would be the first of many World Series delivered by
the Splendid Splinter and friends. There was no hint, no signal that the
1946 Series would one day represent nothing more than a disappointing
aberration in a fifty-year, post-Ruth period of frustration.

In 1946, there were still plenty of breathing, working New Englanders
who remembered the 1918 World Champs. The Red Sox had never
lost a World Series, and these 1946 fence-busters were 20–7 favorites
over the St. Louis Cardinals.

After waiting twenty-eight years to get back into the Fall Classic, the Sox had to wait a few extra days to find out who they'd be playing. The Cardinals and Dodgers tied for first and had a best-of-three playoff for the right to face Boston. Cronin worried about this delay. His stardust club had grown stale in September, losing six straight before clinching in Cleveland. Now the start of the Series was delayed four days while the Cardinals and Dodgers dueled. Cronin decided that the only way his group could regain its sharpness was to play some more hardball, so a team of American League All-Stars was assembled for a three-game series with the Red Sox. In the fifth inning of the first superfluous game, diminutive Senator lefty Mickey Haefner threw a pitch that hit Williams on the right elbow.

Williams came out of the game and skipped the rest of the senseless series. There are those who believe the bruise contributed to his subsequent silent World Series. The Kid's morale was further dented when a big-splash trade rumor claimed he would be shipped to Detroit after the Fall Classic.

The Cardinals beat the Dodgers, then went to work on a plan to stop Boston's MVP. St. Louis manager Eddie Dyer devised his own Williams shift and moved his third baseman to the first-base side of second while shifting shortstop Marty Marion slightly to the right of his normal position.

The first two games were in St. Louis, and the Red Sox won the opener, 3–2, then dropped Game 2, 3–0, when 160-pound lefty Harry Brecheen blanked them on four hits. Williams had only one single in the two games.

The Series finally came to Boston on October 9, and the inimitable Ferriss shut out St. Louis, 4–0, allowing only six hits. Williams was 1–3 and his hit came when he grudgingly foiled Dyer's strategy with a bunt single to the third-base side. Fans cheered as if Williams had homered, and at least one Boston paper ran a headline that screamed "Williams Bunts."

The Cardinals routed Hughson in Game 4 and evened the Series with a twenty-hit, 12–3, victory. A catcher named Joe Garagiola had four hits for the Cardinals while Williams went 1–3 again, managing nothing more than a single. The favored Red Sox began to question themselves slightly, but felt much better when Dobson beat the Cardinals, 6–3, in Game 5. The Red Sox were going back to St. Louis and planned on bringing the World Championship home for the first time since 1918. Cardinals players took the train home while the Sox went out in style, flying west so they could get an extra night's sleep at the Chase Hotel.

Brecheen beat the Red Sox again in Game 6, 4–1, forcing a seventh and deciding game. One day before Game 7, the *Boston Globe* ran a page-one cartoon by Gene Mack. The sketch showed a Red Sox player bouncing out of the dugout to do battle—while the ghosts of past Sox series entries (1903, 1912, 1915, 1916, and 1918) exhorted him to victory with this war cry: "Don't forget, Boy, we've never lost one." The headline read: "Don't Let Us Down," right below, "Sox favored 10 to 7."

This cartoon no doubt today would cause gales of laughter among Boston baby boomers and their progeny, but in 1946 the Red Sox still were expected to win the Big One. These Red Sox were the heirs of that first generation of world champions and there was no reason to expect anything would be different this time around. The public perception was that the Sox were unbeatable. Fortified by Messrs. Williams, Doerr, Pesky, DiMaggio, and a raft of young arms, the Yawkey Red Sox appeared to be on the threshold of a decade of dominance. Game 7 of the 1946 Series was to be the first of many triumphs as the Red Sox returned to their rightful place atop the American League.

All of the above was shattered by the ghastly events of Game 7, and since this day the legacy of the Red Sox has been that of the under-achieving loser. The Red Sox are usually competitive, sometimes good enough to make it to the postseason, but in the end they will always let you down. Tuesday, October 15, 1946, was the turning point. This was the first time the Red Sox took their fans to the edge, then failed.

Cronin had his ace, Ferriss, ready for the finale and was applauded for manipulating his rotation so adroitly. Meanwhile, Dyer had to go with Murray Dickson, who'd been beaten by Rudy York's homer in Game 3.

Williams went out on a couple of long blasts in the first and fourth. Meanwhile, the Cardinals rocked Ferriss and took a 3–1 lead in the fifth. The Red Sox stayed silent until the eighth, when DiMaggio doubled home two runs against Brecheen, who was pitching in relief. In the excitement of watching the Red Sox tie the game on DiMaggio's clutch hit, few noticed the Little Professor limping into second base. He'd suffered a charley horse and could not continue. Backup Leon

Culberson went in to run for DiMaggio and would play center in the bottom of the eighth. Take note.

"Evidently when he turned the base, he hurt it," said Pesky. "It was very noticeable. In those days they didn't drag the infield in the middle innings, which had an effect. When that happened, Dom had to come out of the game. Culberson replaced him. He could play a little infield, a little outfield. He was a pretty good player. A good hitter. I think that year he hit .310. He was all right."

With Culberson on second and two out, Williams had one last chance to do something, but hit a weak pop-up to second baseman Red Schoendienst. Bob Klinger came in to pitch the bottom of the eighth.

Enos Slaughter led off with a single and was still standing on first after outs by Whitey Kurowski and Del Rice. Harry "The Hat" Walker came up and hit a sinking shot to left center, and Culberson gave chase. Shortstop Pesky went out for the relay, but did not notice that Slaughter hadn't stopped running. Third-base coach Mike Gonzalez gave Slaughter no sign. Pesky took the relay throw, turned to his left and hesitated, ever so slightly (grainy film footage is fairly conclusive on this), before making a desperate heave home to get the streaking Slaughter. It's been said and written that Pesky turned toward second when he got Culberson's throw, but the footage doesn't show this and Pesky denies it.

It is interesting to note that in official box scores and newspaper accounts of this play, Walker was credited with a double. Oral history has been more convenient and less kind, and for forty-four years Pesky and the Red Sox have heard that Slaughter scored from first on a single. He didn't. He scored from first on a double. It's a little like "Play it again, Sam," a phrase that Humphrey Bogart certainly *did not* utter in *Casablanca*. Bogey might as well have said it because that's the way it's been passed down, just as Slaughter might as well have scored from first on a single because Walker's hit has shrunk by one base in millions of retellings.

Forty-two years after the fact, Pesky remembered it this way.

> Slaughter was on first. He was stealing. Harry Walker was the hitter. Bobby [Doerr] gave all the signs and I was covering. Klinger was pitching and he didn't really hold him. He got a helluva jump. Slaughter could run. He was a good runner. I went to the bag,

and when I got to the bag the ball was hit. Now I got to get out into left field. I wasn't really, really deep. There's a film of it and I've watched that a hundred times and I thought I was out deeper than I actually was after watching it. But the throw I got was a lob. No one dreamed that Slaughter would try to score. I'm out in short left center field. It was late in the afternoon and Christ, when I picked him up he was about twenty feet from home plate. I'd have needed a rifle to get him. You look over your left shoulder. You're not going to turn this way [turns right]. A lot of people thought I went this way and said that I dropped my hands and went "Oh, gosh." I was just getting ready to throw the ball. I've got the ball like this and I'm looking. I was just going to flip the ball into the infield so the ball wouldn't be mishandled. And he just kept on going. I couldn't hear anything. Everybody was screaming and hollering.

The funny thing about that. I got accused that I hesitated and I watched the movies and I didn't think that I did. That Arch McDonald, who was announcing, said that I held on to the ball too long. I felt terrible about it because really and truly I should have got the ball quicker and he'd have never have scored. But he just kept on going and he got a helluva jump and Culberson had to go for the ball in left center and I'm sure he felt the same way I did.

Clif Keane, of the *Globe,* said, "They blame Pesky. I don't blame Pesky. I saw the play. The guy threw the ball and Pesky got the ball up here and brought it down. And then he went back up. Some people claimed that Doerr never yelled 'home.' You had to sense, I think, that Slaughter was gonna run. Johnny brought the ball down and he brought it back up and didn't have anything on it."

There was one final frustration for the Red Sox. York and Doerr led off the ninth with singles, and with one out the Sox had runners on first and third. Catcher Roy Partee went out on a foul pop to Stan Musial. Pinch hitter Tom McBride hit a tough-play grounder to Schoendienst, who flipped to shortstop Marty Marion at second. The throw beat a sliding Pinky Higgins by the narrowest of margins, and the Red Sox had lost a World Series for the first time in franchise history.

In the loser's clubhouse, Williams was as silent as his bat had been.

In the heat of the moment Pesky chose to shoulder all the blame. "I'm the goat. It's my fault. I'm to blame. I had the ball in my hand. I hesitated and gave Slaughter six steps. . . . I couldn't hear anybody. There was too much yelling. It looked like an ordinary single."

Teammates put a stop to the self-flagellation. Someone said, "Sit down, Johnny."

Legally, he was still John M. Paveskovich. His father immigrated from Yugoslavia after the turn of the century, and young Johnny was one of six children. His parents could neither read, nor write, but his father found work in an Oregon sawmill. Oregon kids, not accustomed to Yugoslavian names, didn't bother saying Paveskovich, and John M. Paveskovich became Johnny Pesky on all but the most official documents. Even his teachers called him Pesky.

His father discouraged baseball and told him, "If you play ball, you'll be a bum. All your life, you'll be a bum." The Tigers, Indians, Yankees, Browns, and Cardinals were interested in young Johnny, but Mr. and Mrs. Paveskovich liked Red Sox scout Ernie Johnson, and Johnny signed with Boston. He signed in 1939, just as Williams was making his big splash in the majors. Pesky was in the big leagues three years later and cracked 205 hits at the age of twenty-one when he replaced Cronin at short. After his rookie season, he went off to war with Williams, DiMaggio, and the rest. He broke the 200-hit barrier again in 1946 and was a table-setter for Williams throughout the golden days of the late forties.

Pesky was just another Series role player struggling to contribute when the Curse of the Bambino tapped him on the throwing shoulder. In subsequent years he moved to third base to accommodate slugging shortstop Vern Stephen and became more than adequate at the hot corner. He was the first Red Sox player to have three straight 200-hit seasons (Williams never did it, he walked too often) and hit .307 in ten seasons with the Sox. Since retiring as a player he's served the BoSox in every department except concessions and ground crew. He's been a coach, a radio and television broadcaster, an advertising salesman, and managed the team in 1963. He was named assistant general manager after the 1984 season but continued to help on the field, swatting fungoes and offering advice to young players seeking help. Pesky has served the Red Sox faithfully and loyally for well over forty years and is one of the great gentlemen of the game. Perhaps he was chosen to carry the weight because he was one of the few strong enough to survive.

Generations of fans have blamed Pesky for hesitating, for holding the ball.

"I don't think I did," Pesky said a lifetime [forty-three years] later. "I was just turning to see it all in one motion because anytime you're a cutoff man you've got to get rid of the ball.

"At first I was a little sensitive to it. I didn't like the insinuations. People made me feel like I was insignificant and that I did it on purpose, which is far from the truth because, Christ, no one ever wanted to win a ball game more than I did, or any of us for that matter. After a few years, you know, you get used to the idea. And I said well, if people wanna blame ya they're gonna blame ya. And those that are sympathetic say, 'Gee, John, it's just one of those things that happened,' and I say, 'Yeah, but it happened in the World Series.'

"I used to get mad when I was asked about it. Now I just take it in stride. Time heals a lot of wounds. If a guy is honest about it and says, 'Well, Johnny, I think you did,' what am I gonna say? I can't change it. I respect opinion. If he wants to blame me, that's his right. I don't think I held on to the ball that long."

Doerr remembered it this way: "Higgins was at third and he might have a play and he can't leave his position. I might have a play at second base and I can't leave my position. There were thirty-three thousand people yelling. Everybody said, 'Well, why didn't you call out the play?' Well, I could have yelled my lungs out and he never would have heard me. It was just one of those split-second things. I say that if the ball had been hit to right center and I had the play, the same thing probably would have happened to me. It was just one of those unfortunate things and Johnny got more blame in that than he should have. He didn't hesitate all that much. It was just one of those daring things that Slaughter got away with. He would have been a bum if he got thrown out. . . . We just didn't play the kind of ball we were capable of playing."

Pesky said he never had nightmares about the play but continued to replay it in his head. He was forced to think about it when asked, but admitted there were times when he thought about it even when he was alone. "But not so much in the last fifteen years," he added.

That's a comfort. A guy *maybe* makes a tiny mistake in 1946 and by the time 1975 rolls around, he's just about stopped dwelling on it.

"That happened forty-three years ago. I'm an old bastard," the little big man said between cigar puffs. "There are so many guys that throw cold water on everything. It's a terrible way to be remembered and I wish I could have done something of importance that was involved in winning the ball game, like a base hit or a good play or whatever. Stealing a base. It just didn't happen in my case and I thought sure we'd be in four or five World Series."

There were no more World Series for Pesky, Doerr, Dominic DiMaggio, and the great Ted Williams.

◇

Pesky still wears the horns, but the true goat of the 1946 World Series was the Splendid Splinter, Ted Williams. After the final out in 1946, Williams wept in the showers, gave his World Series check ($2,077.06) to clubhouse man Johnny Orlando, then got on a train from St. Louis and cried some more.

"He felt very bad," Pesky remembered. "He actually cried. He had his head down. They had a picture [an Associated Press photo that ran worldwide] that didn't show the tears, but I know he cried. He wanted to win so badly for Mr. Yawkey. He had a great love for that man."

It was an awful couple of weeks for Williams, starting with the bruise on the elbow in the senseless exhibition game. Against the Cardinals, he went 5–25, all singles, one a bunt. He walked five times, struck out three times, and fouled out or flied out eleven times. He scored only two runs and knocked in one. In Game 7 he was twice stung by sensational catches—one by broken down Terry Moore and one by Walker.

Babe Ruth sounded like a man who knew something. When Ruth was asked about the 1946 Sox, the first Red Sox World Series team since his 1918 edition, the Bambino said, "Bobby Doerr and not Ted Williams is the number-one man of the Red Sox in my book." Doerr had at least one hit in every Series game and batted .409, more than double Williams's .200.

"We had quite a spell between the time we clinched the pennant and the World Series," Doerr remembered in 1989. "I really wasn't hitting good going into the World Series and I was quite concerned about it. But just a day or two before I just felt real good. It just happened to be a lucky deal. I can't really explain it other than it was just one of those cycles or periods of time that I felt good. Brecheen wasn't tough to look at. We should have tried to take him more to the opposite field or through the middle. He had great command of mixing his speeds, a little scroogie, and I think that if we could have just gone the other way more with him we would have done much better with Brecheen. He wasn't really that tough. He had good command of everything, but he was nice to walk up and hit at.

"We were flat for that Series. I have to say you have a letdown after you clinch the pennant, and we had too much time. And of course Ted, a lot of people didn't realize he'd get that virus once or twice a year and he had that little virus where he wasn't that sharp and then he got hit in the elbow. They said they knew how to pitch him and that they scouted him and all that. Well, you could scout him forever, but if you throw the ball over the plate, there was no way you were going to get him out. He didn't have that real good Series, but he wasn't up to par really and I never heard him say he had the virus. He never did alibi on that and of course I admire him for it."

"We just didn't hit that Series," remembered Ferriss, the Game 7 starter. "We had to wait for St. Louis and Brooklyn to play it off, and Williams got hit in the elbow. We didn't think he swung as good after that. He was in the whirlpool every morning with that thing. He never made anything to do with it, never used it as an excuse, but you know, he didn't hit in that Series. The really great ones can have a bad series in a short series and the Cardinals had a good ball club."

"I'll be damned if I know how they stopped Ted," Pesky said. "And the thing of it is, those Cardinals had a couple of rabble-rousers over there and Eddie Dyer told them, 'Don't say anything to Williams. Just leave him alone. Don't get him mad.' "

Clif Keane remembered, "Brecheen, of course, stopped Williams cold. I always felt, ever since that Series, that umpires become pitcher's umpires during the World Series. Brecheen would throw inside and Williams would back away and during the season those were balls, but during the World Series they became strikes. Umpires work better with pitchers during the World Series."

Williams still wouldn't use the elbow alibi in 1989 when he spoke of the Series. "I can't really say," he said. "I've never made that excuse and I'm not really sure whether it hurt me that much or it didn't. I'm not sure at all that that was the reason I didn't hit. Hell, they didn't pitch me any different. I got 1–9 against Brecheen in the World Series and the next year in Chicago I got up against him twice and hit two bullets to right field—doubles. Just hot and cold."

The train ride home was a twenty-five-hour funeral procession. Williams sat alone in his roomette and glanced at books on saltwater, trout, and fly fishing. Teammates tried to cheer up Pesky in the dining car and friendly scribes flashed stats that showed past Series flops by Joe Gordon, Billy Herman, Bill Dickey, and Red Rolfe. General Manager Eddie Collins, a veteran of nine World Series, said this was the toughest of them all.

There was a little action on the quiet procession. According to Keane, the Sox manager went after one of the writers.

"Maybe three hundred writers had voted on who would win the Series and two hundred ninety-eight voted for the Red Sox," said Keane. "Roger Birtwell and Huck Finnegan voted for the Cardinals in seven games and the Cardinals won in seven. We get on the train coming home after losing and Joe Cronin went after Finnegan with a bread knife at the table. Went after him with a knife. Believe me."

As the train got closer to Boston, there were some Red Sox fans gathered on platforms in western Massachusetts factory towns. There were three hundred loyalists waiting at the Huntington Avenue stop and another fifty at South Station. Bobby Doerr got off the train and packed his car for the long drive to Oregon. Ruth Pesky came in from Lynn to greet husband, John. Williams was whisked away by a policeman friend. Mayor James Michael Curley had planned a win-or-lose reception for Boston's team, but it was called off. Losers didn't ride in floats in the forties.

"It was a great letdown," said Doerr. "Every time I see the Super Bowl or a World Series now I always have a feeling of what the losing part of the thing is, and I always felt that was the one thing I look back on. You can't do anything about it. Looking back, that's the one thing that you miss."

"It was a good ball club, but I thought our '48, '49, and '50 clubs were better," said Pesky. "You can't win without pitching. We had great power, and the guys who didn't hit for power were good players. That was a series that we should have won, but it didn't work out.

Brecheen was a guy like [Mike] Boddicker, but he was left-handed. The only left-handed hitters in our lineup in those years were Ted and myself."

In one final, telling bit of housekeeping, Thomas A. Yawkey scheduled appointments with his fallen heroes, and a parade of players filed through the owner's chambers where they were presented with salary raises for 1947. "I did not give the boys bonuses," said Yawkey. "It was just a salary increase. Judge Landis made a rule against giving bonuses for winning the pennant. I didn't give them all the same sized check. After all, a fellow who sat on the bench all year hardly deserved as much as one who won twenty-five games. But they all got something."

Ernest Lawrence Thayer's "Casey at the Bat" was quoted on the front page of the *Globe* the day after the stunning loss. It would not be the first time Boston would take on the joyless characteristics of Mudville, USA.

In 1947, John M. Paveskovich walked into a Massachusetts probate court, plunked down $75, and officially changed his name to Pesky. He might just as well have changed his name to Denny Galehouse, Joe McCarthy, Luis Aparicio, Jim Burton, Mike Torrez, or Bill Buckner. He was immortal, a man with no need for a name. Fair or unfair, he was, is, and forever will be the man who held the ball. He still stands in shallow left-center, holding the ball and waiting . . . waiting for the Game 7 World Series victory that never comes.

FIVE

Babe Ruth died in August 1948. It's been estimated that two hundred thousand mourners passed his coffin at Yankee Stadium. Another seventy-five thousand, most standing outside, attended the funeral at St. Patrick's Cathedral, August 19.

Joe Dugan and Waite Hoyt, a pair of former teammates, served as pallbearers. It was a brutally hot day, and walking down the steps of St. Patrick's, carrying the Great One, Hoyt said, "Boy, I'd give anything for a cold beer right now."

Dugan motioned to the casket and said, "What do you think the Big Fella would give?"

The only larger funeral in Ruth's lifetime was Franklin Delano Roosevelt's. Columnist Jimmy Cannon wrote, "What Babe Ruth is comes down, one generation handing it to the next, as a national heirloom. . . . It is part of our national history that all boys dream of being Babe Ruth before they are anyone else."

In New England, the betrayal of the Bambino remains a regional embarrassment, and it was clear that the Sox were still paying for the sins of Frazee when Boston's powerhouse teams of the late forties failed in the clutch. Never was this more painful than in 1948 and 1949 when the Boston Red Sox won 192 baseball games, compiled an aggregate winning percentage of .621, drew 3,155,448 fans to Fenway Park, yet failed to win a pennant. Boston finished second both years, one game out of first place. These Red Sox were no longer a laughable lot. Instead, they were muscle-flexing silver medalists. They were the forefathers of a new device that would torture Boston fans into the 1990s. This is when the groundwork was laid for a macabre series of near misses.

The fabled 1948 and 1949 disappointments were set up by the stunning World Series loss to the underdog Cardinals. The 1947 Red Sox were forgettable. Still fat and happy with their World Series pay raises (the trained eye begins to see a disturbing pattern there), they played the first night games at Fenway, suffered a chronic and contagious breakout of sore arms (Ferriss, Hughson, and Harris went from sixty-two wins in 1946, to twenty in 1947), and finished third, fourteen games behind the Yankees. In September of this disappointing season, Cronin went upstairs to take over the general manager's job in place of the ailing Eddie Collins, and Yawkey brought former Yankee skipper Joe McCarthy out of retirement to manage the Red Sox. McCarthy was sixty years old and the winningest (.614 percentage remains tops) manager in the history of the game. He won seven World Series with the Yankees and never managed a second-division team. He had declined an offer to manage the Red Sox in 1931.

Yawkey's hiring of McCarthy was just one more example of the Red Sox trying to get the upper hand on the Yankees pirating some greatness. After all, early in the century the Yankees had taken Ruth and a raft of Boston starters. Eddie Barrow, the last man to manage the Red Sox to a World Series victory, became business manager of the Yankee dynasty that Ruth delivered. Even Bob Quinn, the only Red Sox owner between Frazee and Yawkey, would eventually have Yankee ties. In 1988, Bob Quinn's grandson became general manager of George Steinbrenner's Yankees.

And, of course, there was McCarthy, the man who couldn't lose in New York, then couldn't win in Boston. McCarthy had never won a *close* pennant race, but that hardly seemed his fault. His Yankee teams had dominated the league for more than a decade. When the Red Sox acquired this baseball giant, it was considered a coup. Who bothered to point out that in the only two tight races of his career, 1940 and 1944, McCarthy had seen his Yankee team lose in the final week of the season? It seemed only a meaningless footnote at the time—like a hairline crack in a bolt that eventually reduces a skyscraper to rubble.

It certainly wasn't something you could get McCarthy to talk about.

"McCarthy would never talk about the decisions he made," remarked Clif Keane, longtime *Globe* baseball scribe. "You couldn't get McCarthy to say anything. Nothing. You'd look in and he'd be smoking a cigar and you'd say 'Hi, Joe' and that was it. He wouldn't tell you a fucking word. Nothing."

McCarthy was a strong personality, and there was early doubt about his ability to get along with the volatile Williams. McCarthy had taken over the Yankees when Ruth was the established star in 1931 and the two men never hit it off. Ruth thought McCarthy's lack of playing experience disqualified him from managing, while McCarthy believed that Frankie Frisch and Honus Wagner were better ball players than Ruth. When he joined the Red Sox almost twenty years later, it was known that McCarthy had always been a dress-code guy, and there was speculation that this would lead to a feud with the ever-casual Williams. McCarthy defused the situation immediately. Knowing that Williams would rather stick needles in his eyes than wear neckties, McCarthy showed up without a necktie when he first appeared at the club's spring training site in Sarasota. Williams and McCarthy got along, and to this day Williams says only good things about his controversial (now deceased) skipper.

McCarthy left all of his players alone and there were few problems. He was a passive manager who stayed out of the way of his talent. He was also a hard drinker who favored White Horse scotch. He didn't like pipe smokers, blond-haired Poles, or telephones in the clubhouse. He didn't particularly like reporters, and he hated to see his players reading about themselves. In exchange for this quirk, he was protective of his troops and would never publicly rip a player. Williams said later than no manager got more out of his players than Joe McCarthy. Pesky agreed. Meanwhile, Doerr was a little nervous under McCarthy.

"He didn't say much," remembered Doerr. "He was a very sharp guy. I didn't know quite how to take McCarthy. I played for Cronin my whole career. He was a wonderful guy to play for. McCarthy was very reserved, never say anything to you. It was a little harder for me to play for him, but I had to respect him for his brilliance as a manager."

Like Doerr, Stephens was uncomfortable with McCarthy, and Hughson would eventually say, "The only man in baseball I completely disliked was Joe McCarthy." Williams disagrees:

> Cronin I felt I was pretty close to. He was wonderful to me. I loved him. I had great respect for McCarthy. I'd like to think I

could look into what he was doing, understand what he was doing a little bit better than most guys. He was a helluva manager, boys. He knew the players. He knew how to handle them, individually. He never did talk that much. He was always friendly. Some of the guys were afraid of him a little bit. I don't know what the hell it was, but they were a little afraid of him a little bit. When they first announced he was coming, I thought, "Well, I won't be with the Red Sox anymore." But it couldn't have worked out better. I feel that I was more concerned about my overall play when McCarthy was there than with any other manager. He'd just instill that businesslike attitude to me and to all the players as far as I'm concerned. In fact when I managed four years I tried to instill that in all the young kids. That this was business and this was the most important thing you were gonna do and you'd better get with it.

The 1948 Sox got off to a great start in November of 1947 when new General Manager Joe Cronin (he'd failed to win a World Series in thirteen years as manager) made two stellar trades with the St. Louis Browns. The Sox plucked right-handers Ellis Kinder and Jack Kramer from the Brownies, along with slugging shortstop Vern Stephens and utilityman Billy Hitchcock. In return, Boston sent $375,000 plus a truckload of chattel (ten players, mostly minor leaguers) to St. Louis. It was a heist like some of the ones Jake Ruppert pulled on financially strapped Harry Frazee in the boring twenties.

Ruth visited McCarthy at the Red Sox spring training site in 1948. For the Babe, it was the last spring. The Sox came north and got off to a rotten start, falling eleven and a half games out May 31. Boston lost its first game, 4–2, as the Sox were shut down by a war hero lefty named Lou Brissie. Brissie had taken some German shrapnel in the left leg during the war and wore a shinguard to protect the war wound. Nobody knew it then, but six months later the Red Sox would lose their last game of the year in Fenway, and again the rival pitcher would be a southpaw war hero.

The 1948 Red Sox had enough pitching to dig out of their spring slump. Kramer was en route to an 18–5 season and was joined in the rotation by Kinder, Dobson, and Parnell. The Sox started to win and joined a three-team race with the Yankees and Indians.

Boston led the league from August 26 to September 26 (Cleveland trailed by four and a half on Labor Day) and held sole possession of first with nine games left, five at home, but couldn't hold the lead. With seven games to play, the Sox, Indians, and Yankees were all 91–56. The Sox fell two games back with four to play and had to win their last four (eliminating the Yankees on the next-to-last day of the regular season) to force the first playoff game in American League history. On September 30, 1948, the Red Sox beat the Yankees, 10–5, before 31,354 at Fenway while Hal Newhouser and the Tigers were beating Bob Feller and the Indians, 7–1, in front of 74,181 by the shores of Lake Erie.

Playing on a bad leg, Joe DiMaggio cracked four hits for the Yanks and was awarded the longest and loudest ovation any enemy player had received at Fenway since the Babe's last game in 1934. DiMaggio later said the Fenway ovation was the greatest thrill of his career. "He deserved it," said brother Dominic. Joe stayed in Boston to watch the playoff and attend Dominic's wedding.

In Cleveland, Feller, who had beaten Newhouser in seven of eight previous meetings, lasted less than three innings, and flamboyant club president Bill Veeck admitted, "We couldn't have beaten Newhouser if we had played for two days." A photographer asked Veeck to pose with a "bewildered" look on his face and Veeck said, "What the hell do you think this look on my face is, anyway?" The Indians got on a train at 9 P.M., due in Boston at 10 A.M., scheduled to play in Fenway at 1:30 P.M.

The Sox and Indians were both 96–58 when the Tribe set out for the sudden-death overtime finale. Ironically, it was the Boston Braves who waited for the winner. The Hub of the Universe had never played host to a subway Series.

"Oh sure, we'll be the favorites tomorrow, you can bet on that," said Williams. "We want to get that dough too, you know."

Williams's words reflect a more innocent, hungrier time in baseball. These were the days when a World Series share meant a player might be able to buy a new car or maybe even take a month off before starting a winter job selling sporting goods at a department store. In the 1980s and 1990s, the postseason "dough" amounts to little more than tips and soy sauce for financially-fat ball players. Guys making the minimum still care, and the greedy players still care, but the financial incentives of postseason play aren't the same as when Williams and Company prepared for Lou Boudreau and the Cleveland Indians.

Both managers kept their pitching plans secret. In Cleveland, the player/manager Lou Boudreau said, "I don't know who'll pitch against the Red Sox tomorrow. It could be any one of three men. Yes, it could be any one of six men. It could be among Bob Lemon, [Bob] Feller, and Gene Bearden."

Williams and teammate Wally Moses figured Lemon would start for the Tribe.

Boudreau chose Bearden, a rookie southpaw with a 19–7 record and a 2.43 ERA, a war veteran with aluminum plates in his head and left leg. Bearden was twenty-eight years old and had been presumed dead after his battleship was torpedoed in World War II. Gordon and Johnny Berardino argued with their manager, but Boudreau wanted to go with the kid.

After beating the Yankees Sunday, McCarthy said, "I can't name my pitcher for tomorrow's game. I haven't had a chance to get my thoughts together." Reporters pressed the tight-lipped manager. "Maybe I'll get the word tonight in a dream," said McCarthy. "Or better still, just find some nice little man and rub his curly head."

Parnell and veteran Kinder were the best guesses. Parnell was 3–2 against the Tribe in 1948 and seemed anxious to get the nod when he spoke with reporters on Sunday. He had pitched against the Yankees Saturday but claimed he was ready to go. Kinder was 0–1 against Cleveland in 1948, but hadn't pitched in four days and would be working with a full complement of rest. Plus, a right-hander like Kinder figured to do better against a Cleveland lineup stocked with righty sluggers like Boudreau, Ken Keltner, and Joe Gordon. The Sox were 11–11 against the Indians in 1948, 6–5 at Fenway.

McCarthy's choice remained a mystery up until game time, and the decision to pitch journeyman Denny Galehouse remains one of the giant blunders in Red Sox history.

Baseball writer Clif Keane said, "Birdie Tebbetts claimed that the old man, McCarthy, called him into his office after the last game and said 'I want you to go out and ask all the pitchers which one would like to start this game tomorrow.' So he went to Parnell, and Parnell said something about a sore arm. He went to Jack Kramer. He went to Kinder. He went to four or five guys. And he went to Galehouse. Galehouse was a very nice man. A high-class guy. He had pitched six innings in relief against Cleveland during the season. He said, 'I'll pitch the game.' Tebbetts went back to the old man and he told him Gale-house was willing to pitch the game. And according to Tebbetts, the old man had a piece of paper on his desk and he turned it over and it was Galehouse's name."

"That's not a true story," Parnell said in 1989. "Dave Egan [columnist for the *Boston Record*] started it. No one had a choice. You didn't have a choice with McCarthy. He designated who was going to pitch and that was it. I thought I was going to pitch. We all wanted to pitch because if we win that ball game, it means at least $5,000 to us and that was big money at that time. McCarthy came to me in the clubhouse and said, 'Son, I've changed my mind. I'm going with the right-hander. The elements are against the left-hander today because the wind is blowing out.' Hell, I'd pitched a lot of games with the wind blowing out. Kramer wanted to pitch it. Dobson wanted to pitch it. No one expected Denny Galehouse to pitch it because Denny was at the end of his career."

"Parnell and Kinder would have pitched," said Pesky. "To me, McCarthy was just a fine man and knew baseball. He figured Galehouse had plenty of rest."

Doerr, the Hall of Famer, looked back forty years later and said, "I know when we came out there we all expected that Parnell would be pitching. It was just a surprise when we heard Galehouse was gonna pitch. It was really a surprise. I talked to Parnell after that and he said he felt he was ready to pitch and he had had fair success against Cleveland. But it was one of those things where McCarthy felt he might surprise the other ball club."

Denny Galehouse in the spring of 1989 said, "It's never come out because it would hurt some people. I knew it the night before. Birdie Tebbetts told me. He said that he was pretty sure. He mentioned it to my wife and to me after the ball game, out in the players' parking lot."

While all of baseball wondered what McCarthy was thinking, Gale-house and his wife drove to their home in Newton Center and had dinner. He thought about the game, about the success he'd enjoyed against the Indians, and he slept well. Denny Galehouse wasn't going to make too big a deal out of one ball game, even if it was a playoff.

Meanwhile, Parnell went home to his wife, in Wellesley. His parents were visiting and everybody encouraged him to get to bed early. Parnell was in bed by 9 P.M.

When Galehouse got to the ballpark the next day, a shiny white baseball was in his locker. Tebbetts was right. Galehouse was the man. The 8–7 journeyman got dressed and went to the outfield to stand around with the other pitchers. None of the Indians knew which pitcher was starting for Boston, and McCarthy wanted to keep it that way. Most of the Red Sox still didn't know.

"I came to the ballpark assuming I was pitching," said Parnell. "Normally the starting pitcher takes his time getting dressed because there's nothing to do while batting practice is going on. And I'm sitting around the clubhouse just taking my good old time. That's when McCarthy came up and told me he had changed his mind. I couldn't say anything. I was stunned by it. And then when I went out on the field I think the ball club was stunned too because they asked me what I was doing out there and I told them I wasn't pitching. I think it had a mental effect on us, I really do, because I think everybody was under the assumption that I was going to be the pitcher on that day."

Don Fitzpatrick was a nineteen-year-old batboy from Brookline in 1948. He was the messenger sent to retrieve Galehouse from the outfield. In 1989, Fitzpatrick remembered, "I was told to go out and get Galehouse. He was outside. I think he was out in the field, but he wasn't working hard or anything, but I came out and told him that he was wanted inside. He kind of looked and he just went in. It was a very secretive thing. I guess they felt if I slid out and told him it wouldn't look as obvious as if the coach went out."

Galehouse went to the locker room to lie down for a few minutes then started warming up in front of the grandstand as fans slapped one another upside the head. Across the field, Boudreau was similarly stunned. He saw Galehouse warming up and assumed the Sox had another pitcher getting loose somewhere beneath the stands.

"It looked like he [Galehouse] had good stuff warming up, but they just hit him," said Pesky.

They just hit him. The ordinary righty was probably tired. The home plate ump told him he had good stuff, but it looked too good to the Indians. Galehouse had warmed up several times in Sunday's crucial victory and didn't have much left. He was routed in the fourth. Boudreau had four hits including a pair of homers, and knuckleballing Bearden beat Boston, 8–3, to bring Cleveland its first pennant since

1920 (the same year Frazee sold Ruth). Bearden threw 135 pitches and became only the second lefty to go the distance in Fenway in 1948.

Bearden had some help. The Cleveland trainer was Lefty Weisman from Chelsea, Massachusetts, and according to Fitzpatrick, Lefty was giving him little shots of brandy between innings. Perhaps Galehouse could have used some liquid relaxation.

MVP-to-be Boudreau homered in the first, and it was 1–1 in the fourth when Keltner broke it open with a three-run homer off Galehouse. Kinder came out of the pen, but the rout was on and the pennant was lost. Red Sox fans awarded Boudreau a standing ovation when he came to bat in the ninth.

The game ended at 3:53 P.M. Indian owner Bill Veeck, wooden leg and all, vaulted over the rail and embraced his players. In Cleveland, factory whistles sounded and police and fire engine sirens split the autumn air. According to a UPI report, "Shrieking girls were kissed on the street. Men poured out of bars waving glasses and offered drinks to passersby under the approving eyes of policemen. Confetti swirled down from every office window and grew ankle-deep in the streets."

Boston was hit by a killing frost later that night. The only hot spot was the Kenmore Hotel where Boudreau and his players danced on the ceiling. Boudreau and his coaches left the players' party at 3 A.M. and went to get Chinese food at Ruby Foo's. Two weeks later, they celebrated again in Boston after beating the Braves in the World Series.

Galehouse pitched only two big league innings after the 1948 playoff game. "You feel bad about it naturally," he said forty-one years later when he was living in Doylestown, Ohio, scouting for the San Diego Padres. "But life goes on."

Life went on. Galehouse barely made the team in 1949, pitched once, then was released and retired. He hasn't been in Boston in forty years and has little realization that he's still better remembered than the great molasses flood of 1919. The man entrusted with Boston's hopes in the first playoff game in American League history never won another game in the major leagues.

"I was the guy that should have pitched it," said Parnell. "I had the most rest. I should have been the pitcher of that ball game, without a doubt."

◇

Sox fans showed their resilience and came back for more in 1949. They were rewarded with another great pennant chase . . . but no flag.

The Boston 49ers might have been the strongest Red Sox entry. Like the team that came along twenty-nine years later, they scared everyone in baseball, yet failed to win the pennant.

After the playoff loss of 1948 Dick O'Connell was brought in as assistant GM and changes were made in the farm system. Boston went 5–6 in April, 15–10 in May. The Sox won ten of eleven in late June . . . then the Yankees came to town on June 28, 29, and 30. New York had a new manager, Casey Stengel. A second-division finisher in nine of nine managerial seasons, Stengel had been a member of the Braves and was considered something of a buffoon around Boston. Few remembered that he hit .364 for Brooklyn when Ruth and the Red Sox beat the Dodgers in five games in the 1916 World Series. New Yorkers regarded him with some suspicion, and many Yankee players were bitter over the firing of Bucky Harris.

The 1949 Yanks had played in Boston once already, drawing 100,000 fans to Fenway for the opening series of the season. Joe DiMaggio did not play in that first April series because he was recovering from surgery on a bone spur in his right heel. Joltin' Joe waited until June to make his comeback, and it was like watching the unveiling of Michelangelo's *David*.

This was the Great DiMaggio who inspired Ernest Hemingway's Santiago in *The Old Man and the Sea*. He'd missed all of spring training and the first sixty-five games of the regular season. He'd played in an exhibition game against the Giants and worked out about eight times when he was penciled into Stengel's lineup June 28. DiMaggio singled and homered to win the opener, 5–4, as 36,228 watched. He hit two homers, one a three-run clout in the second game of the series, then hit another three-run homer to win the finale. He batted .455 with four homers and nine RBI in the three games, and a plane circled Fenway with a trailer message that read, "The Great DiMaggio."

The Red Sox had won ten of eleven prior to the Yankee series, but DiMaggio's bat sent them reeling, and Boston lost eight straight before snapping the streak July 5 at Yankee Stadium. By that time, the Sox trailed by twelve and a half games.

Boston sent five players—Williams, Parnell, catcher Tebbetts, short-stop Vern Stephens, and first baseman Billy Goodman—to the All-Star game in Brooklyn. The Sox were in fifth place, twelve games out at the halfway point. But in July and August the Red Sox won twenty-six of thirty-four to move to within five and a half games of the Yankees. Doerr returned from a back injury, Parnell was a stopper, and brother Dominic carried the Sox with a thirty-four-game hitting streak, still the best in Red Sox history. The streak ended when Joe DiMaggio made a shoe-top grab of Dom's sinking liner in the eighth inning of a 6–3 victory over the Yankees August 9. On September 26, before 67,434 at Yankee Stadium, Boston came from four runs back and beat New York, 7–6, thanks to an eighth-inning squeeze bunt by Doerr. Pesky scored the winning run, sliding safely under the tag of Yankee catcher Ralph Houk. The comeback was complete, and McCarthy's Sox were in sole possession of first place with a week to go.

This was no fall fold. The September Sox won eleven straight and fashioned a 19–5 record in what was usually Boston's worst month. They won their last twenty-one home games and finished with a 61–16 Fenway record. Kinder, a twenty-two-game winner, was 15–1 at home. The Sox won fifty-nine of seventy-eight games after falling behind by twelve and a half July 4. A Parnell wild pitch cost the Red Sox a ball game in Washington and broke an eleven-game winning streak, but the Sox beat the Senators, 11–9, at Griffith Stadium on Friday, September 30, and took their one-game lead to New York for the final (two-game) series of the season. Boston needed only one victory to win the pennant, and the Sox had bookend twenty-game winners Parnell and Kinder set to throw.

The Yankees dropped into second place on Friday, losing a 4–1 decision to the Philadelphia A's, but manager Stengel said, "We're going to win two, boys. We're going to keep you here all winter."

In a page-one story from New York, *Boston Globe* baseball writer Harold Kaese led with, "Unless some heartless tragedian gets his slimy paws on the script, the 1949 baseball season is about to have its fairy tale ending for Boston baseball fans."

The Yanks had lost six of nine, and Joe DiMaggio was weakened by pneumonia. The Yankees gave him a "day" prior to the first game of the crucial series, presenting DiMaggio with three hundred quarts of ice cream and a car. Mrs. Rosalie DiMaggio, mother of the brothers

DiMaggio, was flown in for the occasion and announced her impartiality. Sox wives were told to start packing because Mr. Yawkey would send them down to New York on a special train as soon as the Sox clinched.

Bobby Brown was a Yankee infielder who would later become president of the American League. In 1946, when he came up as a rookie, he had arranged to buy World Series tickets through Red Sox second baseman Bobby Doerr. He cut a deal with Doerr that said he would let Doerr buy some Series tickets if his Yankee teams ever made it. Brown and Doerr met before the first game of the final weekend set in 1949 and Brown gave Doerr the name of a friend who would need World Series tickets in Boston. Doerr didn't give Brown any name. Doerr was going to be in the World Series and wouldn't be needing any favors.

The Red Sox took a 4–0 lead in the Saturday game. Yankee starter Allie Reynolds was lifted, trailing 2–0, in the third, and New York reliever Joe Page walked home two runs before getting a man out. Page settled down after that and allowed only a single by Doerr in the final 6.2 innings. It was Page's longest outing of the 1949 season. The Yankees had won forty-two of the sixty games Page had appeared in, and this was a weapon the Red Sox didn't have.

And then there was the Great DiMaggio. Still weak from a bout with viral pneumonia (he'd lost eighteen pounds), DiMaggio led off the fourth with a double off Parnell. New York scored two in the fourth. When Yogi Berra singled home Phil Rizzuto to cut Boston's lead to 4–3 in the fifth, Joe Dobson relieved Parnell. DiMaggio greeted Dobson with a single that loaded the bases, and the Yanks tied it on a double play groundout. With two out in the eighth, Johnny Lindell homered off Dobson to give the Yankees a 5–4 lead. The Sox went out feebly, and both teams were 96–57, with one game to play. DiMaggio called his teammates "the gamest, fightin'est bunch of guys that ever lived."

Bobby Doerr gave Bobby Brown a World Series ticket request before the Sunday game. There was doubt where there had been no doubt.

"We were tough," said Brown. "We were a tough team against tough teams and against tough pitching. We didn't have the statistics that Boston had, but we had guys who, in big games against good pitching, could hit. And we had awfully good pitching. We always felt that in a big series we had a damn good chance of winning it. It wasn't like it was a lead pipe cinch, but we just thought we could win. It was a heckuva lot easier being in the stadium than being in Fenway. We always thought we had a damn good chance. We never thought that we were going to lose."

McCarthy and the fans of Boston turned to Kinder, a hard-drinking, twenty-three-game winner who was unbeaten in his last twenty starts. Kinder was 5–0 against the Yanks in 1948 and 1949, however McCarthy had been using him in relief, and the thirty-five-year-old righty had pitched in four of the previous seven games, seven of the last fifteen. The Yankees had Vic Raschi, working on four days of rest.

With the Yankees leading, 1–0, in the eighth, McCarthy lifted Kinder for a pinch hitter. The Sox had one out and nobody aboard when Tom Wright, a kid up from Louisville where he had led the American Association in hitting (.307), went up to bat against Raschi in place of Kinder. Wright walked, but was erased when Dominic DiMaggio grounded into a double play.

With Kinder gone, McCarthy went back to Parnell, who'd been routed on Saturday (Kinder and Parnell started ten, and relieved seven of the final nineteen games), and Parnell was greeted by a Tommy Henrich homer. Yogi Berra singled after the homer, and Parnell was yanked in favor of Tex Hughson. Hughson got DiMaggio to ground into a double play but then gave up a pair of singles and a walk that loaded the bases. Jerry Coleman came up.

Globe writer Clif Keane remembered the play: "Jerry Coleman was at the bat. And we had a guy in right field playing out in North Dakota somewhere. Coleman was a little banjo hitter. He was like Marty Barrett, he'd tap the ball to right field a lot. And he hit a ball to right field. The guy came in. Al Zarilla. He tried to make a shoestring catch of the ball. The ball bounced and went over his head for a double and all the runs scored."

Forty years later, Zarilla talked about the ball. "People don't realize that after that I was in the hospital for ten days. I popped my knee. All the blood vessels broke. With two outs, bases loaded, if I play back they're going to get two runs. I was more in on him. Bobby Doerr threw him out at third base, so you know it wasn't hit very deep. It was just one of those things where you do or die. I had a chance and I made a couple good plays before. You either do or die. It was tough. When grown men cry, it hurts."

"I didn't think he was playing too deep," remembered Brown.

Trailing 5–0, the Red Sox rallied for three in the ninth. Doerr tripled home two runs and Goodman scored Doerr with a single strike. But Raschi hung on and got Tebbetts on a foul pop to the first baseman. The three-run rally served only to incite Sox fans, who were still steaming over McCarthy's decision to lift Kinder.

When Tebbetts popped up, Bill Dickey, sitting in the Yankee dugout, leaped in jubilation and cracked his head on the dugout roof. Joe DiMaggio said, "I've had a lot of thrills in baseball, and of all of them I'll take this victory. It's the spirit of this whole darn bunch that gets me. So this is it, and this it'll be, because I just couldn't be happier about anything as long as I'm in the game."

There was no honor or glory back in New England. In Lawrence, Massachusetts, a mock funeral procession wound down Elm Street. Twelve pallbearers, dressed in black, carried a flower-covered casket that supported a two-word placard: RED SOX. Behind the casket, thirty mourners kept pace with the funeral strains of a five-piece band. The casket was delivered to a Lawrence funeral parlor. Outside Fenway Park, close to five thousand fans who'd been in a ticket line, which started on Jersey Street and snaked down Van Ness and Lansdowne streets, broke formation and went home with full wallets and empty hearts. Some of the fans had been there forty hours, waiting for the box office to start selling World Series tickets, waiting for the clinch victory that never came. Many walked home muttering about McCarthy's decision to pinch-hit for Kinder.

Kinder told Al Hirshberg, "Goddamit, if the old man had let me bat for myself that day, we'd have won the pennant."

Doerr disagreed.

"I don't think so. That was one thing that McCarthy was sharp at— knowing the situation of pulling pitchers. He didn't miss much on that."

A day later, the subheadline over the boxscore in the *Globe* read, "No Joy in Mudville." For the second consecutive year, a parade was canceled. This time the Boston chamber of commerce had planned a parade, rally, and brunch at the Hotel Bradford, but everything was scrapped after the sad Sunday news. Sox wives never made it to New York for Yawkey's clinch party gala. Somebody else would have to eat the leftover crabmeat sandwiches.

This is where it starts—the stuff the Red Sox of the 1980s and 1990s have come to hate. These were the forefather sins that the Red Sox of today are still paying for—until a championship is won. The Red Sox were punished with twenty-eight years of ineptitude after Ruth was sold, but in the 1940s a new form of denial took hold, and it has proven to be a far worse strain on the fragile psyche of the New England region. The Red Sox have the best team, but still manage NOT to win. "Wait 'til next year" has become "How are they NOT going to win it next year," and today's Red Sox can thank the teams of the late 1940s for this perverted legacy. The fact that the 1949 Sox folded in the face of the Yankees made the pain particularly unbearable and fortified the theory that larger forces were at work.

Williams who hit "only" .305 lifetime at Yankee Stadium went 0–4 in the final weekend, and that cost him his third Triple Crown. He finished with a league-leading forty-three homers and 159 RBI, but his .34275 average was a sliver under George Kell's .3428. He went 7–34 (.206, all singles) in the 1946 World Series and the final three games in 1948 and 1949. "Certainly those were important games," Williams told Bob Costas in 1988. "I did poorly in that '46 Series and I was always just sick and probably the biggest disappointment of my career was that I didn't get back in some more Series. In Yankee Stadium, I was up eight times and walked four times. I went zero for four, and I just missed hitting a couple of home runs, at least one, but I went zero for two in each game."

The walks were no accidents. Allie Reynolds said, "I didn't pitch to Ted Williams. I couldn't fool Ted Williams. The only weakness I ever found he had was that he was a little slow on the bases, so I just walked him. It was simpler."

The 1949 Red Sox had five .300 hitters, two 20-game winners, the MVP, home run and RBI king, and three players with more than 100 RBI. The infield of Goodman, Doerr, Stephens, and Pesky still ranks as one of the best-hitting infields in baseball history. This team had the greatest home-road disparity (61–16, 35–42) of any team in the history of 154-game seasons. Boston's 19–21 record in one-run games was another bad sign, as was the fact that the Sox led the league in runners left on base, 1,284.

Doerr remembered, "The thing I look back on in '49, we lost a few games in the first part of the season that we shouldn't have lost. We had leads of like six to four and then couldn't hold 'em in the eighth or ninth inning."

On this final day in 1949 there was additional intrigue because as the Red Sox were failing after taking their fans to the edge for the third time in four years, a young man named Jackie Robinson was winning the National League flag for the Brooklyn Dodgers. Robinson led the NL with a .342 average and was voted Most Valuable Player. One can only wonder what prizes Robinson would have brought to Boston if the Red Sox had been brave enough to employ the first black player in baseball when they had the chance back in 1945.

The Sox returned to Boston Sunday night, riding the rails for five long hours. Williams described it as the longest train ride of his life, longer than the twenty-six-hour haul back from St. Louis after the 1946 World Series. In the Sox tradition, there was an ugly scene when Kinder went after McCarthy and berated the manager for blowing the season. At 10 P.M., the sad, soggy Sox rolled into Back Bay Station, where 3,000 fans waited for them. McCarthy got a little choked up at the sight of the fans. Williams just wanted to pack and go fishing. Many of the players were inebriated, and who could blame them? No doubt many Sox fans were also bombed.

Pesky said, "We came home on the train, but I don't remember getting off at South Station. I'm not a drinking man, but I was blind. My wife had to lead me to the car. Half of us were almost in tears. The thing in those years, we had so much affection for Mr. Yawkey and he treated us all so well. He was like your big brother or like a parent and that's the way we looked at him. He'd come in and he'd talk to you all the time and if you lost a tough game, he'd say you've got to give the other guy credit. He beat you at what you do best. That's part of the frustration of this damn game. Truthfully, I always thought that our overall team was better than the Yankees."

But even Yawkey admitted, "If we can't win one out of two, we don't deserve it."

McCarthy's two-year contract was up and his tenure had produced two colossal near-misses. There was media speculation that the old man might not be coming back, but Yawkey and Cronin said the decision would be McCarthy's.

Bobby Doerr was elected to the Hall of Fame in 1986. Reflecting on his career, he said, "Not being able to be on a winning World Series team is something you can't go back and do anything about. It's one of the big things. For the rest of my lifetime I'll wish I could have been on a winning, championship team in a World Series."

Williams, visiting the Hall of Fame to watch the induction of Carl Yastrzemski, in 1989, said, "To get that close every year and not do it, or to get that close and then not do it in the Series, was tough. Everything should have been there, but then from there, our club started to degenerate a little bit. Those were frustrating years, but certainly the best years of baseball in my life. Forty-nine was the toughest. To get there and have the lead coming into the last week and have our good pitchers all lined up and to lose every possible way that you can do it, that was tough. I knew it would be tough going to Yankee Stadium for two games. And their pitching was all set up. Damn right. That is the most disappointing year."

SIX

The fifties and early sixties brought more unhappy days for the Boston Red Sox. The core of the powerhouse teams from the late forties started to crumble after the 1949 playoff disappointment, and Williams was left alone to be the star player on very average teams. In New York, Yankee dominance continued as Joe DiMaggio handed the torch to a young switch-hitter named Mickey Mantle. Meanwhile, the Red Sox fortified their image as lead-footed sluggers, rewarded by an indulgent owner and mocked by the baseball community. Red Sox players were too comfortable and it showed. These were the years when New England fans rarely tasted the thrill of the race after Memorial Day. You followed the Sox to see if Ted Williams or Pete Runnels or Carl Yastrzemski could win another batting title, but there was little hope of a pennant race. The last gasp losses in the great races of 1948 and 1949 drained the team and the fandom and there was not much to cheer about for the next seventeen seasons.

The 1950 Red Sox hit .302 and scored 1,027 runs, an average of 6.67 runs per game. They compiled more hits, runs, and total bases than any team in Boston's bashing history, and they did it in a 154-game season. They scored 104 runs in one 7-game stretch. Williams became Boston's first $100,000 ball player but suffered a career-threatening injury when he cracked his left elbow while making a catch in an All-Star game. Billy Goodman won the batting crown with a .354 average and Walt Dropo hit thirty-four homers to win the Rookie of the Year award, but it was all in vain as McCarthy resigned in midseason and the Sox finished third, four games back in a race they were never really in.

The Red Sox were out of the running in each of the next sixteen summers. The Sox played sub-.500 ball the year Dwight Eisenhower was elected president (1952) and didn't get back into a pennant race until Richard Nixon was warming up for his second Oval Office bid, in 1967. From 1951 through 1966 the Sox never finished closer than eleven games out. Boston had the best player in Williams, the best announcer in Curt Gowdy, and the best ballpark in Fenway, but the team became fat and sloppy. Yawkey's millions produced a country club atmosphere that catered to big-swing, one-dimensional ball players. Williams went off to fight in the Korean War early in the 1952 season. Lou Boudreau was brought in to manage, but as ever, the Sox seemed to acquire people after their magic had been used up against Boston. Boudreau dumped his veterans and the Sox played sub-.500 ball in two of his three seasons, finishing nineteen, sixteen, and forty-two games out of first. Fans saw plenty of Green Monster mashing, but far too little good baseball. The Braves left Boston after the 1952 season and the Sox had sole rights to the marketplace, but attendance declined. The Red Sox were just plain bad, as they had been in the years after Ruth, before Yawkey. Meanwhile, the Yankees were in their latest phase of dominance, finishing first eight times in the fifties and five times in the early sixties.

It's difficult to access which form of failure has been tougher on the psyche of the Red Sox fans. New York always led Boston, but was it worse to lose in the final weekend of the season, or to fall hopelessly behind and view New York's success from afar? In the fifties and early sixties, the Red Sox were not frustrated by the Yankees as much as they were humiliated by them.

Real tragedy struck the Sox in June 1955 when Boston first baseman Harry Agganis died of a large blood clot. One of the greatest native New England athletes, Agganis had been an all-American schoolboy in Lynn, Massachusetts, then went to Boston University, where he was an all-American quarterback. He was drafted in the NFL's first round by the Cleveland Browns while he was still a junior. He signed with the Red Sox, played one season of minor league ball, then hit .251 with eleven homers in his first season in the majors in 1954. On the following June 2, he had to stop playing because of fever and chest pains, and golden boy Harry Agganis died June 27 at Sancta Maria Hospital. He was twenty-five.

"Agannis was right on the verge, boy, and you can believe me, of really doing it," said Williams. "That was a real tragedy of talent."

It would not be the last tragic episode involving a homegrown Red Sox star in the prime of his career. Outfielder Jimmy Piersall, a Connecticut native, checked into a mental hospital during his Red Sox days. Piersall came back to lead a normal life. A decade later, Tony Conigliaro, a young Swampscott slugger of infinite promise, was felled by a fastball to the head. In 1982, Conigliaro was permanently paralyzed by a heart attack. He was not yet forty.

Apart from true tragedies, the Red Sox seemed to specialize in good young pitchers who'd develop sore arms and wind up driving forklifts by the age of thirty. In 1954, the Sox had an eighteen-year-old "can't miss" pitching prospect named Frank Baumann. After dazzling hitters in the American Association, Baumann went into the army, gained weight, hurt his arm, then won only thirteen games in five seasons for the Red Sox. The names change, but the Frank Baumann story has been played out dozens of times in Sox history, and very few Boston pitching prospects (Roger Clemens, for example) have survived to deliver the numbers they promised.

Bad, but rarely boring, the Red Sox had enough money, flamboyance, and hitting to keep some fans interested during this long stretch of noncontention. The future was permanently altered when Boston outbid the Yankees for a strapping Florida schoolboy catcher named Haywood Sullivan. Zany outfielder Piersall never failed to entertain the fandom with his defense and his antics. Jackie Jensen was acquired and won an MVP, but he didn't want to fly on airplanes and had to retire. Parnell pitched a no-hitter in Fenway. Williams came back from another war, then was fined $5,000 for spitting at Boston's fans. He engaged in a duel for the batting title with teammate Pete Runnels and accidentally conked Cronin's housekeeper on the head when he flipped his bat into the stands in a regrettable gesture of disgust. Cronin left to become president of the American League. The Sox were the last major league team to put a black man on the field when Pumpsie Green played second base in 1959. Williams homered in his last at bat, and local novelist John Updike responded with a timeless essay on the clout. Carl Yastrzemski replaced Williams in the spring of 1961, and only 10,277 showed up for the Red Sox home opener. While future All-Star Jim Fregosi was left unprotected in the 1960 expansion draft, a clumsy shortstop named Don Buddin became symbolic of Sox buffoonery. Sportswriters said Buddin's license plate should read E-6. Runnels won a couple of batting crowns, and righty Don Schwall was rookie of the year. Bill Monbouquette and Earl Wilson pitched no-hitters in the same season, and pitcher Gene Conley and Pumpsie Green got off a hot team bus in New York and Conley bought a plane ticket for Tel Aviv. Dick Stuart hit seventy-five homers in two seasons but earned the nickname Stonefingers around first base. Stuart was the latest in a line of Clydesdale righty sluggers (Rudy York, Jake Jones, Walt Dropo, Dick Gernert, and Norm Zauchin were some predecessors) who were considered an essential ingredient to take advantage of Fenway. Dick Radatz became the "Monster" relief pitcher, and for two seasons was as good as any late-inning closer in the history of the game. Yastrzemski won a batting title, and local kid Conigliaro homered in his first Fenway at bat.

Things bottomed out in September 1965 when Dave Morehead (soon to be the latest Frank Baumann) pitched a weekday afternoon no-hitter in front of 1,247 fans, minutes before Mike Higgins was fired as general manager. The 1965 Red Sox drew only 652,201 fans (roughly 8,000 per game), lost 100 games, and finished a whopping 40 games behind the Minnesota Twins. Boston drew 461 for a game against the Angels on September 28, 1965. The Sox hadn't drawn fewer fans in any season since the final year of World War II, and 1965 marked Boston's first 100-loss season since 1932—the first such embarrassment in the long Yawkey reign.

The Red Sox finish ninth under Billy Herman in 1965 and ninth again (one half game out of the basement) when Herman was fired in 1966. Boston had played sub-.500 ball for eight straight seasons. But there was a ray of light at the end of the dismal 1966 season. On September 28, 1966, a crusty former utilityman named Dick Williams was hired to manage. No one knew it at the time, but this was the beginning of a new era for the Boston Red Sox.

◊

When Williams went to work in the spring of 1967, American cities were burning, flower power was blossoming on the left coast, the Smothers Brothers were taking on the network censors, and Stephen Stills was singing "paranoia strikes deep, into your life it will creep." Structure was collapsing all around, but it was in this new age of permissiveness that the Red Sox profited from the arrival of a right-wing, crew cut dugout despot.

In any essay dealing with the history of the Boston Red Sox, there is no way to minimize the contribution of the 1967 edition. This single year is a part of the Sox story just as *The Wizard of Oz* is a part of the Judy Garland story. It can be argued that the fortunes of the franchise would have turned positive regardless of 1967. A crop of young stars was ready to blossom, and with strong new management the Red Sox were bound to return to the glory days sometime in the late sixties or early seventies. Incredibly, it all happened at once. There was no transition. The skinny little girl next door became a *Playboy* centerfold overnight.

The 1967 Red Sox season permanently returned the Olde Towne Team to the place of prominence that it held in the days of Ruth and (prefifties) Williams, and forever established the baseball team as Boston's Number One sports heartthrob. Nothing electrifies New England summers more than the Red Sox in a pennant race, and it took the 1967 ball club to awake the slumbering masses and recruit a new generation of disciples who'd known nothing but batting titles and bouts for eighth place featuring the Red Sox, Senators, and Kansas City A's.

It was as if the Curse of the Bambino was lifted for one benevolent season. The Red Sox became the photo negative of everything they'd come to represent. In 1967 Boston had the team of underpaid overachievers. Never-feared pretenders, destined to disappoint, the 1967 Sox instead were a ragtag youth group with hungry hearts and endless vision. The men-who-know in Las Vegas listed them as 100-to-1 underdogs to win the American League pennant and that seemed generous enough. Williams's spring training prediction/mantra was "We'll win more than we lose," and it sounded bold, honorable, and somewhat laughable. This was a team that hadn't seen .500 since the salad days of Elvis, and the waterline of mediocrity seemed unreachable for the forseeable future.

The 1967 Red Sox did far more than play .500 baseball. They got entwined in the tightest four-team race in baseball history, and they won it. There were no damn Yankees to worry about in this stardust summer of love; it was the White Sox, Tigers, and Twins who dueled with Boston. There was little hint of the Curse during this magical tour.

The only dark hour came when Conigliaro (the youngest big-leaguer to hit a hundred homers) was struck and nearly killed by a Jack Hamilton fastball on the night of August 18. The Sox lost their twenty-homer right-fielder for the rest of the season, and for Conigliaro it was the beginning of the end of a brilliant career. "He was the one who could have broken Ruth's home run record," Oriole ace Jim Palmer said. "With his swing in that ballpark, given the number he hit at an early age, he might have been the one to do it."

Little else went wrong. When the Sox needed a big game pitched, they got the big game even if they were depending on a journeyman named Gary Bell or Lee Stange. A twenty-one-year-old no-name lefty named Billy Rohr came within one out of pitching a no-hitter in his major league debut in Yankee Stadium. Rohr settled for a 3–0 victory over Whitey Ford, who would win 233 more big league games than Billy Rohr (Rohr won three). Catcher Bob Tillman conked pitcher John Wyatt on the skull with a low throw in an attempt to catch an enemy base-stealer. En route to Boston's first Cy Young Award, Jim Lonborg won ten games before the All-Star break. The Red Sox won ten in a row in July, and 15,000 greeted the team when it arrived home from Cleveland. Two days after Conigliaro was felled, Boston beat the California Angels after trailing 8–0 in the fourth. On September 7, the four contenders were tied for first, separated only by a single percentage point. A wiry outfielder named Jose Tartabull made a throw to win a ball game. A part-time hit man named Dalton Jones hit a homer in Detroit to win a game. Yastrzemski appeared on the cover of *Life* magazine on September 7. The first-base coach was Bobby Doerr, the sole standout from the 1946 World Series. The third man in the broadcast booth was Mel Parnell, the man who didn't pitch the 1948 playoff game. The team payroll was $825,000, far less than what Mrs. Yawkey would pay Bob Stanley to go 4–15, twenty summers later.

The final weekend of the 1967 season featured the Red Sox playing host to the Twins, needing wins in both games to overtake Minnesota. The White Sox were eliminated Friday night, but Detroit was tied with Boston going into the final two days and the Tigers had two double-headers to play against the Angels. This was a little like 1948 and 1949, but the 1967 Red Sox didn't inspire any flashback fears because they were not heavy favorites.

All of the new fans were too young to remember Ruth, and many were too young to have seen Ted Williams. These people didn't worry about Rico Petrocelli holding the ball as Pesky had in the 1946 World Series. Nobody suggested that Dick Williams would have trouble finding men willing to start the final two games against the Twins. And there was no irrational fear that Williams would lift Lonborg for a pinch hitter if the Red Sox were trailing, 1–0, in the eighth.

Through it all, the Red Sox were carried by a left-fielder who was en route to the Triple Crown and the MVP award. Carl Yastrzemski never had the size, the strength, or the gifts of Ted Williams, but for one summer he was every bit as Splendid as the Splinter, and Yaz would not have to grow old answering questions about his inability to hit in big games. Williams, in seven World Series games, the 1948 playoff, and the final two games in 1949, hit .206 (7–34, all singles). In the final two weeks of the 1967 regular season, Yaz hit .523 (23–44) with five homers and 16 RBI, including .875 (7–8) in the final two games of the best pennant race in history.

"My concentration was just fantastic," Yastrzemski remembered when he went into the Hall of Fame in the summer of 1989. "I'd probably have to attribute it to being in a pennant race. We'd finished last or next to last in my first six years and we used to joke about throwing raw meat into the stands. You wouldn't hit anybody. Going to the ballpark was drudgery. But then we went from losers to winners and changed the attitude of the whole Red Sox organization. Suddenly, it was a joy to go to the ballpark."

There was much joy in that final weekend in 1967. Boston had won only five of sixteen games against the Twins in 1967. This wasn't like 1946 or 1948 or 1949 because the Sox weren't *supposed* to win in 1967. This time, it was the Red Sox who were underdogs; it was the Red Sox who capitalized on lucky breaks; it was the Red Sox who benefited from freak injuries to the opposition; it was the Red Sox who hit in the clutch; and it was the Red Sox who stole the flag on the final day of the season. Fans in the Twin Cities and Tigertown would have great moments in the decades ahead, but as September turned to October in 1967, it was the Red Sox who were finally the fortunate sons.

In the first game against the Twins, on Saturday, September 30, Minnesota lefty Jim Kaat dominated Boston batters, fanning four of the first seven he retired. In the third inning, Kaat blew out his left elbow and had to come out of the game. Minnesota led, 1–0. The Sox rallied for two in the fifth, getting unusual help when Dalton Jones bounced a bad-hop single off Rod Carew's shoulder, and veteran Twin pitcher Jim Perry (a man who'd always been a Sox killer) neglected to cover first on a tapper to the right side by Yastrzemski. These were the things that usually happened *to* the Red Sox and now they were breaking in Boston's favor. If ever there was a time when the Curse of the Bambino appeared lifted, this was it.

A three-run homer by Yastrzemski, number forty-four, put the Saturday game out of reach, and the Sox won it, 6–4.

The matchups for the finale were ominous. Lonborg was 0–6 lifetime against the Twins, while Minnesota's Dean Chance was 4–0 against Boston in 1967. The early innings justified the fears of those who remembered the folds of the forties. A couple of misplays by Gold Glovers Yaz and George Scott helped the Twins to a pair of unearned runs.

But there would be no excuses, no memorable flops, no tear tracks streaming from Fenway's green gates. Losing 2–0 in the bottom of the sixth, Lonborg led with a perfect surprise bunt single. Red Sox fans can recite this inning faster than their own telephone numbers. Adair singled. Jones singled. Yaz singled to center to score two runs and tie it. Ken Harrelson hit a chopper to short and Zoilo Versalles fired late to the plate. 3–2. Al Worthington uncorked two wild pitches, good for a fourth Boston run. Harmon Killebrew's error allowed the Sox to take a 5–2 lead into the seventh. Lonborg stayed in the game and got a timely assist when Yaz erased Bob Allison going for a double in the eighth. Pinch hitter Rich Rollins went out on a shallow pop to shortstop Rico Petrocelli for the final out, and New England experienced joy not felt since the end of World War II. This sounds like exaggeration. It is not.

In Lyme, Connecticut, twenty-five-year-old Robert Craig was arrested for painting "Boston Red Sox" on Route 161 in East Lyme. In West Roxbury, a man with a transistor in his ear and a power mower in his hands accidentally mowed down his wife's prize marigolds. In Newark, New Jersey, former Bostonian Kent Stile backed his car into his neighbor's privet hedge.

The flag didn't officially fly over Fenway until Bill Rigney's California Angels beat the Tigers in the second game of a Detroit doubleheader later that day.

"We weren't going to go anywhere," remembered Rigney.

We were going to be fourth or fifth no matter what we did. But we played really hard up in Minnesota and beat them two out of three. We got rained out the first night in Detroit, so we had to play back-to-back doubleheaders, Saturday and Sunday. In that second game Sunday, when we finally got the lead, I had the best reliever I had in the game, Minnie Rojas. George Brunet had pitched the day before and it was his nineteenth loss and I had a feeling that Saturday night George Brunet might have touched a few bases around Detroit, cuz he was from there. And I can remember about the seventh inning of the second game Sunday I said, "How bad were you last night?" He gave me one of those "Who me?" looks. He said, "I wasn't too bad." I said, "Do you think you can get a hitter out?" and he said, "Yeah," so I told him to go down and warm up. Rojas was having trouble in the ninth and we were still leading so I had three pitchers warming up and I've never done that in my life. Three pitchers warming up in the bullpen, including George Brunet. They got two men on, and Dick McAuliffe was the hitter. I brought in Brunet. We got a two-run lead and if McAuliffe airmails him, Brunet's going to lose his twentieth game, cuz he's the winning run and George Brunet made one pitch and Dick McAuliffe hit a rocket one-hopper to Bobby Knopp—over to Fregosi to Mincher—and Boston was going to the World Series.

The Boston clubhouse radio told of the wondrous happening in Detroit, and Yawkey announced that it was the happiest moment of his life and promptly doubled Yastrzemski's salary to $100,000. Just like the old days. There was sadness in Tiger Stadium, and ancient Detroit owner John Fetzer called the visitors' clubhouse and asked manager Billy Rigney if he would join him for a drink. Fetzer, a sportsman to the finish, was pleased that Rigney had done his best to uphold the integrity of the game.

California's victory averted a one-game playoff against the Tigers in Detroit. In those hours when a playoff was still possible, Dick Williams did not pull a Joe McCarthy and state that he didn't know who'd pitch the big game. There were no plans to start Darrell Brandon, the 1967 equivalent of Denny Galehouse. Lee Stange would have pitched the playoff game. Stange was 8–10 in 1967, but had a 2.77 ERA.

On October 2, 1967, New York Senator Robert F. Kennedy led President Lyndon Johnson, 51–39 percentage points, among Democrats responding to a Gallup presidential poll. At Cambridge Police headquarters, three hundred hippies protested the drug arrests of twenty-one fellow flower children. Mia Farrow was thinking of joining the Beatles, Donovan, and other disciples of Maharishi Mahesh Yogi in New Delhi, and "The Flying Nun" and "Gomer Pyle" were in the top-ten television shows. But it was hard to find any news that wasn't cloaked in Red Sox hysteria. The front page of the *Herald Traveler* ran a banner headline "Pennant Is Ours!" over a half-page color team photo of the Sox. The tabloid *Record American*'s front page was simply "Champs!" and a pair of red Red Sox. The inimitable Bud Collins of the *Globe* wrote, "Karl Marx, who said religion is the opiate of the people, would have revised himself had he watched the Red Sox unite to throw off their ninth-place chains. The Red Sox are the opiate right now, Karl, baby, although you might classify them as a religion."

The Series was billed as an anticlimactic event, but that didn't sap any of the local enthusiasm in a town that hadn't made it to the big show in twenty-one years. Many schools and offices allowed radio broadcasts to be piped into the classroom/workplace. A sign in front of Merrimack College (which had awarded a degree to Yastrzemski) read "Yaz studied here." Massachusetts town clerks made Tom Yawkey an honorary member of their association. Yawkey planned his first road trip in seventeen years. Flanked by sons Bobby and Ted, seventy-nine-year-old Joseph P. Kennedy attended the World Series opener—Jose Santiago versus Bob Gibson.

The Red Sox lost the World Series in seven games against the St. Louis Cardinals, but there were few regrets. St. Louis had won a hundred and one games and had taken the National League pennant by ten and a half games. St. Louis's manager was Red Schoendienst, the man who fielded the final grounder in the 1946 classic. The Cards had the better team and had a rested big-game pitcher in Gibson. The Cardinal ace blinded Boston in games 1, 4, and 7, allowing only fourteen hits in twenty-seven innings, and had enough to offset the heroics of Yastrzemski (.400, three homers, five RBI) and Lonborg. The Sox fell behind three games to one before Lonborg rescued them in Game 5 and a kid pitcher named Gary Waslewski got them into the middle innings of Game 6. Williams had to start Lonborg on two days' rest for Game 7. There was no other way. When first asked who he was going with for Game 7, the fiesty manager replied, "Lonborg and champagne." It made for a good headline and gave the Cardinals some extra incentive.

Lonborg had nothing for the finale. It was obvious from the start when Lou Brock led off with a long fly to left center. Yastrzemski caught up with the clout, but it was the kind of drive that a lead-off man couldn't achieve in the first inning if Lonborg were strong. St. Louis scored two in the third, two in the fifth, and three in the sixth before the Red Sox were able to dent Gibson.

How could there have been regrets? The Red Sox hadn't played a World Series game in twenty-one seasons and hadn't been over .500 in the decade. The Sox were clearly overmatched in the Series and handicapped by the very event that provided the most drama—the pennant race. Lonborg's complete game effort on sudden-death Sunday pushed him back a day in the Series, and when Williams was forced to match aces in the seventh game, St. Louis had a rested flamethrower while the Sox had Gentleman Jim pitching on heart, desire, and only two days of rest. This was a Series the Red Sox were never supposed to win. They never led in games, and it says something that they were able to stretch the duel to a seventh game.

But there was no drama in the Fenway finale. It was a Thursday afternoon, Columbus Day, a day when the sons of Italy march proudly through the crooked, cozy streets of Boston's North End. Twenty-eight bands marched, but police estimates said the crowd was less than half of the usual 200,000. In some areas of the Back Bay, the marchers outnumbered the spectators, and many of the parade-watchers were gathered in front of televisions set in appliance stores along the route. A sales rep at Jordan Marsh downtown reported that seven hundred people jammed the aisles on the ninth floor when the Sox and Cardinals dueled. *Housewives on Call* and *Tortured Females* played at the X-rated Mayflower Theatre, but manager Charlie Schultz said that there were few who gave in to temptation during the World Series games. Because it was Columbus Day, there was no school in Massachusetts, and this was a fitting reward for the thousands who would have been forced to play hookey.

Gibson was indomitable, and Cardinal banjo hitters like Dal Maxvill were banging shots off the green walls in deep center. Julien Javier hit a three-run homer into the screen, and Gibson, adding a Ruthian touch of his own, hit a towering solo homer into the triangle in center. Fenway was stone silent for most of the day, and the most excitement for the locals came when a railway freight car fire sent smoke rising beyond the fence in left center. Williams paraded Jose Santiago, Dave Morehead, Dan Osinski, and Ken Brett to the mound in the late innings. Brett was nineteen years old, symbolic of the youth and innocence of New England's beloved baseball team in 1967.

The day after the Series ended was Friday the thirteenth, and the *Globe* front-page headline read, "The Slipper Wouldn't Fit."

The only sadness attached to the seventh game of the 1967 World Series was that the event, by its very definition, signified that the season was over. During the summer of 1967, Boston's born-again baseball fans wanted to postpone winter forever. This was the summer when radios stayed tuned until one of the forty-four New England Sox carriers announced the final score. It was when daring teens perched on the Old Grand Dad billboard beyond the fence in left center, and when grown men stormed the field and grabbed handfuls of Fenway dirt (to be placed in urns like ashes of a loved one perhaps?) after Petrocelli caught Rollins's pop-up at 4:36 P.M. EST October 1, 1967.

Looking back, it strikes one how little is remembered from the World Series compared with the retention of details involving the long summer pennant fight. Petrocelli hit two homers in Game 6 of the World Series, but the lasting image is that of him catching a weak fly ball as thousands poured onto the sacred Fenway lawn. Lonborg pitched a one-hit shutout, facing only twenty-nine batters in Game 2 of the World Series, but is better remembered for his bunt single in the sixth inning of the last regular season game. Dalton Jones hit .389 in the Series, but his greater gifts were the extra-inning homer in Detroit and the Sunday single past the draw-in infield against Dean Chance.

The Red Sox have blown many pennant races, lost the only two playoff games in American League history, dropped an American League Championship Series in four straight, and lost the seventh game of the World Series four times since Ruth was sold to the Yankees seventy years ago. In all these disappointments, only the 1967 team is immune from criticism, ridicule, and regret. They are spared the second-guessers and the harsh historians who have scrutinized and plagued all other Sox teams since 1918. Nobody held the ball, nobody tripped rounding third base, nobody threw an ill-timed wild pitch, nobody made a hideous and regrettable hunch, nobody let a ground ball slip between his legs and into history.

It was okay for the 1967 Red Sox to lose the seventh game of the World Series because they'd already performed the great service of bringing a moribund franchise back to life and registering millions of new members to the party of the long-suffering. The 1967 Red Sox were not a great team. Their .568 winning percentage would place them third most seasons, and the club ERA was 3.35, eighth in the league. Only one pitcher won more than thirteen games and no catcher hit higher than .203. But they put the Sox in the World Series for the first time in twenty-one years and inspired books, record albums (*The Impossible Dream* was a Christmas must in December of 1967), and Big Yaz Bread.

Lonborg was going to be the anchor of the pitching staff for many years, but less than three months after his World Series heroics, Gentleman Jim came crashing down a California ski slope near Lake Tahoe and crushed ligaments in his knee. Lonborg's injury was the first indication that the Red Sox were in for bad times in their defense of the American League pennant. This has been a problem of all Sox flag-winners since Ruth left; they usually play the following season as if still hungover from October's champagne fest. The 1946 winners finished fourteen games out in 1947, and the 1967 champs fell to seventeen games out in 1968. Manager Dick Williams, still under forty, couldn't be a genius without a healthy Lonborg (6–10 in 1968, 27–29 in the four seasons after 1967) and a Triple Crown winner. Yastrzemski in 1968 won the batting crown with a .301 average, but his numbers were way off the Impossible Dream pace. George Scott's average dropped from .301 to .171 while his weight went the other way, and Conigliaro could not play at all because of the eye injury he sustained in August 1967. Jose Santiago and Ken Brett developed arm problems, and the Sox pitching leaders were a couple of National League retreads named Dick Ellsworth and Ray Culp. Yawkey began to think that the hard-headed Williams didn't communicate enough with the players while Williams grew to resent the owner consoling players who had been chewed out by their manager. Despite all of the above, the Sox in 1968 were still living off the euphoria of the previous summer and drew a franchise record 1,940,788 to Fenway.

"I was disappointed after '67," said Yastrzemski. "I thought we really had something for a while, but you lose Conigliaro and Lonborg and Santiago. Right then and there you knew. There goes the nucleus right down the drain."

◇

The Red Sox continued to play better than .500 ball and draw fans, but from 1969 through 1971 they were no match for a minidynasty in Baltimore. In those three years Boston won respectively eighty-seven, eighty-seven, and eighty-five games, but finished third each year as the Orioles became the third team in baseball history to win a hundred or more games in three consecutive seasons. Williams was fired at the end of the 1969 season, the immensely popular Ken Harrelson was traded to Cleveland early in that same season, and Yastrzemski started to hear boos after he hurt his hand and his production dropped to .254, fifteen homers, and 70 RBI in 1971. Conigliaro made a miraculous comeback, then was traded after the 1970 season, and in July 1971 the clubhouse was torn by a childish dispute pitting Billy Conigliaro vs. Yastrzemski and Reggie Smith. Conigliaro felt he was being criticized by the two star outfielders, and he blamed them for getting his older brother traded. He said he didn't want to play in the same outfield with Yastrzemski and Smith. Only in Boston or New York would this have been headline news, but the Sox still had a grip on the community, and clubhouse dissension has always been a seductive item for readers of the sports pages. Manager Eddie Kasko naturally was unhappy with the situation and Billy Conigliaro was traded to Milwaukee after the 1971 season.

The Sox picked Luis Tiant off the scrap heap on May 17, 1971, and this should go down as one of the shrewdest moves in the jagged history of Boston transactions. Cleveland had traded El Tiante to Minnesota in 1970, but his career was considered over after he sustained a serious arm injury. Boston plucked him from the Atlanta organization and assigned him to Louisville. He was called up to the majors in June and staggered (1–7, 4.88 ERA) through the end of the season as the Sox finished eighteen games behind the Orioles.

◇

The Red Sox were back in a pennant race in 1972, but the confidence of 1967's success was shaken when a couple of unlikely and untimely mistakes cost Boston a chance to win the American League East. Luis Aparicio, a Hall of Famer who made his living with his legs, fell down twice rounding third base in the crucial game of the season and the Sox were denied a playoff berth.

The 1972 season got off to a bad start when the Red Sox traded lefty reliever Sparky Lyle to the Yankees for right-handed hitter Danny Cater. Cater had always hurt the Sox in Boston and was considered a prototype "Fenway hitter." Unfortunately, he turned out to be one of the many who used up his best games before he was traded to Boston. Cater's average plummeted to .237 in his first year in Boston and he never hit more than eight homers in his three seasons with the Red Sox. Meanwhile, Lyle went on to win a Cy Young Award for the World Champion Yankees. So much for the Boston–New York, Frazee-Ruppert pipeline. After this tragic transition, the Sox and Yanks did not deal with each other again for fourteen years.

A two-week strike at the start of the 1972 season created an unbalanced schedule and lopped eight games off the Sox season. The Red Sox were seven games under .500 June 24, fell eight and a half games back, but rallied behind Tiant in August and spent twenty-four days of September in first place. As always, the Sox lacked pitching. Unknown, untested Mike Garman had to start a game against Detroit on the next-to-last week of the season. Boston eliminated the Orioles on the final weekend in Baltimore, and on Saturday, September 30, Yastrzemski's homer off Jim Palmer put the Red Sox a game and a half ahead with four to play. Earlier that day, the box office opened on Jersey Street and 15,000 playoff tickets were sold.

Junkballer Mike Cuellar, backed by the vacuum/glove of Brooks Robinson, beat the Red Sox 2–1, on the final Sunday of the season, and Kasko's kids went to Detroit for the final three games of the season, needing two victories to win the American League East. "The Red Sox have the best ball club," said Palmer. Kasco had John Curtis, Tiant, and Marty Pattin lined up against Billy Martin's troika of Mickey Lolich, Woody Fryman, and Joe Coleman. Kasco wanted to pitch Sonny Siebert in the opener, but Siebert couldn't go because of a bad ankle. The Sox were 1–5 in Motown going into the final series.

Left-handed rookie John Duffield Curtis II faced Detroit's 1968 World Series hero (three victories) Mickey Lolich in the first game of this series. Curtis had some impressive baseball bloodlines. His great uncle had laid the original sod in Fenway Park and his uncle was Tom Yawkey's roommate at Yale.

Curtis gave up a homer to Al Kaline in the first inning, but the Sox had Lolich on the ropes in the third when the Curse of the Bambino struck. Trailing 1–0, Boston had Aparicio on first and Tommy Harper on third with one out when Yastrzemski hit a rocket over Mickey Stanley's head in center. Harper scored easily. Aparicio held at second to make sure the ball was over Stanley's head then broke for third and fell down twice after rounding the corner bag. Wet turf was part of the problem. Tiger Stadium sewers backed up two days before the series opener and the field was unusually muddy. Yastrzemski's drive might have been an inside-the-park homer under drier conditions, but Stanley was able to get to the ball when the mud stopped it from rolling. Meanwhile, Aparicio was not helped by the soft footing on the baselines. After falling the first time, he scrambled to get back to third, cutting his right knee open with his own spikes. He found Yastrzemski waiting at third and Yaz was out when he retreated to second. Then Reggie Smith fanned, the big inning was over, and Lolich was off the hook. Detroit's portly southpaw tightened the screws after Aparicio's blunder, fanning fifteen in a 4–1 complete-game victory.

Third-base coach Eddie Popowski took Yastrzemski off the hook, saying, "I told him [Aparicio] to go back to third and there was no way to hold Yaz at second. He saw me wave Luis in and he has to think he has an easy triple."

Luis Ernesto Montiel Aparicio was born April 29, 1934, in Maracaibo, Venezuela, and joined the White Sox of the American League in 1956. He led the AL in stolen bases in each of his first nine seasons, a major league record. He was on a pair of pennant winners and anchored the Oriole infield when they won their first World Championship, in 1966. In eighteen big-league seasons he played 2,581 games at shortstop, more than any player in history. In Chicago and Baltimore he is remembered as the premier shortstop of his day, "Little Looie," a slash-hitter with great range at short and the best base runner in the American League. In Boston, he is remembered as the man who blew the 1972 division flag by stumbling around the third-base bag like some drunk fumbling around a dark hotel room after the furniture has been rearranged. The Red Sox have had scores of bonehead base runners and men with plowhorse agility, yet the most famous basepath blunder in franchise history belongs to a man whose legs carried him into the Hall of Fame in 1984.

"I had to hold up at second on Yaz's ball, because Stanley is one of the best center fielders and he almost got to it, but that was not why I fell," Aparicio said moments after his double tumble. "When I hit the base I landed right on top of it and that threw me off, and when I hit the wet grass beyond the base I went down. I didn't think of trying for home then. I spiked myself. I screwed up the play."

Yastrzemski's version, seventeen years later: "It's like it wasn't supposed to be. I hit the ball off Lolich and when I was rounding first, I saw it hit the center-field fence. It hit right on top and bounced back toward center field. I was thinking inside-the-park home run because it bounced so far back. It hit that top steel. Then I'm heading into third base and I see Aparicio laying on the ground and I was in shock. He comes back to third and I'm on third and I'm still thinking I'm going to go. So I pushed him off the bag and said, 'Luis, you can still make it.' And he started running and gets halfway and falls down again. I was all set, even watching the relay, before he fell down the second time, to still go for an inside-the-park home run and follow him in. I just couldn't believe it. One of the greatest base runners who ever lived. You don't mind getting beat, but not to have the best base runner the game had ever seen fall down twice going from third to home."

The years gave Yastrzemski a vision that most Sox players don't have. Long after his playing days were over, the Hall of Famer was able to see that perhaps larger forces were at work. It's easy to explain things away until you see the unexplainable happening over and over again, and Yastrzemski's tired eyes have witnessed as much as any Sox historian.

The loss to Lolich was the second of three straight games in which the Red Sox were able to score only one run. They hit only .231 in September and finished 33–44 on the road. Cater, the big name in the big Yankee trade, would finish with 39 RBI, while Lyle saved a league-leading thirty-five games for the Yankees. Detroit manager Billy Martin said Sparky Lyle deserved the MVP award.

It was Tiant versus Woody Fryman the next night. Tiant, one of the premier "big game" pitchers of his time, was the American League ERA champ (1.88 going in) and had won four in a row, eleven of twelve since August first. In less than two months he had beaten Bert Blyleven,

Dave McNally, Doyle Alexander, Tom Bradley, Jim Lonborg, Fritz Peterson, Dick Tidrow, Mike Cuellar, Woody Fryman, and Jim Palmer. In his final outing, he was again facing Fryman, a journeyman lefty the Tigers had snatched from the Phillies off the waiver wire.

. As always, the Sox left themselves open to second-guessing. With the score tied, 1–1, in the seventh, Kasko elected to let Tiant pitch to Tiger star Al Kaline with first base open, Dick McAuliffe on second, and one out. Kaline singled to left, scoring McAuliffe with the winning run. Boston's best play was made by a twenty-year-old kid up from triple-A named Dwight Evans. Making a prorated $13,500 minimum salary, Evans opened some eyes with a sliding catch of a Duke Sims drive to left with two men on in the fifth inning. It was not enough. The Red Sox couldn't hit Fryman, a pitcher Boston let slip through the waiver wire.

The Sox were Avis rent-a-cars once again. It was not totally unlike the final weekend in 1949 when Boston needed only one victory in New York but lost both.

Red Sox fans have grown accustomed to chanting, "We're number two," but this time there was an added twist to the near miss. Since the Red Sox won the final game in Detroit, 4–1 (a meaningless duel featuring many triple-A players, and who knows what would have happened if the game had meant something?), Boston finished 85–70, a half game worse than Detroit's 86–70 record. Since both teams lost the same number of games, it could (and surely has been) argued that the Red Sox were cheated by the baseball strike, which allowed them to play one less game than the Tigers. The game the Sox didn't play was against the Indians. During the April strike, Boston's two-game series with the Indians was stricken while Detroit's three-game series with the Yankees was canceled. The "missing game" theory is a weak excuse because anyone who knows anything about the Red Sox knows that if the Sox and Tigers had played the same number of games, and if the final game in Detroit had meant anything, certainly Boston would have found a way to lose again. The Sox came to Detroit needing two of three and lost the first two. Case closed.

The 1973 Sox finished second again, eight games out, and that gave the front office enough ammo to fire Eddie Kasko and replace him with Darrell Johnson, a man who'd been groomed for the job since 1972.

In Johnson's first season, the Red Sox teased New England fans with another red hot summer, followed by a September collapse. To all but the most devout disciples, details of this fold are fuzzy, yet it serves nicely as a blueprint for the image the Red Sox have carried into the 1990s. On August 23, 1974, Tiant blanked Vida Blue and the Oakland A's, 3–0, winning his twentieth in front of Fenway's biggest crowd (35,866) in eighteen years and pushing the unstoppable Red Sox seven games ahead of the second-place Orioles and Yankees. Incredibly, when the season ended, the blind-sided BoSox were in third place, seven games behind the Orioles. Too many Mario Guerreros. It remains one of the classic flops in franchise history and explains today why every New England baseball fan over the age of twenty-five worries that "they'll blow it" whenever the team is in first place in late August.

Catfish Hunter dueled Bill Lee on Saturday, August 24, and New England hardly trembled when the A's made off with a 4–1 victory. The weekend series with the two-time World Champs was merely a playoff preview, a chance for all amateur scouts to get a good book on the A's. You never know what might work against them when the games really count in October. Other than that, the only issues seemed to be whether it would be Tiant or Hunter for the American League Cy Young Award; Tiant or Reggie Jackson for MVP. The *Globe* was running a daily box comparing the Red Sox 1974 team with the 1967 team at each juncture. Ken Holtzman blanked the Sox in the series finale, but still there was no regional alarm. Few listened to the great Jackson, who looked at the Red Sox and wondered, "Who are all these Mario Andretti guys?"

No one was paying much attention to the Orioles. Baltimore trailed the Red Sox by a whopping eight games on Friday, August 30. When the Sox landed in Baltimore on Labor Day (September 2), the Yankees were still considered the threat. New York trailed the slumping Bostons by only two games. The Sox suffered severe Labor pains September 2. A couple of junkballing Oriole lefties, Ross Grimsley and Mike Cuellar, blanked Boston in straight sets, 1–0, 1–0, and the bookend beatings sent a tremor through New England. *It was happening again.* Rookie manager Darrell Johnson said, "It's not the low point," but the nervous legions back home knew that only meant more trouble on the horizon. The *Globe*'s Leigh Montville wrote, "The Red Sox fan, of course, is mad mostly at himself. He finds he was tricked again by those beguiling storm-door and aluminum-siding salesmen from Lansdowne Street. He bought their whole damn package. . . . The Red Sox fan had forgotten his inbred pessimism, his rooting heritage. He had stuffed it in a drawer."

After a day off, the Sox went back to Memorial Stadium and got shut out again, 6–0, victims of Jim Palmer. The tired Townies had lost six straight while being blanked five times in eleven games, including twenty-nine consecutive innings. They scored zero runs on eight singles in twenty-seven innings in Baltimore. The punchless wonders returned to Boston still holding a piece of first place (tied with the Yankees), but the proud old Orioles were roaring down the back stretch, two games out with twenty-seven to play.

For the first time in fifty-three days, Boston was not in sole possession of first place. The Sox went home and took some extra batting practice before playing Milwaukee. Boston led, 3–2, in the ninth when young Gorman Thomas beat them with a two-run homer off Diego Segui. The tumble down the stairs was complete. The Red Sox had dropped out of first place for good. They were shut out again the next night, their eighth straight loss. Manager Darrell Johnson told his team to turn up the volume on the clubhouse radio after the eighth straight loss. The first-year skipper didn't want any appearance of panic, so he instructed his nervous team to act as if they were still carefree division leaders. Danny Cater offered a reason for the slump, claiming it was part of a cyclical ten-year curse. Cater was a member of the 1964 Philadelphia Phillies, a fold-up team against which all others are measured. In truth, the Sox slumped because they didn't have hard-hitting catcher Carlton Fisk (knee problems) and because veterans Petrocelli, Tommy Harper, and Yastrzemski stopped hitting.

The 1974 Sox weren't eliminated by the eight-game free-fall. One day after ending the losing streak, they vaulted back into a first-place tie with the Yankees. The Yankees came to town that same night. New York had lost twenty of its last twenty-one games at Fenway Park, but this was September and these games meant something and, well, grizzled Sox watchers knew something bad was probably going to happen. Bingo. In the first game, both second baseman Doug Griffin and short-stop Guerrero (playing instead of slumping rookie Rick Burleson) neglected to cover second when Roy White attempted to steal. Bob

Montgomery's throw hit the base, skipped into center, and the hated Pinstripes were on their way to a 6–3 victory. "We got screwed up on the play," said Griffin.

The save went to former Red Sox reliever Sparky Lyle. Perfect. The Yanks, helped by former Red Sox players, were back in first place. The choking Red Sox were in second, and all was right with the universe. The planets were all in line.

One night later Tiant dueled Pat Dobson in front of 33,174. Tiant led, 1–0, in the ninth when Chris Chambliss hit what appeared to be a ground rule double to right. Pinch runner Larry Murray was on first and would have been stopped at third, but umpire Marty Springstead ruled that there had been fan interference and decided that Murray would have scored if the ball hadn't been touched. The Yanks went on to win the game, 2–1, when Alex Johnson homered off Diego Segui in the twelfth. Gaylord Perry beat Boston in Cleveland the next night, and the Sox, losers of fourteen out of eighteen, fell two and a half games out.

The Red Sox were not front-page news during this collapse. On Thursday, September 12, 1974, desegregation came to Boston's public school system, the oldest in America. Resistance to Boston's school busing put the region's long-standing racial disharmony on top of the national news. It was violent and ugly and photos of police motorcycles accompanying buses of small children exposed the Hub of the Universe as a bastion of racism. It was somehow fitting that the Red Sox, never forerunners in the area of race relations, would be unraveling at this same moment.

Two and a half games out of first place on September 18, the dead Sox drew 12,213 for a night game with the Tigers. In that series, the Sox were beaten by Vern Ruhle in his major league debut, and Luis Tiant failed to win his sixth consecutive start.

The Orioles came to town and won two of three, prompting the *Globe*'s Peter Gammons to lead his Monday morning game story with an italic quotation from the Requiem Mass. A fan whipped out a bugle and blew taps behind the Red Sox dugout during the 7–2 series finale, and Baltimore's Bobby Grich said, "Except for Burleson, Yaz, and a couple of others, the Red Sox didn't act like it was a life-or-death series. They seemed resigned."

The Red Sox were officially eliminated in Detroit September 29 and finished third, seven games behind the white-hot Orioles. Boston went 14–24 after August 23, while Baltimore won twenty-eight of its last thirty-four.

◊

This was the beginning of the new identity of the Sox—one that exists today. Boston's baseball fans have not been comfortable with any first-place team since the collapse of 1974. Prior to that, the Red Sox of the Yawkey era had no reputation for losing summer leads. The Sox had disappointed in the final stretches of 1948, 1949, and 1972, and they'd dropped the seventh game of the World Series in 1946 and 1967, but they hadn't blown midsummer leads. The 1974 Sox toughened New England fans for what was to come. From 1972 through 1988, the Red Sox nine times led the American League East after the All-Star game yet won the division in only three of those years. There are people in all walks of life who would rather do the chasing than be chased. The Red Sox and their fans today are more relaxed when the team is behind than when the team is sitting on a first-place lead. Let the record show that the foundation for this inverted logic was poured during the summer of 1974.

Hardball historians pinpointed the cause of this trauma immediately. When the 1974 Olde Towne Team was on the brink of elimination, the *Globe*'s Ray Fitzgerald wrote a whimsical piece asking, "What happened to the Red Sox," and listed twenty-five explanations for the fold. Number twenty-five was, "They should have never sold Babe Ruth."

The man was on to something. The Curse of the Bambino was taking on new dimensions, causing pain and heartaches in ways not yet imagined.

SEVEN

The summer of 1975 was relatively uneventful worldwide. The Suez Canal reopened after eight years; Americans and Russians hooked up in space for the first time; no one could find Patty Hearst or Jimmy Hoffa; and Squeaky Fromme and Sara Jane Moore failed in separate attempts to assassinate President Ford. In New England, it was a hotter summer than most, and Judge W. Arthur Garrity's public school busing edict sparked demonstrations and increased tension throughout the city.

At Fenway Park, the Red Sox wore two-toned caps and tore up the American League thanks to the greatest rookie tandem in the history of major league baseball. Fred Lynn and Jim Rice were the Gold Dust Twins and delivered the Red Sox to another seven-game World Series, Boston's third since 1946. Lynn batted .331 with twenty-one homers and 105 RBI while Rice hit .309 with twenty-two homers and 102 RBI. Lynn won a Gold Glove and was voted American League Rookie of the Year and Most Valuable Player. Fast Freddie was the cool California kid, a year and a half out of USC, and everything seemed to be easy for him, even his smile. Rice, a South Carolina native, was never comfortable with the New England climate (racial and otherwise) and inevitable comparisons with the graceful, gracious Lynn. Jim Ed Rice silently glared back at the bright lights and went about his work.

This was a wonderful team, a team that was loved right from the start when Tony Conigliaro, making one final comeback, hit the first home run of the season in Baltimore. New Hampshire's Fisk came back to hit .331 and Burleson established himself as a premier shortstop. Yastrzemski hit .310 in the first half and Cecil Cooper picked up the slack in June, becoming one of the most dangerous hitters in the American League. Petrocelli (with Yaz, the only returnees from 1967) was better than average at third and Denny Doyle came off the scrap heap to hit .310 while playing second base. Right-fielder Dwight Evans was still only twenty-three and filled out what looked like Boston's best outfield since Tris Speaker, Duffy Lewis, and Harry Hooper.

The 1975 Red Sox won ninety-five games, their best since 1946. They hit only 134 homers but led the league in average (.275), slugging, and on-base percentage. They were an awful 10–21 in spring training, and there were doubts about their ability to recover from the fall of 1974. Despite the splashy, almost daily heroics of Lynn (he hit three homers and knocked in ten runs in a single game in Detroit in June), there was nothing remarkable about the Red Sox start in 1975. Darrell Johnson was trying to get his pitching rotation in order as the Sox hovered near the top in early June. A 9–4 road trip in mid-June put the Townies in a good spot to make their run, and Boston trailed the first-place Yankees by one and a half games when the New Yorkers came to Fenway for four games starting June 23. The Sox won three of four and moved into first place for good.

A month later, the first-place Sox went to New York holding an eight-game lead over George Steinbrenner's team. The rivals split the first two games, but the Red Sox buried the hated Yanks for good by sweeping a Sunday doubleheader in Shea Stadium (Yankee Stadium was undergoing renovation). Bill Lee dueled Catfish Hunter in the first game and was protecting a 1–0 lead in the ninth when Graig Nettles hit a gapper to left center. Lynn raced to his right, dove, speared the drive, went into a double somersault, and popped up holding the baseball as if he were the Statue of Liberty. Sox third-base coach Don Zimmer, a man who'd been in baseball for twenty-seven years at the hour, called it the best catch he'd ever seen. It still ranks Number One on Lynn's list. Rogelio Moret blanked the bombers, 6–0, in the nightcap, and the Yankees were toast. It was the first time the Yankees had been shut out in both ends of a doubleheader since 1958.

Attendance lagged in the early months, and veteran publicist Bill Crowley noted, "People, I think, remembered last year and felt they didn't want to get burned again. Do you know what I think was the one day when they finally started to believe? When Fred Lynn had that night in Detroit. I think that was the most important day of our season. The team came back on June 23 and, bingo, here were the people."

The final challenge, a mirage of a threat at that, came from the Orioles. Baltimore manager Earl Weaver, exploiting the fears planted one year earlier, said, "I still want to see what happens starting around the twenty-fourth of August. It may be wishful thinking, since the Red Sox certainly did well, but I'm still waiting for the fall that came a year ago." The Orioles trailed the Sox by seven games with thirty-three to play when Weaver uttered those words.

When the Sox, leading the AL East by six games, got to Baltimore on September 3, a Crabtown columnist called them the "Great Boston Chokers" and compared them with Albert DeSalvo, the infamous Boston Strangler. Orioles fans chanted "choke, choke, choke" when Baltimore took a lead in the sixth inning of the first game, but the Sox came back and Cecil Cooper won it, 3–2, with a homer off Jim Palmer in the tenth. Dick Pole and Dick Drago combined to shut down the defending division champs the next night, and the Sox led by eight with twenty-five to play.

Boston fans took the challenge seriously. This was a Baltimore team that had won five of the American League's first six division titles. Veterans Brooks Robinson, Mark Belanger, and Palmer never made plans for October. They always figured they'd be playing well past Columbus Day, and usually they were. And so it was no surprise when the Orioles managed to close the gap to four and a half games and put Sox fans back on the rack September 16.

Baltimore is a provincial, semisouthern city with a deep-rooted inferiority complex, but its citizens knew they had something on those New England nabobs. Babe Ruth was born in Baltimore, and it was only fitting that the ancestors of his first professional team were fulfilling the Curse of the Bambino. Jack Dunn III was a top Orioles executive in 1975, and it was his grandfather who signed Ruth to his first contract. After what the Orioles did to the Red Sox and Boston fans in 1974, it was very believable that it could happen again. Baltimoreans did their best to exploit the irrational fears of the Boston fandom. Johnny Walker, a disc jockey for WFBR in Baltimore, flew to Nairobi to ask a witch doctor to put a hex on the Red Sox. Walker claimed the voodoo man was a sports specialist, Kenya's top practitioner of spells on soccer teams. Walker paid the witch doctor $200 and two cases of beer to put the whammy on the Red Sox. An autographed baseball was incanted over, wrapped in human hairs, and placed in a monkey's paw.

Weaver, the inimitable manager of the Orioles, had a field day with New England's panic. He popped out of the Fenway runway and into his dugout before the first game of the crucial series and said, "We've crawled out of more coffins than Bela Lugosi."

Luis Tiant put a stop to the nonsense with a five-hit, eight strikeout, 2–0 shutout. This remains one of the most memorable regular-season Fenway games since World War II. Homers by Fisk and Petrocelli provided the offense, and Boston's magic number was reduced to seven with eleven games to play as 34,724 (treasurer John Harrington later estimated this crowd to be 47,000) filed out of the park chanting "Loo-ie, Loo-ie," a refrain that became Tiant's trademark. As ever, the Orioles were more gracious in defeat than the Red Sox were in victory. Loser Jim Palmer admitted, "You can talk about anybody else on that team you want to, but Tiant is The Man."

The Sox announced plans for playoff ticket sales, but the next night Oriole righty Mike Torrez (his name would come up again in a few years) beat Rick Wise, 5–2, enabling the O's to creep back to four and a half. Weaver tried to capitalize with more psychological warfare.

"Do you realize," said the midget manager, "we may just win the rest of our eleven games? If we win the rest of our games, Boston still has to win seven of ten to win this thing, and it's awfully difficult to do that."

This made no sense, of course, since the premise was that the Orioles would win *all* of their games, but Baltimore had gone 28–6 down the stretch in 1974, and Weaver's teams were traditionally fast finishers, and the manager knew that his little snowball could turn into an avalanche. "Lolich'll beat 'em," said Weaver. "Hunter, Eckersley, Bibby."

It didn't happen. The Orioles were old and weak, while the Red Sox were driven by their own talent and the memory of 1974. A man is more careful with his new wallet the day after his old one is stolen. Tiant and Reggie Cleveland swept the Indians with a pair of shutouts Friday, September 26, and the next night the Red Sox clinched their first American League East title at 7:35 P.M. when the Yankees' nightcap victory over the Orioles came across the Teletype. In New York, Weaver could say only, "They've finally driven that wooden stake right through our hearts."

The Red Sox were matched against the three-time World Champions from Oakland in the playoffs, and *Sports Illustrated* summarized its

ALCS preview with this tagline: "Strange things can happen in so short a series, but no one is better equipped to deal with things strange than the feisty young men from Oakland. Expect Boston to suffer their wrath."

The 1975 A's were Charlie Finley's last great team (not coincidentally), the last team assembled before free agency forever changed the rules of baseball. Reggie Jackson was the American League home run champ, and they had premier reliever Rollie Fingers, bluechip starters Vida Blue and Ken Holtzman, veteran stars Joe Rudi, Sal Bando, and Gene Tenace, and roadrunners Bert Campaneris, Billy North, Claudell Washington, and Phil Garner.

Tiant beat the handlebar-mustache guys with a three-hit, eight-strikeout, 7–1 victory in Game 1 of the playoffs, and the Sox were rolling. Oakland set the tone for the entire series by making three errors in the first inning of the first game. There was no beating Tiant in a big game. Yastrzemski later said, "We always believed we were the best team in the world when Luis started strolling in from the bullpen."

Game 2 pitted Reggie Cleveland (he won five straight in September) against twenty-two-game winner Vida Blue. Yaz inhaled all the Wall's rebounds and turned several doubles into singles, then smashed a two-run homer into the screen off Blue in the fourth. Yaz doubled in the sixth and scored the go-ahead run on a single by Fisk. Petrocelli homered in the seventh, and the Sox were en route to a 6–3 victory and a 2–0 series lead as the teams flew 3,000 miles for one final game.

Oakland manager Alvin Dark was forced to come back with Ken Holtzman on two days' rest, and the Sox took a 4–0 lead in the first five innings of Game 3. Rick Wise had a 5–2 lead when Jackson hit a sinking shot to left center with two men on base. Yastrzemski dove for the ball and got it on the short hop to hold Jackson to a single and keep a second run from scoring. Dick Drago came in and got Rudi to bounce into a double play. The final batter in the ninth was pinch hitter Jim Holt, and he went out on a weak tapper to Doyle at second. Oakland's three-year reign atop the baseball world (the A's are the only team in the last three decades to win three straight World Series) was over. Rudi, Bando, and Tenace would never play in another postseason game. The Red Sox were 5–3 winners and American League Champions for the third time since 1918. Thomas A. Yawkey, having made his first trip to California in forty-five years, drank Jacques Reynaud champagne from a Jack-in-the-Box paper cup. He would not live to see another October. Yastrzemski, the hero of the series, had an honest beer. In the three-game sweep, Yaz (he had hit .212 for two and a half months of the 1975 season) hit .455 while playing left field for the first time in a year, and playing it with the brilliance he showed in 1967. Reggie Jackson (Yaz robbed Mr. October twice in the finale) said, "Yastrzemski is a superstar and you can keep on saying that all night." The *Globe*'s Gammons wrote, "One night, maybe in 1992, you and I will flash at the same time and remember that this man could take himself beyond the realm of his body as supernaturally as any man we could remember." Yawkey, the owner who'd purchased Cronin and worshiped Williams, said that Yastrzemski was the best all-around player he'd ever had.

"We were a strong club, but there's no doubt that it was the year of the Red Sox," Jackson said later. "They couldn't do anything wrong. Yaz was the perfect player at that time."

Sox manager Darrell Johnson never left his clubhouse office for the victory celebration. He sipped beer and enjoyed a quiet conversation with his winter hunting pal, Joe Rudi.

Red Sox rookie lefty Jim Burton celebrated by drinking milk. Who could have guessed that big things were still ahead for Burton?

An estimated 1,500 fans greeted the Sox when they arrived at Logan Airport at 7:20 the next morning, and former National Leaguer Reggie Cleveland said, "Bring on the Little Red Tinkertoy."

The Sox were matched up against the favored (7–5) Reds in the World Series. There was some nice symmetry to this duel: Boston and Cincinnati were the first professional baseball towns. The beginning of baseball's new popularity would begin with a World Series featuring charter members.

The 1975 Reds won 108 ball games, clinched the National League West on September 7 (earliest in history), and went an unthinkable 64–17 at home. Cincinnati had a rare balance of speed (168 stolen bases) and power (124 homers). It was a team with two certain Hall of Famers—Johnny Bench and Joe Morgan—plus the all-time major league hit leader, Pete Rose, and manager Sparky Anderson. Despite all of the above, the Reds had a lot to prove. They were on the verge of going down as one of the great underachieving teams of any era, and cynics were poking fun at the Big Red Machine. Where were the championships? The Reds had lost the World Series in 1970 and 1972 and dropped a playoff set in 1973. The town of Cincinnati hadn't won a World Series since 1940, a long dry spell, unless you'd been stranded in the New England desert.

As in 1967 when the Red Sox had to play the Cardinals without Tony Conigliaro, the 1975 Sox were forced to face the Reds without one of their primary offensive weapons. Rookie slugger Rice was felled September 22, victim of a bone-cracking fastball to the wrist that was tossed by the immortal Vern Ruhle.

Bill Lee could feel the skepticism of New England fans and said, "Even if we won we'd get picked for third place in 1976."

Was it sheer coincidence that the National Trust for Historic Preservation was holding its convention in the Hub the weekend the Series started at Fenway? Baseball was in a relatively dormant period prior to the 1975 World Series. Despite all their color, the champion Oakland A's had been representatives of a remote city with little baseball tradition and no natural rivals. Oakland beat the Reds, the Mets, and the Dodgers in 1972, 1973 and 1974, but there was little to remember about those Series other than the pitiful final days of Willie Mays. Television had taken its toll, and the NFL (a game that surely would cease to exist if no one bothered to wager) was flexing its muscles with Super Bowl hysteria and a weekly national television holiday known as the Monday Night Game of the Week. This was a time when action and violence constituted entertainment for America. These were the days that spawned disco dancing, John Travolta, and *People* magazine. Baseball was old, slow, and boring. Richard Nixon was a football fan and Gerald Ford was a former football player. Football was chic. Baseball was something your father talked about—a game loved when all the men wore straw hats and all the children walked ten miles in snowdrifts to get to school in the morning.

The 1975 World Series changed the way Americans felt about baseball. Watching these games was like blowing the dust off a favorite book and reading it for the first time in twenty years. The nation rediscovered its pastime. NBC did a wonderful job with its telecasts, and the marquee names and freeze-frame plays were chiseled into a nation's consciousness. Soon, it would be hip to be a baseball fan again. Carl Yastrzemski still says, "I've always thought baseball was the winner of that World Series."

Johnny Bench doesn't say that. "The ring I have on my finger says, Reds, four, Red Sox, three," Bench said when he was elected to the Hall of Fame in January 1989.

Sox fans can only wince. The 1975 Series, unforgettable and revered throughout the land, is yet another example of the Curse of the Bambino. It was an event littered with drama, heroism, and reversal, but the bottom line is that the Red Sox should have won and they didn't.

"We should have won that Series in the first five games," said Yastrzemski.

He's right. There can be no denying the power and immortality of the 1975 Reds, but a close inspection of the games reveals that this was another Series the Red Sox lost more than the opponents won.

Tiant was the master in Game 1, allowing only five hits in a 6–0 victory. He threw Bench thirteen pitches before getting the star catcher to pop up in the fourth. Man of Machismo Pete Rose said, "In the National League we don't face anyone who throws a spinning curve that takes two minutes to come down."

Bill Lee was selected to pitch the second game of the Series. Lee won seventeen games in 1975, but elbow problems and ineffectiveness put him in the bullpen late in the season, and he did not pitch in the playoffs against the A's. He hadn't started in over a month and hadn't won since August 24. Ironically, the man who convinced Johnson to use Lee was third-base coach Don Zimmer. Lee and Zimmer would scribble their own chapter to this macabre book three years later, but that's another story.

Game 2 was played on a cold drizzly Sunday, and with Henry Kissinger sitting in the high-priced seats wearing a Red Sox cap (one can't be diplomatic about everything), the Reds beat the Sox, 3–2, in Fenway. This was a game Boston should have won. Lee took a 2–1 lead into the ninth, then watched Bench double to right on the first pitch of the inning—a screwball, two inches outside and one inch above the knee. Drago came in to pitch and got Tony Perez to ground to short, Bench moving to third. George Foster popped out to shallow left, and the Sox were one out away from taking a 2–0 Series lead. Dave Concepcion chopped a 1–1 pitch back over the mound. Doyle gloved the ball but had no play, and it was tied. Concepcion stole second and scored on a double to left by Ken Griffey.

The Sox could only look back in anger at the mistakes they made in the early innings. Cecil Cooper ran down the third-base line in the first and was nailed trying to return. Dwight Evans was picked off second in the second. Boston had six runners aboard in the first two innings and only one of them scored. Lee's pitch to Bench and Drago's pitches to Concepcion and Griffey were questioned.

And so the Series moved to Riverfront Stadium, dubbed by Lee, "A concrete jungle made by a pharmaceutical company." This was where the Reds played .790 baseball in 1975. Thomas A. Yawkey made the trip, but he was too ill to attend any of the games.

Game 3 produced one of the great umpiring controversies of this century. Home plate umpire Larry Barnett, a mediocre arbiter from the American League, failed to rule interference on Ed Armbrister's tenth-inning bunt, and Sox fans have been howling ever since. Young Sox fans are trained to spit on the ground at the mere mention of Harry Frazee, Lou Boudreau, Denny Galehouse, Luis Aparicio, and Bucky Dent. Larry Barnett, a native of Nitro, West Virginia, who was thirty years old when he umpired his first World Series game behind home plate in 1975, is the only umpire with a plaque in this Hall of Shame.

It was 5–5 in the bottom of the tenth when Cesar Geronimo led with a single off Jim Willoughby. Sparky Anderson sent Armbrister up to bunt, and the utilityman did his job, bouncing a bunt off the plate and into fair territory. Armbrister took two steps, then stopped as Sox catcher Carlton Fisk lunged forward to make the play. Fisk collided with Armbrister, grabbed the ball, and threw, while still off-balance, toward second. The throw went into center, Geronimo went to third, and Armbrister took second. Rogelio Moret relieved Willoughby and intentionally walked Rose, then fanned Merv Rettenmund. With the outfield drawn in, Morgan hit a shot over Lynn's head in center to win the game. Fisk flung his mask into the screen behind home plate as. Geronimo trotted home with the winning run.

The Red Sox were down, 2–1, and easily could have been up, 3–0. Again, mistakes made earlier in the game came back to spook the Townies. In the fourth, Lynn singled and was picked off by Concepcion after taking too wide a turn at first. Lynn's gaffe killed a potential big inning, and the Sox fell behind, 5–1. But Bernie Carbo hit a pinch homer and Evans tied it with a dramatic two-run smash in the ninth. Doyle led the tenth with a single, then Yastrzemski (the Sox were hurt for eschewing the bunt here) crushed a drive to the wall in center.

Geronimo, back to the wall, caught the ball, and the Reds were in position to win in the bottom of the tenth. Sox fans over the years have found it convenient to blame this loss on Barnett, but the fact remains that Fisk made a terrible throw.

Fisk was still catching (at the age of forty-one) in 1989 and said he was never involved in a similar play. "It [the collision] definitely threw me off balance, off stride," he said. "It affected my timing when I threw. Burleson was there to catch the ball, and he kind of tried to catch it and tag him and the ball went over his head, too. It's still all a matter of interpretation and how he interpreted it. The runner did start toward first and back up and hit me as I went over to get the ball. It doesn't say whether you mean to or not, it's whether you do or not."

Barnett's interpretation was that there was no interference because, "It was simply a collision. It is interference only when the batter intentionally gets in the way."

Years later, when the Baltimore Orioles were playing a game at Cleveland, Baltimore catcher Rick Dempsey was blocked by a batter who had bunted the ball in front of the plate. When no interference was called, Oriole manager Earl Weaver sprinted from the dugout to confront the home plate umpire. Barnett was working at second base and came in toward Weaver, saying, "Easy now, I've handled this one before."

Weaver screamed, "I know you have. And last time you fucked it up I kicked in my TV set!"

Ah. What a comfort to know that the Earl of Baltimore had been rooting for the Red Sox after doing his best to torture Boston fans only a month earlier.

Some of the 1975 Sox didn't think Darrell Johnson put up enough of an argument on the night of L'Affaire Armbrister. Bill Lee said, "If it had been me out there I'd have bitten Barnett's ear off. I'd have van Goghed him."

According to rule 2.00(a): "Offensive interference is an act which interferes with, obstructs, impedes, hinders or confuses any fielder attempting to make a play." According to rule 7:09(L): "It is interference if the batter fails to avoid a fielder who is attempting to field a batted ball or intentionally interferes with a thrown ball." It was later revealed that the umpires had been working with a supplemental instruction governing interference that read, "When a catcher and a batter-runner going to first have contact when the catcher is fielding the ball, there is generally no violation and nothing should be called." None of this was explained after Game 3.

"As far as I'm concerned, it's a double play," said Fisk. "I know I had to tag that Armbrister."

Lee added, "We'd be better off on the honor system. Let's bring the game back to the players and the fans. . . . There's going to be a great outpouring of sympathy for us. The country is going to go crazy. The people of Fairbanks, Alaska, are going to start sending letters to Bowie Kuhn, start calling his house. There's going to be such an outcry that they're going to have to play the game over tomorrow. You wait and see."

They did not play the game over; instead, America was treated to another virtuoso performance by El Tiante the next night. Boston's rumba righty had nothing in Game 4, but like a wobbly champion prize-fighter, he went the distance and won on points. Tiant threw 163 pitches in a 5–4, Game 4 victory at Riverfront to tie the Series at 2–2. The Sox scored all of their runs in the fourth inning, then watched their gutty Cuban righty hang on by force of will. It was a Karl Wallenda act all the way. The Reds slashed three hits and cut the lead to 5–4 in the fourth. Tiant gave up two walks in the fifth, a single in the sixth, and a single in the eighth. He got out of each jam. NBC informed its massive audience that the Reds had won twenty-three games in their final times at bat. Geronimo opened with a single, and there was Arm-brister, bunting again. Rose walked, and Griffey hit a 400-foot shot to center, which Lynn snared. Everyone was exhausted by then, and Morgan popped up to end it.

The Reds won a 6–2 blowout the next night, the only truly dull game of this starfest. Tony Perez snapped out of his (0–15) slump with a pair of homers, and Don Gullett shot down the Sox, retiring sixteen straight in one powerful stretch. This was the first of the five games that left the Sox and their fans with no regrets. The Reds finally played like the Reds, and Boston trailed 3–2 when the teams came back to rainy New England to settle things.

The rain hurt the Red Sox. Lee was scheduled to pitch Game 6 on a Saturday afternoon, but the game was postponed due to rain Saturday, Sunday, and again on Monday. Johnson, figuring he had to pitch Tiant to assure a seventh game, took advantage of the extra time and moved Tiant into Game 6. Lee ripped Johnson for the switch, saying, "The biggest reason Johnson is going with Tiant in Game 6 is to satisfy certain elements of the media." This was the same Bill Lee who said, "Darrell's been falling out of trees and landing on his feet all season."

Where was this rain when the Sox needed some rest for Jim Lonborg in 1967?

Each day the commissioner considered playing, but there was no hope. The most memorable moment arrived Monday when a Bowie Kuhn spokesperson hopefully offered, "The commissioner would like to announce that it has stopped raining in New Jersey." Some newspapers ran out of cash and called writers home while those who stayed resorted to features on Bill Lee's father and Fenway groundskeeper Joe Mooney. The Reds went to Tufts University to work out, and some Medford residents still remember the sight of Sparky Anderson, in full uniform, hopping off the bus to get directions to the urban campus. Seventy-two hours of nonstop downpour and drizzle created considerable anxiety among the players. Lynn was happy to have Sunday off because, he said, "I can watch the Juice." (Fellow Trojan O. J. Simpson was doing his thing for the Buffalo Bills.) But Lynn admitted, "It's incredible how much of the edge is taken off this thing now. It just doesn't seem the same as it did a few days ago. Now it's just like any regular season game. The atmosphere and excitement sure have changed."

Tuesday, October 21, was a brilliant autumn day in New England, and the Red Sox and Reds finally resumed the soggy Series. It was clear from the outset that the layoff had done nothing to diminish the intensity or execution of play, and what unfolded was arguably the best World Series game of all time. Game Six has taken on a life of its own in the years since it was played, and it gets larger and more thrilling in each retelling. Some distance allows that there may be other contenders for the title of the Greatest Game Ever Played, but by any measure 1975's Game 6 will stand as one of the top ten games in World Series history, and one that came at a time when baseball needed it most.

The estimable Roger Angell wrote, "Game Six . . . what can we say of it without seeming to diminish it by recapitulation or dull it with detail?"

◊

Let us then be brief:

Under a hunter's moon, Lynn stroked a three-run homer to get things started in the first. The Reds took over from there and bled Tiant for six runs over eight innings, snapping El Tiante's string of forty consecutive scoreless innings in Fenway. The Boston crowd (not to mention the 62 million watching at home) got a scare when Lynn crashed into the center-field fence in the fifth. It was at this instant that Yawkey pledged to pad the green perimeter. Geronimo delivered the knockout punch with a first-pitch, solo homer in the eighth, and Boston's grand master walked from the mound as Lonborg had walked off in Game 7 against the Cardinals. It was simply too much to expect Tiant to shut the Reds down for a third straight time.

Boston trailed, 6–3, with two on and two out in the bottom of the eighth. The game was seven outs from being over, and there would have been little remarkable about Cincinnati winning the Series in six games with a 6–3 finale in Boston. In the press box, *Globe* columnist Ray Fitzgerald, the best New England wordsmith of his time, a Springfield native and a former Notre Dame left-hander who knew the feelings of the fandom, put a clean sheet of paper behind his typewriter cylinder, twirled the scroll bar, and wrote, "You could feel it slipping away . . ."

The world changed when pinch hitter Bernardo Carbo, a former Cincinnati kid, barely fouled off a 2–2 pitch, then crushed a three-run homer to center off Rawley Eastwick. They played into the morning after that. The Sox failed to score after loading the bases with no outs in the ninth (George Foster threw out Denny Doyle at the plate when Doyle thought coach Zimmer said, "go, go, go" instead of "no, no, no"), and the Reds were foiled by Dwight Evans's legendary over-the-shoulder grab of Joe Morgan's drive in the eleventh.

At 12:34 A.M., Wednesday morning, facing Pat Darcy, the twelfth pitcher of the game, Carlton Fisk ended it with a twisting shot off the left-field foul pole. An NBC camera placed inside the left-field Wall caught Fisk gyrating, waving and somehow *willing* the ball into fair territory. This tape can be inspected at the Smithsonian Institution or any time NBC plugs an upcoming postseason game. Fisk's pole shot and his tour-de-bases has become synonymous with the thrill of victory.

And thus, Game 6 1975 took its place alongside Game 8 in 1912, Game 4 in 1947, and Game 7 in 1960.

In 1989 Doug Green proposed to Lori Barrington of Brunswick, Maine. They selected October 21 as their wedding date, and the engraved invitation featured a photo of Fisk hitting his homer. The invitation read, "October 21, 1975, A Great Moment . . . October 21, 1989, Another Great Moment."

"I always wanted to be married on that date," said Green.

Fisk: "Freddie Lynn was on deck. He was hitting after me that game for some reason. I don't know why, but he was and I can remember standing in the on-deck circle before the inning started, and you just had a feeling something good was going to happen. And I told Freddie, 'Freddie, I'm going to hit one off the Wall. Drive me in.' And that was the way it ended."

Fenway legions did not want to leave the ancient yard after Fisk's historic shot, and they stayed to watch him gallop across the field for a television interview under the left-field stands. Venerable organist John Kiley kept things shaking with the "Hallelujah Chorus," followed by "Stout-Hearted Men," followed by "Beer Barrel Polka," followed by "Seventy-six Trombones." In Kenmore Square young people poured out of bars and celebrated as if a war had been won. Down Brookline Avenue, the girls from Emmanuel, Simmons, and Wheelock hung out of dorm windows, squealing and toasting strangers in the night. To the north and west, church bells rang and car horns blared.

The Red Sox won the Greatest Game Ever Played, so what did it matter what happened in Game 7? This was the type of thinking that hurt the Red Sox in 1967 (World Series as anticlimax), and it came into play again after Game 6. More than one hardball historian suggested that the Series be called off and declared a draw; just toast each other and let it be decided by infinite mind games. Indeed, euphoric Boston lost sight of the fact that the objective of this event was to win the Series, not just the best game of the Series. And so it was that the Red Sox 1975 Game 7 loss was greeted without sting, without a trace of regret. The Sox blew a 3–0 lead and lost, 4–3, when the Reds scored a run on a broken-bat single in the ninth, but the headline in the next day's *Globe* was "Reds win—but what a year we had!" Peter Gammons, the official keeper of the flame, wrote, "It was like the death of a favorite grandmother, a season whose life was beautiful and full and gave everyone from Southie to Stonington, Connecticut, from Groton to Charlestown, New Hampshire, a year they will reminisce about until Olde Fenway calls them back again.''

The *Globe* proudly inserted "Wait'll next year" iron-on transfers into weekend editions after the loss.

Once again, we see the glee of almost winning. This is why Johnny Bench has the ring and Carl Yastrzemski doesn't.

The autopsy on Game 7 is grim and revealing; it can only leave Sox fans with regret. The Sox blew a chance in the first when Carbo failed to go from second to third on a fly to right. Boston scored three in the third, but couldn't go for the kill. Rick Burleson struck out with the bases loaded to end the inning and give the Reds hope. The Red Sox left nine runners in the first five innings, always a bad sign. Boston still led 3–0 in the sixth, but with the indomitable Rose on first (the Series MVP, Rose reached base in eleven of his last fifteen plate appearances), Bench hit a potential double-play grounder to short. Rose went into second like the wild man of Borneo and Denny Doyle's relay throw to first wound up in the dugout. Doyle later claimed the cover of the ball had been almost torn off when Bench hit it to short (teammate Bob Heise retrieved the ball in the dugout and presented it to Doyle after the game). Bench took second and Tony Perez was allowed to bat with two out.

Then it happened. There are, in life, a few moments which all of us would like to have back. A man in a rental car, searching for an office building in an unfamiliar neighborhood, glances down at his map, then looks up and sees his hood crashing into the rear end of a station wagon. Too late. Visiting your in-laws for the first time, attempting to break the ice at a tense family dinner, you blurt out an ethnic joke, and the attempt is greeted by stony silence and forced coughs. Too late.

Catcher Fisk called for a curveball. It was up to Lee to decide what kind of curveball it would be. Lee thought he had a great idea. He'd try sneaking a blooper pitch past veteran slugger Tony Perez. Too late. The ball approached Perez in slow motion as Lee's teammates and Sox fans held their breath. When the insult fell to earth, Perez sent it into orbit, way over the screen in left. Boston's lead was cut to 3–2. It was happening again.

The sting and the shame were still there fourteen years later when Lee admitted:

> I was annoyed with that botched double play and I hung a breaking ball out of a stretch. It was a terrible pitch. I'd gotten him out all the time, but I'd never hung it. I'd gotten him out with a good curveball, but I'd lost my concentration after we fucked up the double play. I'm going, 'How the fuck did we not turn the double play on that fucker?' I was really pissed off and I just lost concentration. But we still had a 3–2 lead. What got me was, you look back at that game and look at the runners we left on base early in the ball game. We could have blown 'em away in the seventh game and we didn't blow 'em away. The thing I remember most is after we didn't score; I remember how the fans got progressively and progressively quieter. It was an eerie feeling how everybody . . . they were just so nervous. They've got a history, a premonition of the past and they allow that to influence their decision. They're not positive people in the stands. They're very negative-oriented because they settled in New England on a fucking rocky place where you can't grow shit. It wouldn't have happened if they settled in the Midwest. The people in New England are hardy and they're hard-nosed and tough and provincial. Why are they that way? Cuz they landed on the worst part of the shore.

With one out in the seventh, Lee had to leave because of a blister. Rose tied it with a single off Moret and Willoughby came in to stall the Red Machine.

Evans walked to start the bottom of the eighth, then Burleson came up and tried to bunt. He failed on two pitches (it would be too easy here to say, "typical Red Sox") then grounded into a double play. With two out and nobody on, Johnson sent Cecil Cooper up to hit for Jim Willoughby (0.00 ERA in 6.1 Series innings). Willoughby had faced four batters, and none got the ball out of the infield. Cooper was 1–18 at that point and went out on a foul pop to third baseman Rose. Cooper finished the Series with a .053 batting average. Sox fans again cursed their hard luck. The injured Rice was dearly missed.

Dick Drago had pitched three innings the night before and rookie lefty Jim Burton got the call. This was the same Jim Burton who was not trusted to pitch against the Brewers in August, the same young Burton who drank milk instead of champagne the night the Sox eliminated the A's in Oakland.

Burton walked Griffey to start the inning, then Geronimo sacrificed Griffey to second. Griffey moved to third when pinch hitter Dan Driessen grounded out, and Rose walked. On a 1–2 pitch, Morgan broke his bat and blooped a single to center. 4–3.

"A couple of years ago, I would have struck out on the pitch he threw me," said Morgan. "It was a good slider and I got it off the end of the bat."

Burton said, "I felt it was the right call for the manager to bring me in. I wasn't any more nervous than in any big game. Just concentrating on the batters. I threw Morgan my best pitch, a slider low and away. He got a piece of it and when I looked back and saw that Lynn couldn't get to it, I had that empty disappointed feeling."

Jim Burton was born in Royal Oak, Michigan, in October 1949, just after the Red Sox dropped those final two games to the Yankees in New York. He pitched in twenty-nine games for the Sox in 1975, compiling an ERA of 2.89 to go with his 1–2 record. He was just a few days shy of his twenty-sixth birthday when he came in to the seventh game of the World Series. It was his moment. He pitched in only one big league game after losing the seventh game of the 1975 World Series.

The Sox went down in order in the ninth, with Yastrzemski making the final out on a routine fly to center. Twenty-two hours after their greatest victory, the 1975 Red Sox suffered a disappointing defeat. In effect, the Sox had split a morning/night doubleheader, and it cost them a World Championship.

Burleson, ever the competitor, didn't buy the kind words that were tossed about the loser's clubhouse. "We haven't played well since the playoffs and we beat ourselves again with mistakes," said the Rooster.

"I thought we should have won that Series in five games, I really did," Yastrzemski said in 1989. "The change-up that Lee threw to Perez hurt. The one thing that our scouting reports said was you don't throw anything off speed to him. My theory is in a short series, you can't make mistakes. They'll come up and bite you."

Lee denied any wrongdoing, and said, "Why does everybody ask me about that pitch to Perez? Why doesn't somebody ask me about the pitch I threw to Johnny Bench to get a double play that we botched? I have lived by the slow curve. I die by the slow curve. That home run didn't beat us. We made some mistakes that beat us."

Willoughby said, "There is no such thing as poetic justice in baseball. Just luck."

It was a remarkable Series. In six of the seven games the winning team came from behind. Five games were decided by one run, two games were settled in the ninth, and two others went into extra innings. There were thirteen lead changes and/or ties in the seven games. The Sox led in every game, but made too many base-running mistakes (six Boston base runners were tagged out at the plate) and allowed the Reds to steal nine bases. The Sox allowed the Reds to keep coming back, and the Reds did keep coming back, and that is why they, not the Red Sox, deserved to be World Champions.

◇

There was a widespread perception that the Red Sox were a dynasty-in-the-making. Of course, this is what everybody thought after the 1946 World Series. In both instances, the Red Sox were a young, slugging unit tabbed as the team-to-beat for the rest of the decade. It didn't happen either time.

Nine months after the palpitating 1975 World Series, the Red Sox, way out of contention in the 1976 race, traded Carbo to Milwaukee for Bobby Darwin, and Evans greeted Darwin with this: "You're going to enjoy the Fall Classic."

"What classic is that?" asked a stunned Darwin.

Evans said, "The Fall Classic. The World Series."

Darwin, of course, was right. While Evans and most Red Sox fans looked into the future and saw an endless string of postseason appearances, the reality was that the rules of baseball changed after the 1975 World Series, and it took the Red Sox several years to adjust to the times. In the months immediately after the 1975 Series, independent arbitrator Peter L. Seitz ruled that baseball's reserve clause was not renewable and was good for only one year. Any player who didn't sign for the 1976 season would be a free agent at the end of that season. Fisk, Burleson, and Lynn, three of Jerry Kapstein's clients, were not signed when the 1976 season started, and the controversy and disharmony that accompanied this uncertainty drove a pipe through the ball club. The Red Sox are nothing if not predictable, and just as they flopped in 1947 and 1968, they fell on their fresh young faces in 1976, one year after losing the seventh game of the World Series.

They lost ten in a row early in the season. Lee blew out his shoulder in a Yankee Stadium brawl. Trade rumors regarding Fisk, Burleson, and Lynn flew around the yard like fly balls during batting practice. Carbo was traded. On June 15, General Manager Dick O'Connell agreed to send Charlie Finley $2 million for Joe Rudi and Rollie Fingers. Yawkey was undergoing chemotherapy during this time, and it has never been clear how much input he had into these decisions. Commissioner Kuhn voided the Rudi-Fingers deal two days later. Meanwhile, Johnson was second-guessing Fisk's game calling and gradually losing control of the team. Eight times they got to within a game of .500, then lost. Captain Yastrzemski said, "With the talent we have on this team, playing .500 is a disgrace."

Yawkey didn't live to see the end of the dismal title defense. Weak from a year-long battle with cancer and hospitalized at New England Baptist, the venerable owner died in his sleep at 4:20 P.M. on Friday, July 9. Since this date, Red Sox ownership has displayed the smarts and stability of a Banana Republic.

Manager Darrell Johnson staggered into the summer. He stayed at the Bellevue-Stratford when he managed the American League in the 1976 All-Star game in Philadelphia. Members of an American Legion convention shared the hotel space, and many later died of a mysterious disease. Johnson lived to manage the Sox for a few more days, then was fired after losing five out of six. The Sox were in fifth place when Don Zimmer took over as manager. The Sox stumbled into September, then won fifteen of their last eighteen to finish third, four games over .500 and fifteen and a half behind the beefed-up Yankees.

Clearly, New York was going to be the competition for the next couple of years. Yankee owner George Steinbrenner was intent on bringing back the glory days and had the instincts and the money to do it. It was no surprise when the Yankees and the Red Sox battled it out in 1977. The Baltimore Orioles were the surprising intruder in the 1977 race, but the Sox and the Yanks were the centerfold teams of baseball. Fisk and Yankee catcher Thurman Munson developed a Kennedy-Nixon rivalry, and fans in Boston and New York reveled in the rebirth of the Athens-Sparta feud. For the first time since 1949, both teams were very good at the same time.

The 1977 Red Sox featured one of the most explosive lineups in baseball history. They had a number nine batter (Butch Hobson) who hit thirty homers. They hit sixteen homers in three games against the Yanks and thirty-three in a ten-game stretch. They hit eight homers in one game against the expansion Blue Jays, and eight times hit five or more in a game. Five players hit more than twenty-five homers, and more than two million filed through Fenway for the first time in franchise history. As ever, the Red Sox had the sluggers, but the Yankees had the pitching. Zimmer had to start rookie Mike Paxton against Ron Guidry in Yankee Stadium in September. In the end, former Sox reliever Sparky Lyle won the Cy Young Award, Boston finished in a second-place tie with Baltimore (two and a half games back), and the Yankees won the World Series while the Red Sox went home to think about 1978.

EIGHT

Nineteen seventy-eight. Nothing compares. The New England baseball fan is paralyzed at the mere mention of the year. The mind calcifies. This was the apocalyptic, cataclysmic fold by which all others must be measured.

The year was ushered in by Boston's greatest blizzard of the century. Twenty-three inches of snow fell on the Fenway lawn, and moonlighting Pawtucket manager Joe Morgan worked twenty-four-hour shifts plowing the Massachusetts Turnpike. Perhaps the great blizzard (plowmen still call it "the big one," an expression usually reserved for veterans of World War II) could have been read as a warning. Just as it was impossible to thoroughly prepare for a storm of such fury and magnitude, no Sox fan could have braced for the horror of losing the flag to the Yankees after leading the hated New Yorkers by fourteen games on July 20. In baseball lore, only three collapses approximate this one: the 1915 New York Giants led the Boston Braves by fifteen games on the Fourth of July and finished ten and a half behind; the 1951 Brooklyn Dodgers led the Giants by thirteen games August 11, got tied on the final day of the season, then lost the playoff; and the 1964 Phillies led the Cardinals by six and a half games with twelve to play, then lost ten straight. The Giants, Dodgers, and Phillies eventually won championships. The Red Sox have not fully recovered and maybe never will.

Nineteen seventy-eight was the year when the Red Sox left scars that will last until a World Series is finally won. After what happened to the 1978 Townies, the oft-burned masses can only conclude that no regular season lead is safe until the pennant has been mathematically clinched. Today's Sox bristle when they surge into first in July and face a sea of skeptics, but they should know that 1978 is the reason. Most Red Sox of the eighties and nineties were not around when it happened and haven't lived with the emotional wreckage that washed ashore after the fall of 1978. The joys and disappointments that a baseball team brings to its fans are trivial compared with life, death, marriage, divorce, health, success, family, and friends, but a good portion of the fandom fawns on the team as a substitute for life's dullnesses or inequities. Others simply follow the Red Sox because their fathers and grandfathers followed, but in either case, Sox fans with their normally high expectations become like four-year-old children on Christmas Eve when it actually looks like the Red Sox are going to finally do it. This was the way the Fenway fans felt in the summer of 1978, and New Englanders will never forget what happened in those final two months. A walk through the 1978 campaign should erase any remaining doubt that the Sox have been cursed since they sold the Babe to New York seventy years ago.

For starters, the Sox went out and signed the Yankees' best pitcher, Mike Torrez, a product of free agency who'd been with four teams in four seasons. Torrez won seventeen for New York in 1977, then won two more when the Yankees beat the Dodgers for their first World Series victory in fifteen years—a long drought by Yankee standards. Torrez was a twenty-game winner for the Orioles when they failed to catch the Red Sox in 1975. Meanwhile, second baseman Jerry Remy, a Somerset, Massachusetts, native was acquired in a winter trade, and the Sox got a final boost when young flamethrower Dennis Eckersley came from Cleveland in a late spring trade that sent four bodies to the Tribe.

The pressure was on, and Zimmer was nervous, right from the start. Yastrzemski recalled, "He looked at me in spring training and said, 'A hundred bucks says you're the manager of this team by the end of the season.' I shook my head and laughed. I told him I never wanted to manage."

They went to Fort Lauderdale two days after St. Patrick's Day and faced a small army of media ranging from David Susskind to Phyllis George (it was pointed out that she had regressed from Miss America to Miss Information in a few short years). An obscure minor league pitcher named Bobby Sprowl was shot in the arm during spring training when a doctor's gun in a next-door apartment went off. Sprowl recovered nicely. He wasn't going to die in some fluke hotel room accident. The diamond gods had other, more torturous plans for Bobby Sprowl. The Sox went to Puerto Rico for a couple of games and happened to be on the scene when Karl Wallenda fell to his death outside their hotel. Another harbinger.

Jim Rice was in MVP form at the start, and the Sox moved into first place on May 13. They won twenty-six of their first thirty Fenway games. In a twelve-game stretch against the Yankees and Orioles they went 8–4 and blew the race open. Seven Red Sox were named to the All-Star team, and Boston led the American League by nine games on July 10, but Burleson hurt his ankle July 9 while sliding into second base in Cleveland, and it would prove costly. It was like the first tiny snag in the sleeve of a sweater; you don't even notice it at first, but once you start pulling the thread, the sleeve falls off.

On Thursday, July 20, the Sox were 62–28 and led the second-place Brewers by nine games and the fourth-place Yankees by a whopping fourteen games. The defending World Champions were not going to be a factor this year, that was for sure. The Red Sox were America's team. All the things that were said about them after the 1975 Series were finally coming true.

Pete Rose was in the midst of his forty-four-game hitting streak when the Red Sox started to unravel in late July. Burleson was still limping, second baseman Remy had a cracked wrist, Evans was dizzy from a beaning, and third baseman Butch Hobson was rearranging the bone chips in his elbow between pitches. Boston lost four straight, and after getting swept in Kansas City the lead shrunk to five games for the first time since June 10. But it was still the Brewers who were threatening, not the Yankees. New York was a mess. Billy Martin was fired after saying of star Reggie Jackson and owner Steinbrenner: "One's a born liar, the other's convicted," and the Yanks were a hopeless ten games out.

After the All-Star break, the Sox went 2–8 through Minnesota, Kansas City, and Texas, and the Yankees had closed to within eight when Zimmer's wounded troupe stumbled home. New York had picked up six games in eight days. The Yanks cut it to six and a half games before the Red Sox swept a doubleheader in New York August 3. Four days later Zimmer said, "I look at us now and we're seven games in front.

We were nine in front at the All-Star game, we lost eleven of fourteen and we're still seven in front. I've got to be happy with that."

They endured their second West Coast trip, and when they got home they were still seven and a half games ahead of the Yankees. Hobson already had thirty errors. Lee had lost his seventh straight while the team was in Oakland and was yanked from the pitching rotation. Meanwhile, Torrez was ripping Zimmer's managerial strategy, and Zimmer was ripping mad at both Lee and Torrez. The manager was keeping a clip file on Lee—consisting of stories in which Lee called him a gerbil. As for Torrez, Zimmer said, "There must be something in his contract that says he's not just a pitcher, but a player/manager." Rice also used the newspapers to blast Torrez, the man teammates called "Taco."

The Sox silenced the barking dogs with six straight victories when they returned to Fenway, then blew a 5–2, seventh-inning lead against Toronto August 31. Oakland followed the Jays to town and won two of three, and the Red Sox were in trouble again. It was the first time Boston had dropped three straight home games in 1978. It would not be the last. On Friday, September 1, Oakland snapped the streak with a 5–1 win. It was on this night that twenty-two-year-old lefty Bobby Sprowl was called up to the big leagues. Pawtucket manager Joe Morgan admitted that Sprowl "might not be ready," but Lee was in the bullpen/doghouse, and Zimmer had plans for the kid.

The Yankees were only five games out. Boston went to Baltimore, birthplace of the Babe and always a chamber of horrors for the Red Sox in September. Zimmer's league leaders lost the first game when Don Stanhouse picked Fisk off first base in the ninth inning. Sprowl lost his major league debut to Jim Palmer the next night, and the Yankees beat the Tigers to close to within four games. The nervous Sox had lost five of six and committed eleven errors in the half dozen games.

While the Red Sox were in Baltimore, Oriole first-base coach Jim Frey had some casual conversations with Red Sox first baseman George Scott. Scott was tossing grounders to his infielders before an inning when Frey decided to tease the Boomer. "Boomer, you guys had this big lead and now it's down to four or five games," said Frey. "What the hell's going on with you guys?"

Scott didn't even look up. He kept rolling grounders to his teammates and said, "Some of these guys are choking, man."

That said, the staggering Sox went home to Boston for a showdown with the surging Yankees. The Yankees had won thirteen of fifteen when they arrived in Boston Thursday, September 7. Moreover, they were 18–7 since the start of a New York newspaper strike that had shut down the *Times, Daily News,* and the *Post.* The combustible Yankees could only benefit from a work stoppage by the ink-stained wretches of New York, and it was Boston's ill fortune to have the New York writers walking picket lines when the Red Sox started to slump. The 1971 Pirates won a World Championship in a season when the Pittsburgh papers were on strike from May to September. Detroit papers were on strike the year the Tigers won their 1968 World Series. The 1978 Yankees were playing in a news vacuum when they made their charge. There were no flammable quotes from Reggie Jackson or George Steinbrenner. The Red Sox, meanwhile, were facing the usual skepticism from the fourth estate.

There is no way to understate what happened to the Red Sox on this September weekend in 1978. The Yankees came to Fenway four games back and pulverized the Sox four straight times, outscoring Boston 42–9, outhitting the Sox, 67–21. Boston made twelve errors to New York's five. Aptly dubbed "The Boston Massacre," this series scarred a new generation of Red Sox fans. New York did it to Boston again.

In the opener, the Yanks pulverized Torrez, pounding twenty-one hits and taking a 12–0 lead in the fourth. Hobson added two more errors to his league-leading total. Thurman Munson had three hits before the Sox number nine batter came to the plate. Natural forces came into play here because Game 1 of the series was a makeup tilt, originally scheduled for the Fourth of July, back when the Sox were smoking and the Yankees were going up in smoke under the fiery rule of Billy Martin. At that time, Thurman Munson was working in right field, and Willie Randolph and Bucky Dent were both out of the lineup with injuries. The Yanks had first baseman Jim Spencer throwing in the bullpen and had summoned double-A pitchers from West Haven (would faceless righty Paul Semall have started?) before the game was washed away. Earth, wind, fire, and rain have not been friends of the Red Sox during this seventy-year trial, and Game 1 of the Massacre serves as one more example.

Panic was evident. While bleacher fans were chanting, "We want

Lee," Zimmer announced that Sprowl would make his second major league start in the Sunday finale.

The Red Sox made seven errors the next night in a 13–2 loss. It was 8–0 in the second inning. Evans had to leave in the second because of dizziness. Tom Boswell of the *Washington Post* led his story with, "Ibid." George Scott admitted, "Of course it's embarrassing."

Eckersley and Ron Guidry were locked in a 0–0 duel in the fourth inning of the third game when Lou Piniella's two-out, wind-blown pop-up fell in the middle of five Boston fielders and led to a seven-run rally in front of a national television audience. The Yankees were 7–0 winners and closed to within one game of first place.

Dick Waterman stood up in a Cambridge bar and stated, "Today was the first time in history that a first-place team was mathematically eliminated."

Mary Kelly of Braintree went to Mass at St. Thomas More that night, and when the priest asked those in attendance to pray for the intentions of the pope, for peace in the world, and "for your own personal intentions," Kelly said, "Lord, hear my prayer. May the Red Sox snap out of it."

Carl Yastrzemski appealed to a different master, but with no more success. Torrez, rookie Jim Wright, and Eckersley had been beaten, and Tiant only had three days' rest. Lee was rotting in the bullpen and owned a 12–5 lifetime record against the Yankees, third best in history (Babe Ruth, 17–5, is number two). Yastrzemski went into Zimmer's office Sunday morning and begged the manager to start Lee instead of Sprowl.

"He opened his desk," Yastrzemski reported eleven years later, "and he tossed all these clippings at me, clippings where Lee had called him 'gerbil' or something else like that."

The stubborn manager was sticking with Sprowl. He kept spitting tobacco juice and saying, "The kid's got ice water in his veins."

Ice water. Sprowl walked the first two Yankee batters, got Munson to hit into a double play, then gave up a single and two more walks and was gone. He never threw another big league pitch in a Red Sox uniform. His jittery heaves flew to the backstop the following spring and he was traded to Houston. Bobby Sprowl never won a game in the majors and retired in 1983 after pitching in twenty-two major league games (0–3, 5.40 ERA). Ice water.

While Sprowl took a shower after failing to break a sweat, the Yankees beat the Red Sox, 7–4, to complete the sweep and move into a first-place tie. New York had won sixteen of eighteen. It was the first time in 109 days that the Sox hadn't been in sole possession of first place, and it also marked the first time since 1943 that the Yankees swept a four-game series at Fenway Park.

Lee was still fuming about the snub in the spring of 1989 and said, "I could have started any game. He wouldn't let me pitch. It was between him and [Haywood] Sullivan. I got in a fight with him and Sullivan. Sullivan was the main heavy in that, not Zimmer. He hated me because a long time ago when they asked me what's the difference between Haywood Sullivan and [club traveling secretary] Jack Rogers, I said, 'Jack Rogers does a nice job, Haywood Sullivan has a nice job.' Then I got in a fight with him when they sold Carbo to Cleveland and he got me in his office and came across the desk and tried to fight me and Buddy LeRoux broke it up. He really wanted to come across the table at me and I said, 'Come on across.' Boy, I'd have killed the son of a bitch. Then I had a helluva year in '79. They really lost because they didn't pitch me."

Three days after the Boston Massacre, Scott extended his slump to 0–34 ("some of these guys are choking, man") and the Sox dropped a 2–1 decision to fall into second place. The staggering Townies trailed by one and a half when they arrived in New York. The *Globe*'s Peter Gammons wrote, "This weekend is more than the pennant. It's a chance to avoid being history. Guys who have it and blow it are history. The '64 Phillies. Richard M. Nixon. Eddie Fisher. It's a chance to avoid going into restaurants this winter and being asked 'What happened?' For guys who live around Boston, like Carlton Fisk and Jerry Remy, it means avoiding being asked that the rest of their lives."

They were greeted by an army of New York fans wearing T-shirts that read BOSTON IS DEAD, RED SOCKS CHOKE, YAZ HAS VD, and the ubiquitous BOSTON SUCKS.

Guidry improved his record to 22–2 with a two-hit, 4–0, win in the first game in New York and Boston dropped two and a half back. Boston bottomed out sixteen hours later, losing 3–2 in the Stadium to fall three and a half back. There were plenty of regrets after the Saturday afternoon loss. Torrez gave up a Reggie Jackson homer on an 0–2 pitch. Yastrzemski got caught playing too shallow on a Mickey Rivers triple (another 0–2 Torrez pitch) in the ninth, then Zimmer let Torrez pitch to Munson with the winning run on third and first base open. Munson scored Rivers with a sac fly to left. Boston had lost fourteen of seventeen, hitting .192 with a 4.58 ERA and thirty-one errors. Rick Burleson broke the silence in the Red Sox locker room with this admission: "It just seems like destiny has taken over. I don't see how we can win this thing. . . . The abuse we have taken and the abuse we must be prepared to take for the entire winter we richly deserve."

Dick Drago said, "This whole thing tears through you. And all you can do is take it. You won't know what humiliation is until you've been through what we're enduring right now."

Sparky Lyle, the man Boston sent to New York for Danny Cater, was asked about his former teammates and said, "I don't feel sorry for them. I pity them."

Remy had trouble sleeping. He'd lie down in his room at the New York Sheraton on Fifty-sixth Street and Seventh Avenue and he'd hear "Red Sox suck." His head pounded. He'd grown up rooting for the Red Sox back when Chuck Schilling was the second baseman. He knew what the Boston fans were feeling because he was one of them. But he suddenly realized how much easier it was to be one of the fans. The fans could go back to their jobs. This was his job, and he knew he was part of something that fans would ridicule for the rest of their lives.

The Sox recovered the next day, finally beating the Yankees, 7–3. Scott ended his slump, which had stretched to an incredible 0–36. Zimmer knew about such things. He once went 0–34 with the New York Mets. Hobson asked out of the lineup September 21 and prepared for postseason elbow surgery. Thirteen games remained—the Red Sox won eleven of them, including the last eight. Tiant, pitching his last game in a Red Sox uniform, beat the Blue Jays, 5–0, on the final day of the regular season, and the Indians blasted Catfish Hunter and the Yankees, 9–2, forcing the second playoff game in American League history.

◊

Yankee manager Bob Lemon was in the bullpen for the 1948 Indians when Cleveland beat Denny Galehouse and Boston thirty years earlier. Yankee General Manager Al Rosen was a Tribe third baseman.

The Yankees had Guidry (24–3) pitching on three days' rest while the Red Sox countered with Torrez (16–12). Guidry's three 1978 losses came against pitchers named Mike (Caldwell, Flanagan, and Willis), and that was considered a good omen. It is also interesting to note that Torrez, Guidry, and Piniella, three men who would play big roles in this game, shared the same birthday, August 28. Torrez had been struggling and said, "Here I've been given a chance to redeem myself. If I win this, this is what people will remember. . . . The history books owe us one."

The Red Sox were in this position because the team had worn down and played shoddy defense in August and early September. Fisk had caught 155 games and played with a cracked rib. Remy had a cracked bone in his wrist, and Hobson's bone chips caused many of his forty-three errors. Evans was still dizzy from a Mike Parrott beaning in August and Burleson's ankle was never right. Boston's vaunted lineup was together for only 38 of 162 games. Relief ace Bill Campbell had a shoulder tendon problem. Bernie Carbo had been sold to Cleveland, leaving Bob Bailey (.191) and Gary Hancock as the pinch hitters of choice. Fred Kendall and Frank Duffy were no more threatening. Boston's nonstarters hit six homers in 1978. George Scott was used as a pinch runner. Zimmer's feud with Lee also took its toll. "I'll tell you when we lost," said Torrez. "We lost when Zimmer took Bill Lee out of the rotation."

The Yankees were in this position because they had won fifty-two of their last seventy-four games and had six (Jackson, Nettles, Munson, Rivers, Chambliss, Piniella) of the best clutch hitters of their era. The Yanks were the defending World Champs, united only in their collective disdain for owner George Steinbrenner. Just as they didn't panic when they fell fourteen games behind the Red Sox, they didn't panic when the Sox tied them on the final day of the regular season. Twenty-nine years earlier, the Yankees beat the Red Sox because the Yankees had the tough guys and the Red Sox had the marquee guys. After losing game number 162, the Yankees packed their bags for Kansas City (where the playoffs were to start) and flew to Boston for a one-game playoff. They were confident, and many of the players gathered at Daisy Buchanan's, on Newbury Street, the night before the epic. It was impossible to stay in a hotel room that evening. Lou Piniella was worrying when he walked over to Daisy's, but when he saw his teammates drinking and laughing, he stopped worrying. Everything was going to be okay.

Years later, Reggie Jackson said "When you were with the Yankees, you just handled the Red Sox. You knew you were going to beat them. They just didn't play well against New York. The papers would get on 'em and the fans expected them to get beat. The Red Sox players didn't expect to play well."

Monday, October 2, 1978, was a crisp, sparkling afternoon in Boston. It was a perfect backdrop in the perfect little ballpark for what many have chosen to term the best game ever. Certainly this Yankee–Red Sox playoff ranks with most memorable, alongside the 1951 Dodgers-Yankees, Bobby Thomson home run game and a handful of World Series classics. Given the extraordinary circumstances and individuals— Boston's fold, New York's surge, the history of Yankee–Red Sox duels, Guidry's 24–3 record, Torrez's defection from New York, Mr. October (Jackson), Boston's tormented thirty-nine-year-old superstar (Yastrzemski), the sale of Ruth to the Yankees in 1920—there was reason to believe this would be a game for the ages. Baseball's Athens and Sparta had each played 162 games and finished with identical (99–63) records. One game was scheduled to determine a winner, and the one game was (naturally) decided by one run, one inning, one out, and one pitch. Real life is more dramatic than fiction. The Yankees won, 5–4. George Steinbrenner, owner of the property once owned by Jacob Ruppert, humbly anointed it "the greatest game in the history of American sports."

Reggie Jackson was foiled by the fickle Fenway winds in the first inning when his high drive to left dropped straight down and into the glove of Yastrzemski. "That was no wind," said Lee. "That was Mr. Yawkey's breath."

Yastrzemski, ever the big-game player, got the Red Sox on the board in the second with a line drive homer just inside the right-field foul pole. It was an extraordinary feat for a thirty-nine-year-old slugger facing a pellet-throwing lefty. The Sox could have scored again in the third when Scott led with a double and was bunted to third, but Burleson grounded to third, failing to get the Boomer home. Typical Red Sox. In the final month of the season, the Sox twenty-four times failed to get a runner in from third with less than two out (this is known as fundamental baseball execution), and in that stretch the Townies lost five games by one run.

It was still 1–0 in the sixth and Fenway was deadly quiet. Red Sox fans are a silent majority in games of this magnitude. History has taught them that something bad is going to happen, and 32,925 sat on their hands waiting for the October sky to fall. In the bottom of the sixth, Burleson doubled down the left-field line and scored on Jim Rice's RBI single to center. It was midafternoon, and the shadows were getting longer. In the office of the *Boston Globe,* as 3:45 approached, day editor Peter Stilla called downstairs to the *Globe* press room and instructed them to insert a one in the Sox sixth-inning linescore. The late stocks edition had to go, and the trucks were rolling by 4:30. The newspaper was in some boxes by 4:45 and the banner headline screamed, "Red Sox Ahead," under a six-inning linescore that showed the Sox up, 2–0, scoring single runs in the second and the sixth innings. The page today conjures thoughts of a weary businessman/Sox fan emerging from a five-hour meeting and seeing this boldface encouragement, while *those who know* have already pledged *never again.*

Sox fans sitting in Fenway October 2 were not fooled by the big tease. It had only been three years since the 3–0 lead in the sixth. Boston led 1–0 and 3–2 in Game 7 in 1946.

Every pivotal Red Sox loss of the last seventy years is sprinkled with moments that shifted the momentum away from the locals, and this one had its first strange turn when Lynn hit what looked like a two-run double to the corner in right with two out in the sixth. Incredibly, Piniella had drifted way out of position and was standing where the ball was hit. Three outs. On to the seventh. Torrez was working on a two-hitter.

Chris Chambliss and Roy White hit one-out singles in the seventh, and after a second out, the number nine hitter, Bucky Dent, came up. Under normal circumstances, manager Bob Lemon probably would have sent Jim Spencer up to hit for Dent, but Willie Randolph was injured, Lemon was short on infield help, and Spencer had already been used. Dent had to hit for himself. Dent fouled the second pitch off his foot, hopped out of the batter's box, and went over to where Mickey Rivers was standing in the on-deck circle. Dent was concerned because he'd had surgery for a blood clot before the season. He shook it off, and while he did, batboy Sandy Salandrea, at the urging of Rivers, brought Dent a new bat and took away the old, chipped bat.

"Bucky and myself use the same type of bat," Rivers explained. "The bats actually belong to Roy White, but he doesn't use them, so he let us have them. I asked our clubhouse guy if he had any of those bats in our bag. The one we had been using was a little chipped. The clubhouse guy looked in his trunk and came up with a new one—a Max 44 model. It was the last one left in the bunch. The clubhouse kid said, 'Mickey, I'm here.' Like that. And I said, 'Thank you. Oh, good, you know?' Cuz I always take care of my bats. I started wrappin' it up, tapin' it up. Then Bucky took the other bat up there because he didn't know it was cracked and he fouled one off. I started hollering, 'Homey, Homey, that bat is cracked, you got the wrong one.' I was on him to change and he wouldn't. Finally, when the ball hit his foot, and he was being treated, I grabbed the batboy and told him to take the bat up and take away the one Bucky had."

Rivers told Torrez the bat was corked when the two met at an old-timers' game in 1987.

"Come on, now," Rivers said when he was later asked about the cork theory. "I'm serious. We didn't have to use no corked bat."

Torrez didn't stay loose by warming up during this interruption. Big mistake. "I didn't throw," he said in 1989. "I should have. I was in the seventh inning and I was up 2–0 and I was just trying to reserve my energy. I didn't realize it was going to be four or five minutes. I thought he was going to get another bat and get back in. Guys were throwing the ball around in the infield. I should have thrown a couple to get myself back because I really had great concentration. I think I should have thrown a pitch or two while he was getting attended to. There's a lot of things you think about now, but that's all part of the game, the history of it. It's gonna be there forever, so you can't do anything about it."

Choking up a good three inches on his bat, Dent went back to the batter's box and hit the next pitch, an inside fastball—the warm-up pitch that Torrez never threw—in the air to left field. Torrez started to walk off the field. He had checked the wind a few innings earlier and this ball had no chance. He was near the first-base stripe when he saw Yastrzemski back against the Wall, looking up.

Larger forces were at work again. The wind had shifted since Jackson's shot in the first. House Speaker Tip O'Neill, born in 1912, was in a box seat and remembered, "He hit that goddamn pop fly. Everybody stood up and I thought it was a simple out. I couldn't believe that it landed in the net."

Across the continent, in California, Max Frazee, a great-grandson of Harry Frazee, was sitting in an art history class, wearing earphones, listening to the game on a tiny radio. In the middle of the quiet classroom, he screamed, "Bucky Dent just hit a home run! The Yankees are going to win the Series!" He'd bet $500 that the Yankees would win the American League East.

"Obvously, it was the jinx," Frazee said later. "Here's a guy who couldn't hit anything and he hits that killer."

Yastrzemski, of course, was the player closest to the ball when it barely cleared the fence. In seventeen seasons, Yastrzemski had seen thousands of baseballs fly toward Fenway's monstrous façade. "Jesus Christ, I still can't believe it went in the net," Yaz said the day he was elected to Baseball's Hall of Fame (1989). "I thought I had a chance at it at first. The wind was blowing from right to left, and he kind of pulled it down toward the corner and it just kept on carrying and carrying and the wind blew it a little more toward the line, and boom. It was just an empty feeling, but there again, typical of our team. We had the lead and blew it."

There is, before a thunderstorm, a dark, dead-air time when the world seems very quiet and vividly clear. Objects that are far away seem close and the slightest motion—a wisp of a wind that reveals the underside of tree leaves—catches the eye. This is what Fenway Park felt like when Bucky Dent crossed the plate, shook hands with his teammates, and jogged to the happy visitors' dugout in front of the third-base boxes. Thousands of people sat in stunned silence, and the only sound was that of a few hands clapping by the third-base box seats, and some whooping in the Yankee dugout. The prestorm hush engulfed the green yard.

It was Dent's fifth homer in 124 games.

"Another half inch in on his hands and I may have broken his bat," Torrez said. "I don't lose any sleep over it. I'm not ashamed of the way I pitched."

"The ball was down and in," recalled Dent. "The first two times up

I had popped up fastballs that were up. I think he was trying to get the ball back in on me and he just made a mistake. . . . I didn't see it. I took off running. I knew from playing there so many years that if a ball is hitting on the Wall and you don't run hard from home, you don't get a double. I never did see the ball go into the net. I rounded first and I looked and the umpire was signaling home run."

On February 13, 1989, Torrez and Dent reenacted the infamous moment at Dent's baseball school in Delray Beach, Florida. It was part of a dedication ceremony for Dent's new "Little Fenway" Field at the school. Dent hit Torrez's fifth pitch into the screen in left center. The wall at Little Fenway is thirty-four feet high and the screen extends fifteen feet over the wall. A replica of Fenway's left-field scoreboard is painted to appear exactly as Fenway's did when Dent crossed home plate October 2, 1978. Like a clock tower struck by lightning—always reading 12:30—the frozen frames forever show the Yankees up, 3–2, in the seventh. The façade is bound to inspire violent flashbacks if you are a Red Sox fan.

Zimmer, perhaps the most tragic victim of Dent's fly ball, lived with the memory daily in 1983. Zimmer worked as a coach with the Yankees in 1983 and rented Dent's apartment in Wyckoff, New Jersey. Dent left all his memorabilia and photographs in the apartment, including a picture of the home run shot that hung on the back of the bedroom door. Every night when coach Don Zimmer closed his bedroom door, the last thing he saw was a picture of Dent hitting the home run off Torrez. Good night, sweet prince.

After Dent's homer, Torrez walked Rivers on a 3–2 pitch. Thurman Munson was next and Torrez had fanned Munson three times but Zimmer went with Bob Stanley.

"I ended up walking Mickey Rivers after he fouled off four or five pitches," said Torrez. "The umpire could have rang him up. One was a borderline pitch. I was surprised that Zimmer took me out. He didn't even ask me. Once he came out, he just went and gave the signal and I was like, 'Wait a minute, it's still a 3–2 ball game.' Looking back, I wish he had come out and said, 'How do you feel?' He didn't even bother. He just called in Stanley."

This was the Steamer's glory year. Stanley went 15–2 with a 2.60 ERA in 1978 and was a fan favorite. In later years he would become the embodiment of the sloppy, hapless victim—an overweight, hardluck pitcher with a fat contract—but on October 2, 1978, there was every reason to believe that he could do the job. With Stanley in the game, Rivers immediately stole second, and hindsight heavyweights believe Dick Drago would have been a better choice with a man on base. Munson rocked a double to left-center, scoring Rivers to make it 4–2.

In the bottom of the seventh, with one on and two out, Zimmer sent right-handed Bob Bailey up to hit for Jack Brohamer. Lemon countered with rocket righty Rich Gossage, and there was no Carbo to bail Zimmer out. Bailey never got the bat off his shoulder and struck out on three pitches. It was his last at-bat in the major leagues. Typical Red Sox depth. The whole season was at stake, and the Sox turned the game over to a man one day away from the Equitable Old Timers' circuit.

Reggie Jackson homered off Stanley in the eighth to make it 5–2. The game had lost much of its bite. A 5–2 blowout was disappointing after 162 games of high anxiety. For a moment, it looked like the Sox season might whimper to a close. No. The Red Sox fought back with great heart and thus put their fans on the rack one more time. Remy doubled off Rich Gossage in the eighth and scored on a single to center by Yastrzemski. Fisk and Lynn turned back Gossage fastballs, pushing Yaz across the plate with a pair of singles. It was 5–4 and the Sox had runners on first and second with one out. Hobson flied out and Scott fanned.

Burleson drew a one-out walk in the ninth. Remy cracked a shot to right. It was late in the afternoon and the sun was setting over the roof boxes behind the third-base line. Piniella had no clue where Remy's ball was. He stood in the outfield flapping his arms, a man praying for some sign from above to steer him toward the baseball that was coming out of the sun. "I went to where I thought it would land," said Piniella. "I saw it when it hit and reacted."

After the ball landed eight feet in front of him, Piniella lunged to his left with his glove hand extended and the ball bounced into his webbing on a perfect hop. Burleson was not able to advance past second. These are the things that have happened to the Red Sox for seventy years.

"When I hit my home run, I thought it was like a sign," Yaz remembered. "But we made a lot of mistakes in that game. Piniella sticks up his hand with the sun in his eyes and gets the ball. You're not talking about the greatest outfielder that ever lived. I thought Burleson should have gone to third base."

Rice went out on a fly ball, advancing Burleson to third, and that brought up Yastrzemski. Two on, two out, the tying run ninety feet from home.

Yastrzemski came to the plate more than 14,000 times during his major league career. This is the one at-bat he'd like over. He has talked about it for twelve years and will be asked about it until the day he dies. His remembrance is well-rehearsed:

"I was trying to hit a ground ball into the open hole between first and second. In the seventh he tried to go up with me and I got a base hit to center. I figured he'd probably go low all the way. The first pitch, he misses low and inside and I've got him 1–0. The next one was down and a good ball to pull and it just exploded on me. I never got the head of the bat out. He beat me that time and all I can do is tip my hat to him."

The pop-up landed safely in the glove of third baseman Nettles. Fenway went stone silent. Drained fans looked at one another. Is that all there is?

John Updike and his wife were en route to a Cambridge dinner date. They parked along Memorial Drive, listening to the last inning on the car radio. When Nettles caught Yastrzemski's pop-up, the author thought of Enos Slaughter rounding third base in 1946.

In New Haven, a bar owner spoke: "They killed our fathers and now the sons of bitches are coming to get us."

Lee was the first to point fingers. "He [Zimmer] lost the pennant," said the veteran lefty. "We should have been home free. A man shouldn't bury veteran ball players. He shouldn't have buried me."

Yastrzemski admitted, "We have everything in the world to be proud of. What we don't have is the ring. . . . Someday, we're going to get that cigar. Before Old Yaz retires, he's going to play on a World Champion."

Burleson looked in the mirror after the heartbreaker. "We just blew it, that's all. We never should have been in this game."

Humberto Cardinal Medeiros, archbishop of Boston, was in the Vatican and said, "We just lost a pope, which is very sad. And now we lose to the Yankees, which is also very sad. I prayed hard for the Sox, but apparently New York is more powerful in prayer than Boston."

◇

A glance at the Red Sox year-by-year chart indicates that it took the Boston franchise eight years to recover from the fall of 1978. In fact, many of those who were there have never recovered, and it's apparent that this was the best Boston baseball team since Ruth left town. Only proponents of the 1946 team could argue. But the sad fact is that the 1977 and 1978 Red Sox won 196 games without winning anything. The Yankees, of course, won the American League East in both of those seasons and, of course, went on to win the World Series each time.

The Sox started to unravel almost immediately after the playoff disappointment. Insulted at Boston's one-year contract offer, Tiant signed with (who else?) the Yankees for $840,000 over two years. It was the first in a series of PR blunders that threatened to return the Boston ball club to the days of abject drudgery that ruled Fenway in the early sixties. Popular Bill Lee was swapped for someone named Stan Papi. While Lee went 16–10 with the Expos, Boston's lefty starters won one game in 1979 and the Sox finished eleven and a half games behind the Orioles. Boston finished nineteen games out a year later, and Zimmer was fired during the final week of the season. After the 1980 season, Burleson and Lynn were traded to California (Lynn brought the whopping package of Jim Dorsey and broken-down Frank Tanana and Joe Rudi), and Fisk was declared a free agent when Haywood Sullivan failed to tender him a contract by December 20, 1980. Sullivan and Fisk were bitter enemies by this time, and the New England-born catcher signed with the Chicago White Sox in the spring of 1981.

The best catcher in the history of the franchise, a future Hall of Famer who embodied the New England work ethic, was lost with no compensation. John Harrington, Mrs. Jean Yawkey's most trusted official, later said that losing Fisk hurt the franchise more than anything during his tenure with the club.

It was sad. The Red Sox were a public relations nightmare. Many of the players fans loved to see were leaving with bitter aftertastes. Yastrzemski later admitted, "When that team broke up, it really took a lot out of me personally because you knew you weren't going to get that kind of talent again."

Ralph Houk was hired to manage the Sox in the strike-torn season of 1981, and the Red Sox made a semblance of a run at the fabricated "second season." There was little excitement during the Houk years. Bruce Hurst, Rich Gedman, Wade Boggs, and Marty Barrett established themselves as major leaguers, and fans filed into Fenway, but the team was only moderately interesting.

The festering ownership squabble exploded at the worst possible moment, on June 5, 1983. In 1982, Tony Conigliaro, ever the tragic figure (he died in February of 1990), suffered a paralyzing heart attack, which left him in a coma. In an effort to raise funds for Conigliaro's round-the-clock care, his teammates from the 1967 Dream Season had gathered on the Fenway roof that day in June. At 4:30 P.M. Buddy LeRoux, one of the three majority owners (with Sullivan and Mrs. Yawkey), interrupted the benefit party with a press conference announcing, in Al Haig fashion, that he was in charge. Twenty-five minutes later, Sullivan held a press conference and announced that he was in charge.

Perfect. While a former star slugger lay motionless on the North Shore, buffoons LeRoux and Sullivan were wrestling on the roof like a couple of little Napoleons. Many days in court would follow, and Sullivan's side won, but everybody looked like a loser. It was Frazee Redux.

On the field, the thrill was gone. Larry Bird was selling out the Garden and leading the Celtics to World Championships and the Red Sox were becoming boring. They also became losers. In 1983, Boston finished under .500 (78–84) for the first time since 1966. That was the year Yastrzemski retired. Perfect symmetry. The Red Sox were losers when Yastrzemski arrived in 1961 and they were losers when he left in 1983. And Old Yaz, still paying for the original sin of Frazee, retired without ever winning a World Series.

The Red Sox finished twenty games out in 1983, eighteen out in 1984, and in the first year under John McNamara, eighteen and a half out in 1985. Eckersley was traded for Bill Buckner. Stanley, Evans, and Rice were signed to long-term, big-money contracts, Boggs was winning batting titles, Oil Can Boyd came off the Mississippi playgrounds throwing big league strikes, and a kid pitcher from Texas named Roger Clemens was considered a "can't miss" prospect. In December 1985, lefty prospect Bobby Ojeda was shipped to the Mets in exchange for pitchers Calvin Schiraldi and Wes Gardner, and diehard Sox fans had reason to believe that the team might contend again in 1986.

In 1988, two-time Pulitzer Prize–winning photographer Stan Grossfeld accompanied a New Jersey teenage, All-Star baseball team to the Soviet Union for some goodwill games against Soviet teams in Moscow, Kiev, and Tbilisi. Andrew Tselikovsry, a nineteen-year-old first baseman for Moscow's D. I. Mendeleyev Institute of Chemical Engineering team, told Grossfeld, "I want to see two things in my life. This *Natural* movie and the 1986 World Series Game 6, Red Sox–Mets. I have heard about this ground ball."

In 1986, *Boston Globe* managing editor Jack Driscoll was in the People's Republic of China, touring a garden with other American journalists. When the guide learned Driscoll was from Boston, he said, "Ah, Boston Red Sox," then spread his feet and bent down like a man watching a baseball trickle between his legs.

That same winter, in West Newton, Massachusetts, Joel Krakow of the Captain Video store unwrapped a shipment that included the Red Sox 1986 highlight film and knew exactly where to catalog the baseball tape: he filed it in the sci-fi/horror section of his store.

Game 6 of the 1986 World Series was the denouement, an unthinkable sequence—sinister and hideous even by the lofty standards of the Boston Red Sox. Lugging sixty-eight years of failure into the bottom of the tenth inning at Shea Stadium, the Sox came within a single strike of winning the World Series, but failed. The Boston uniforms proved too heavy. The Curse of the Bambino was too strong. With two outs and nobody on base, the Mets rallied for three runs, scoring the game winner when Mookie Wilson's Little League grounder dribbled between the legs of Boston first baseman Bill Buckner. An inventor of baseball board-games later calculated that the odds of the Mets scoring three runs in that situation were 279–1. Given the circumstances and the fact that it happened during this age of hype, replay, and videocassette recorders, Buckner's gaffe stands as the most famous error in baseball history—celluloid proof that the Red Sox indeed are cursed, perhaps forever.

It's almost four years since this event, yet it has already taken its place as a permanent regional tragedy. Even nonbaseball fans, and there are some in New England, could not help but be touched by the nightmarish loss. With few exceptions, all New Englanders remember where they were and what they were doing when the ball went through Buckner's legs—just as they remember hurricanes, blackouts, and assassinations.

Former House Speaker Tip O'Neill threw out the first ball in Game 3 of the 1986 Series at Fenway, but he watched Game 6 on television with his wife. "I didn't sleep for three months," said the affable statesman. "I'd wake up every night seeing that ball go through Buckner's legs. Of course we were cursed that time."

Cursed. That comes from the Speaker, speaking for millions of Red Sox fans.

Fifteen months after the error, when the Mets taped a video at empty Shea in the dead of a winter, *New York Times* columnist George Vecsey wrote, "During breaks, crew members peered down at the snow-filled seats and pointed to where they had been when Mookie Wilson's grounder slithered through Bill Buckner's legs, now a moment in history, like Pearl Harbor, Bobby Thomson's homer and the death of Elvis."

There were, of course, several other players and a manager who contributed to Boston's historic Game 6 defeat, but Buckner has become the sad Sox symbol—like the unfortunate skier ABC uses to personify "the agony of defeat" before every "Wide World of Sports" episode. No good theory explains why Buckner was designated to take the rap for decades to come. He would play more than twenty years in the majors and accumulate more hits than Ted Williams or Mickey Mantle and more RBI than Hack Wilson or George Sisler. But despite four decades of appearances, a lifetime average over .290, and more than 2,500 hits in the big leagues, his *Sporting News* obituary is destined to read: "Bill Buckner; missed grounder in Series."

Sorry, Bill. Skillful takeoffs and landings are quickly forgotten, but a plane crash is the stuff of which feature films are made. No one remembers much about Gary Hart's voting record in the United States Senate, but everybody remembers Donna Rice.

Buckner was born December 14, 1949, sixteen months after Ruth died. He grew up in northern California and excelled at baseball and football. Stanford football coach Dick Vermeil recruited him as a wide receiver. Buckner chose baseball and spent the first fourteen years of his career in the National League with the Dodgers and Cubs.

One episode, something that happened very early in his career, connects Buckner with the Curse of Babe Ruth. In 1974, Bill Buckner was the Dodger left fielder who watched Atlanta's Hank Aaron hit a fly ball over his head and into the Braves bullpen for home run number 715, the one that broke Ruth's record. This is probably a reach—the kind you see when historians point out the similarities between the assassinations of presidents Lincoln and Kennedy (both succeeded by a Johnson, Lincoln's secretary named Kennedy, Kennedy's secretary named Lincoln, and so on). We won't try to establish that Ruth cursed Buckner for not catching Aaron's record breaker. It's just interesting that Buckner was *there*, just as he was there when the Sox suffered the worst of their tragic moments.

"I climbed the fence going for that ball," Buckner said fifteen years later. "Everyone was asking, 'Why did you climb the fence?' I was going over to get the ball cuz they were offering thirty-five thousand dollars for that ball and that was more than I was making. I got to the top of the fence and he [Tom House in the Braves' bullpen] caught it. If there had been a pileup, I'd have been right in it."

Buckner served the Red Sox quite well in 1986, hitting .267 with eighteen homers and 102 RBI. Unfortunately, there was a lot of junk in his ankles and he was a hobbling war horse by the time the Sox and Mets dueled in the Fall Classic. He said he felt like a man with a piano strapped to his back and characterized his attempts to run as "moving" rather than running.

The Red Sox had blown pennants before and three other times had lost the seventh game of the World Series, but no team in the history of the game ever got this close to the threshold without actually winning. Losing on a final play that involved a ball going through an infielder's legs provided the perfect lasting image for sixty-eight years of failure.

Most Americans have played baseball or softball and remember the embarrassment of the grounder that scoots between the wickets. Skaters fall on their rear ends, basketball players take shots that miss the basket entirely, and baseball players let a grounder roll between the legs. "Keep your glove down," the coach would say. No play in baseball is more humiliating than the slow grounder between the legs: it is worse than striking out, worse than dropping a fly ball, worse than getting picked off. He who lets a ground ball slip between his legs wants to dig a hole and crawl inside for shelter. It is a Charlie Brown error that calls for the perpetrator to say, "Rats!"

There is little shelter for Bill Buckner.

"I did concentrate on that ball," he said moments after the error. "I saw it well. It bounced and bounced and then it didn't bounce, it just skipped. I can't remember the last time I missed a ball like that, but I'll remember that one."

Four months later, before spring training 1987, Buckner said, "I'm not going to talk to anybody about it. Once I get to spring training, that's it. It's been blown way out of proportion in the first place. This is the last time I'm talking about it, so tell your friends—this is it. I hate to downplay it, but a lot more important things happened than that. Now that I've seen the films, I know that we were not going to get Mookie Wilson at first anyway. [Bob] Stanley was not going to be there [to cover first]. It's just a mistake and it's still being blown out of proportion. What bothers me the most is the way the media has blown it out of proportion. Other people had a tough time in that Series, too. I won't mention names, but other people had as tough a time as I did. . . . The ball went through my legs. I didn't have any trouble getting to it."

On July 23, 1987, with the Red Sox in fifth place, fourteen and a half games out of first, Buckner was released. He said, "I would have to say that things were good for me here, up until after the sixth game of the World Series. After that, it just went down. All the bad media and fan reaction. I think everybody in this town, including the Red Sox, holds that against me. I don't think I lost the World Series. There is no guarantee we would have won that game . . . I don't know whether it's unfair. It's just human nature. People have a tendency to dwell on the negative. But I have no qualms about what I did with the Red Sox. I did the best I could for them and I think I did a good job."

Buckner's unspeakable error capped the most devastating loss in Red Sox history and set the table for a Game 7 that all Sox fans knew the team could not win. It mattered not that Boston took a 3–0 lead in the fatal finale. The 1975 Red Sox led Game 7 3–0 and lost, and it was clear that there would be no recovery from the horrors of 1986's Game 6. It's interesting to note that the Red Sox' darkest hour came during an hour that, technically speaking, took place twice. Dave Henderson's tenth-inning homer, which gave the Sox the lead in Game 6, was struck at 11:59 P.M. EDT, and it was midnight when Henderson crossed home plate. All residents in the eastern time zone were instructed to turn back their clocks one hour. And so the sand for the final hour of October 25, 1986, actually ran out twice, and it was in the second "final" hour of the day that the Sox folded. If only they could replay it one more time.

Moments after the bone-rattling Game 6 loss, red-faced John McNamara stood under the bright lights and bristled at the mention of the obvious curse. Having certified his admission to the Red Sox Hall of Shame with a series of mind-boggling moves, McNamara stared into a sea of reporters and snapped, "I don't know nothin' about history and I don't want to hear anything about choking or any of that crap."

It was the dumb but definitive statement of a team that effectively clamped the nattering nabobs of negativity for seven full months and came closer to winning than any Red Sox team since the days of George Herman Ruth. Unlike their 1946 or 1975 forefathers, the 1986 Red Sox were an overachieving lot, able to perform well beyond expectations while spitting at the cynics who predicted doom. They had an unusually deep pitching staff. They were good and they were lucky. They performed with the energy of the innocent and didn't fully understand what it was all about until the final hours.

◊

The Sox had been a symmetrically boring 81–81 in 1985, and there was little reason to suspect things would be much different in the second year under unimaginative manager McNamara. Boston finished an aggregate fifty-six and a half games out of first place in the three seasons leading into 1986, and the Red Sox were perceived as a dull team, still suffering from ownership squabbles and front office blunders that had effectively dismantled the 1975–1978 machine and eliminated the Townies from annual contention. There were no huge winter deals that promised an end to the snore tour, and 120 of 210 American baseball writers predicted that Boston would finish fifth in the American League East. *Sport Magazine* wrote, "The Red Sox are the most boring team in baseball. . . . This collection of slow and aging vets has been together for too long." This correspondent labeled them "brain dead."

Things changed on Good Friday, March 28, when Don Baylor was acquired from the Yankees in exchange for Mike Easler. It was the first Red Sox–Yankee deal since the infamous Sparky Lyle-for-Danny Cater swap/swipe of 1972, and it meant that the Red Sox were tempting the fates by trading a man of the cloth (Easler was an ordained minister) on Good Friday. No problem. Baylor was a proven winner and a man of great conviction, and young pitcher Roger Clemens remarked, "As soon as he walked into this clubhouse, there wasn't any doubt who the leader was."

Dwight Evans homered on the first pitch of the season, but the Sox lost their opener, then came to Fenway and dropped the home opener to Kansas City. Sad Sack Stanley, by this time a human dartboard ornament for the Fenway legions, was routed and booed in the first home game and responded with: "When I'm standing out there and save the final day of the season and we win the pennant, I'll be waving to my wife and family. The rest of 'em can go to hell."

Things started to pick up April 29 when Roger Clemens fanned twenty Seattle Mariners in a nine-inning game. No pitcher in major league history had accomplished the feat and it was the first hint that Clemens was on his way to an MVP season. He did not lose a game (14–0) until July, and by that time Baylor was among the league homer leaders and the Red Sox were in first place to stay. One by one, they turned back every challenger in the American League East. They went to New York and swept the Yankees. They went to Detroit and won three of four. They won seventeen games while scoring three or fewer runs and won thirty-nine games after coming from behind. They picked up future Hall-of-Famer Tom Seaver June 29 and promoted Calvin Schiraldi from Pawtucket. Seaver filled out the starting rotation and Schiraldi became the bullpen stopper they lacked. The Orioles closed to within two and a half games August 5, but six days later Baltimore was seven back and the Red Sox coasted into the home stretch, ripping off eleven straight victories to turn back a final challenge from the Toronto Blue Jays.

Despite all of the above, the Red Sox listened to doubts throughout the summer. Most of them didn't understand why the fans and the media expected them to fail. Evans, Stanley, and Rice understood because they were survivors of 1978. Like parents and grandparents who lived through the Great Depression, Evans, Stanley, and Rice knew what the locals had been through. Storing money in your mattress seems pretty strange unless you've seen a life's savings dissolve in a savings bank. Catchers Rich Gedman and Marc Sullivan also understood. Gedman is from Worcester and Sullivan grew up in Canton, Massachusetts, watching his father become part-owner of the team.

When the Sox slumped in July, *Sports Illustrated* ran a piece entitled "Poised for another El Foldo?" The *Globe* ran a page-one story, replete with photos of John Calvin and Babe Ruth, and the lead paragraph was, "A fatalistic gloom hangs over Boston. It's August and the Red Sox are in first place."

Sox fans expect something to go wrong. They go to the theater even though they have seen the play before. The cast changes and new liberties are taken with an ancient script, but Hamlet always dies in the end.

Don Baylor had played for proud, successful franchises in Baltimore, Oakland, California, and New York. He was a winner and thought like a winner. He did not understand or appreciate the negativity of the New England mind. "I've had a hard time dealing with that," Baylor said. "I've had a hard time dealing with reporters. I don't care what happened in 1978. This club wants to win so bad. We haven't been swept in our division. And to have people telling you you're going to fail, that the same thing's going to happen that happened in 1978. . . . You can see it; they expect us to choke, just like they expect the Celtics to win."

It was Peter Gammons, arguably the best baseball writer in America, who in 1978 declared that The Who's "Won't Get Fooled Again" had become the official anthem of Red Sox fans, and now clearly it was true. The 1986 Red Sox were an admirable lot, hopeful, hard-working, and harmonious by BoSox standards, and they were forced to pay for the sins of their forebears. This was no 1967 joyride, when fans forgot about Frazee's folly and Pesky holding the ball. No. Fans had seen too much too recently. Only the youngest New Englanders knew nothing of 1978, and the rest of the region resisted the urge to fall in love again. Lucy will always pull the football away from Charlie Brown, and the Red Sox will always do the same, leaving you dizzy, dazed, and staring blankly into the sky.

Author Geoffrey Wolff attacked this perverted fan experience in a *Globe* essay after the Sox clinched the American League East. Wolff invoked the German word *Schadenfreude,* which means malicious joy, or gloating at another's misfortune. Wolff wrote, "If the choke exists, it's nurtured rather than natured. To fail under pressure is not the most notable genetic component of a professional athlete's makeup, but to read in the newspapers and hear on radio talk shows that he WILL fail under pressure is surely one of the principal experiences of a New England athlete's professional destiny. . . . An athlete, hearing often enough that he will choke because once upon a time other athletes from the Boston area choked, which they didn't either, might come to believe such a prophecy."

Sox reliever Joe Sambito, a Long Island native who was an All-Star while pitching for the Houston Astros, predicted, "If we win, it'll screw up this whole town. They'll have to start thinking positive."

On August 17, 1986, the Red Sox traded shortstop Rey Quinones to Seattle in a deal that brought shortstop Spike Owen and outfielder David Henderson to Boston. The Sox were suspicious of Quinones, who was rooming with Oil Can Boyd in Chelsea. Boyd had quit the team in July when he was not named to the All-Star squad, and the Can and Quinones got into a scuffle with some Chelsea police officers during the break. Quinones was a flashy fielder with a big swing, but some of the veterans didn't like him because he hung out with Boyd and he rejected the inflexible instruction of guru batting coach Walter Hriniak. Owen was considered mediocre, but steady—the type of player you could trust down the stretch in a pennant race. Henderson was a sculpted athlete of enormous potential who was buried in Dick Williams's doghouse in Seattle. Henderson batted fifty-one times for Boston, hitting a pathetic .196 with one homer and three RBI. He was veteran insurance in case one of the veteran outfielders got hurt. Nothing more.

Bolstered by the rotation of Clemens (24–4), Bruce Hurst (13–8), and Oil Can Boyd (16–10), the Sox clinched the division with a week to go, beating the Blue Jays, 12–3, on Sunday, September 28, at Fenway. The Sox prepared to meet the California Angels in the American League Championship Series.

The Angels were managed by Gene Mauch, a man described by Earl Weaver as "the greatest manager never to win a pennant." Mauch was manager of the 1964 Phillies, who finished second after leading by six and a half with twelve to play. He also managed the 1982 Angels and had a 2–0 lead in a best of five series, only to watch the Brewers win three straight. It's the only time that happened during the sixteen years of five-game playoff format. Given this long history of sustained failure and hard luck, you know Mauch has to have some ties to the Red Sox and sure enough, Gene William Mauch finished his playing days as the Red Sox second baseman in 1957. The playoffs presented dueling curses—the Curse of the Bambino vs. the shadow of defeat that stalked Mauch for the better part of three decades.

The 1986 Angels had fourteen players over the age of thirty, and this was perceived as the last roundup for Gene Autry's cowboys. The Western Division champs got off to a convincing start, whipping the Red Sox three times in the first four games. Clemens was uncharacteristically flat in the opener, and Mike Witt mastered the Sox with a five-hitter in an 8–1 win. The Sox won a goofy Game 2 at Fenway as both teams made errors and base-running mistakes in a rare weekday game. Out in California, the Angels beat Boyd, 5–3, in Game 3, then took Game 4 after trailing 3–0 in the ninth.

It was in this fourth playoff game, played on a Saturday night in Anaheim, California, that the 1986 postseason first took on a mythical quality. In 648 prior postseason games, encompassing all major league baseball history, no team had ever lost after holding a lead of three runs or more in the ninth inning. It happened to the Red Sox. This game was eventually buried by the skull-imploding episodes of ALCS Game 5 and World Series Game 6, but it serves to demonstrate that larger forces were at work before Dave Henderson, Mookie Wilson, and Bill Buckner got into the act. Clemens led, 3–0, in the ninth inning of ALCS Game 4, and no Angel had reached third base. Remember, this was Roger (24–4) Clemens, the man who would be MVP and win the Cy Young Award and become an autobiographer in upcoming months. Leading 3–0 with Clemens on the mound, the Red Sox clearly were on the verge of tying the series, 2–2. Angel third baseman Doug DeCinces led off the ninth with a home run. With one out, Dick Schofield and Bob Boone hit singles, Boone's coming on an 0–2 pitch. McNamara yanked Clemens and summoned Schiraldi, the floppy-dog righty who had less than ninety-five innings of major league experience. Schiraldi got Gary Pettis to hit a routine fly to left, but Rice lost the ball in the lights, buckled under the glare, and the Angels had another run and base runners on second and third with one out. Schiraldi struck out Bobby Grich, after intentionally walking Ruppert Jones to load the bases. Boston's rookie reliever than got ahead of Brian Downing 0–2, ran the count to 1–2, then threw a curious backdoor slider that plunked Downing in the ribs, forcing home the tying run. Grich won the game with an RBI single off Schiraldi in the eleventh. A day later, the Sox would atone for these sins, but weaknesses had been exposed—weaknesses that would cost dearly in subsequent days. McNamara was afraid of most of the pitchers in his bullpen (Sammy Stewart, Steve Crawford, Al Nipper, Joe Sambito, and Tim Lollar), and Boston's defense was cracking around the edges. It would be difficult to disguise these deficiencies for a full seven games against a good team. The long, heroic season, it seemed, was over. Veteran Rice took things in stride and danced the night away at the Sox hotel headquarters.

The 1986 Red Sox were at their defiant, history-be-damned best on Sunday, October 12. Facing certain defeat, down to the final strike of their heroic season, the Red Sox rallied and won. This one goes alongside Game 6 in the 1975 World Series, but was even more dramatic. It would prove ironic because two weeks later the Mets would do to the Red Sox what the Red Sox did to the Angels, but for a few magic moments the 1986 Sox let their fans feel what winners feel. This time it was the *other* team that folded while the Red Sox took advantage. New Englanders rejoiced and felt something the Sox hadn't allowed them to feel. This was how the people of St. Louis felt in 1946 and how the people of Detroit felt in 1972 and how the people of Baltimore felt in 1974 and how the people of Cincinnati felt in 1975 and how the people of New York felt in 1978.

If the Sox and Angels had met two years earlier, the series would have been over in four games, but baseball expanded its championship format to a best-of-seven games in 1985, just in time to rescue the 1985 Royals (down 3–1 to the Blue Jays) and the 1986 Red Sox.

Boston led Game 5, 2–1, in the sixth inning when Grich hit a drive to deep center. It was at this moment that many first noticed a new Red Sox center fielder in the game, David Henderson. He'd entered the game in the fifth because Tony Armas twisted his ankle. Henderson, a fair outfielder gifted with extraordinary speed, grace, and style, chased the ball, leaped, snagged it, then crashed into the wall. As he hit the fence, the ball popped up, out of his mitt and over the fence. It would not have carried out without an assist from the hustling Hendu. Armas probably would have turned and watched the ball hit the wall and held Grich to a double. Henderson's extra effort cost the Sox two runs, and the Angels led, 3–2.

Groan. The Babe appeared to be finding new ways to torture the Boston fandom. This time, the Sox were going to lose because a reserve outfielder tipped a fly ball over the fence after *almost* making a great catch. Would the Montreal Canadiens lose because they shot the puck into their own net? Only the Red Sox.

California led, 5–2, in the ninth when the Red Sox began to show a pulse. Buckner snapped a single up the middle. Rice struck out on three pitches, walked to the dugout with his head down, and started to unbutton his uniform jersey. Baylor drove a 3–2 Mike Witt curveball over the fence in left to cut the margin to 5–4—the same score the Sox faced when Yaz popped up to end the playoff game. Evans popped up, and Boston was down to its last out. It was then that the dueling curses came into play. Overmanaging to the finish, Gene Mauch came out and lifted Witt, summoning lefty Gary Lucas to face lefty Rich Gedman. Before batting, Gedman stepped out and asked that a banner reading "Another Boston Choke" be removed from the outfield wall. Lucas hadn't hit a batter in over six years, but he hit Gedman with his first pitch and Mauch had to bring in rightie Donnie Moore to face Henderson. Henderson would have had no chance against Witt (Witt struck him out on four pitches in the seventh), but he was able to battle Moore. Looking particularly inept (much like Bernie Carbo in Game 6 of the 1975 Series), Henderson fouled off a 2–2 pitch and stepped out. Moore threw a forkball low and away and Henderson swatted it way over the fence in left center.

Henderson never understood the impact of this dramatic home run. "I was just trying to be out there doing a job," he said. "Everybody else was out there battling with history. I didn't know anything about

Boston history 'til after the fact—all the so-called jinxes and the other crap you guys write about. So it wasn't any big deal to me."

The Sox won it in the eleventh on Henderson's sac fly off Moore and beat the Angels, 10–4 and 8–1, back in Fenway to bring Boston a World Series for the fourth time in sixty-eight years. The Angels seemed beaten by the time they came back to Boston, and the final two games in Fenway were over early. There wasn't much drama, but there was a great sense of relief because the Red Sox hadn't won a seventh game of any kind since 1918. One by one, the jinxes were being erased.

Three years after serving the home run pitch to Henderson, veteran pitcher Donnie Moore took his own life, shooting himself in the head. Moore's agent, David Pinter, said, "Ever since Henderson's home run, he was extremely depressed. He blamed himself for the Angels not going to the World Series."

◊

The 1986 Mets were a formidable foe, winners of 108 regular season games, best since the 1975 Reds. It's interesting to note that the Red Sox' last three World Series opponents (1967 Cardinals, 1975 Reds, and 1986 Mets) were the winningest NL teams in their respective decades. Why couldn't the Sox have hooked up against a team like the 1984 Padres or the 1987 Cardinals?

The Sox-Mets duel marked the first time Boston and New York met in a World Series since 1912. The Mets were 2½–1 favorites, the heaviest favorites since the 1950 Yankees over the Philadephia Whiz Kids. The 1986 Fall Classic opened in New York, and McNamara got off to a bad start on "Good Morning America." Host Charles Gibson gleefully noted that Woodrow Wilson was president when Boston won its last World Series, and McNamara took the heat, saying, "Hey, you're not funny."

Boston took the opener, 1–0, scoring the winning run when a Rich Gedman grounder skipped between the legs of Met second baseman Tim Teufel. Hurst was a hero. The last Sox lefty to win Game 1 of a World Series was Babe Ruth (versus the Cubs in 1918). McNamara lifted Hurst after eight innings and looked like a genius when Calvin Schiraldi got the Mets with little trouble in the ninth. Game 2 was billed as a duel between young aces Clemens and Dwight Gooden, but both were gone by the sixth. The Sox rattled eighteen hits around Shea, cruised to a 9–3 win, and returned to Boston with a 2–0 advantage. The 1985 Cardinals were the only team in baseball history to win the first two Series games on the road then lose the Series. It looked like the Sox were finally the Anointed Ones.

Jim Frazee, a great-grandson of Harry Frazee, Boston's Benedict Arnold, took the moment to defend the family honor. In an article in the *Tacoma News-Tribune,* Frazee wrote, "With the Red Sox now in a good position to win their first World Series since 1918, it seems appropriate to take the wraps off a family tale that has been held in confidence these 68 years since that grand occasion. . . . I think it's time to call an end to the so-called 'curse' or 'jinx' on the Red Sox. It's time to end the excuses and blame, all the specious stuff."

The Mets routed Oil Can Boyd and took Game 3, 7–1, then peppered Al Nipper in Game 4, squaring the Series with a 6–2 victory. Hurst went the route in a gutty Game 5, beating the Mets, 4–2, and sending the Sox back to the Apple with a 3–2 Series lead. It marked the first time a Sox lefty had won a Series game in Fenway since Babe Ruth won the fourth game in 1918. We should have known.

Game Six. It has two connotations around Boston. In 1975, Game 6 was New Year's Eve, Mardi Gras, Fourth of July, and a holy day of celebration. Carlton Fisk put baseball back on the map and left the fandom with a memory that outlasted some of the pains of 1975's Game 7. Game 6 in 1986 stamped itself on the New England mind much like the unexpected death of a loved one. Deprived of a championship for sixty-eight summers, Red Sox fans were taken to the edge, then swatted back.

Some veteran Sox fans recognized bad signs early in the game when the Townies managed to strand five runners in the first two innings. Wide-load Rice was unable to score from first on a two-out wall double by Dwight Evans. Met starter Bobby Ojeda, a former teammate of Rice, shook his head. Ojeda could not believe his good fortune. Rice *had* to score on that ball. In the first two innings, the Sox had four singles, a walk, and a double, yet scored only twice. Longtime Sox watchers nodded sagely, knowing these runs would be needed later. The indomitable Clemens had a 2–0 lead and a no-hitter through four, but the Mets tied it with a pair in the fifth, and it stayed that way until the seventh. Boston took a 3–2 lead when Marty Barrett scored on a force play, but another run was lost when Rice was thrown out at the plate, trying to score from second on a single to left by Gedman. Third-base coach Walk-Away-Rene Lachemann took some blame for this one, but Rice's wide turn at third was a crusher. This was a night when the Red Sox would strand a whopping fourteen base runners.

McNamara made a couple of costly blunders in the eighth. With one on and one out, he sent rookie Mike Greenwell up to hit for Clemens. Clemens had developed a blister on the middle finger of his pitching hand and could no longer throw his slider. While Don Baylor sat and stewed, Greenwell fanned on three Roger McDowell pitches. With the bases loaded and two outs, McNamara let Buckner (.143) bat against lefty Jesse Orosco. Buckner lined to center, stranding his seventh, eighth, and ninth runners of the day. Baylor was steaming and so was Clemens.

Schiraldi came in to pitch in the eighth, and the Mets quickly tied the game. It stayed that way until the tenth when Henderson, a man who clearly had struck a Faustian bargain, led with his midnight homer off the *Newsday* billboard in left. (Isn't it strange that the two most memorable World Series games in Red Sox history both took two days to play—Game 6 in 1975 also went past midnight.) Wade Boggs and Marty Barrett manufactured another run, and NBC's crews went to work setting up staging in the Sox clubhouse. Cameras were wheeled in and plastic was taped to the front of the lockers to prevent champagne stains. Twenty cases of Great Western were wheeled into the clubhouse and foil was peeled back from the tops of the bottles. Bruce Hurst won the preliminary MVP vote by a 4–1 margin (Henderson got the other vote) and the Met scoreboard operator prepared this message: "Congratulations Boston Red Sox." Before the half inning ended, McNamara rejected one last chance to hit for Buckner.

Wally Backman led off the bottom of the tenth and flied to Rice in left. Keith Hernandez was next and went out on a fly to Henderson in center. Hernandez went into the clubhouse, cracked a beer, and sat with Met scout Darrell Johnson—the same Darrell Johnson who brought Jim Burton in to pitch in the ninth inning in Game 7 of 1975. Hernandez wasn't the type to give up, but he couldn't bear the thought of watching the Red Sox celebrate on the Mets' home turf.

Ben Birnbaum, editor of the *Boston College* magazine, woke his seven-year-old young son, Adam, and carried him to the television. This was something no one had seen in seventy years and Birnbaum knew his sleepy son someday would thank him for this momentary interruption.

On Nantucket, Steve Sheppard and Karin Ganga-Sheppard were at the home of friends and taking a lot of kidding. They had been married earlier in 1986, and the last line of their wedding vows was, "Til death do us part, or until the Red Sox win the World Series."

At 558 Dutton Road in Sudbury, Massachusetts, Dennis Gavin was entertaining a few friends in the poolroom/attic of his 250-year-old farmhouse—the former home of Babe Ruth. They had the TV on and they felt the presence of the Big Fella. Gavin was proud. He raised a mug and told his friends that the last time the Sox won the World Series, the pitcher came home to the room they were sitting in.

Max Frazee, a great-grandson of Harry Frazee, was watching the game in the lounge of the River Run restaurant in TriBeCa, New York City. He thought, This is it. Boston's got it. No problem. He wanted the Red Sox to win because he hated the Mets.

Carter was the last, best hope for the beaten Mets. He was determined not to make the final out. He knew Schiraldi, and he knew the kid had a flaw. Schiraldi threw inside under Carter's chin, and the veteran stepped out, glaring at Boston's rookie righty. Both pitches had been fastballs. Carter had caught Schiraldi. He knew the kid was nervous.

All the Mets knew Schiraldi. A lazy, spoiled young man with a great arm, he'd been in the New York organization since he was drafted out of the University of Texas. Many scouts preferred Schiraldi over Roger Clemens when the two were Longhorn teammates, but Clemens would work. Schiraldi wouldn't. The Mets don't give up on many good pitchers, but they gave up on Schiraldi in the winter of 1985–1986. Mets vice president Joe McIlvaine later said, "There are guys you call winners and guys you call losers. You might have to lump Calvin in that loser category. We sure liked his stuff, but there was something missing."

Clif Keane, who saw his first Sox game in 1924 and covered the team for a half century, remembered watching at home on television when Carter came up: "The guy was one strike away, the big relief pitcher. And I'm sitting at home in a rocking chair and I'm yelling, 'Don't let that fuckin' Gedman call for a breaking ball.' I'd like to run out on the field right now and tell him, 'Don't throw a breakin' ball.' Gedman is the catcher who throws two pitches and then he changes. He'd thrown two heatballs right by him. He doesn't throw the third, he's got to change. Gedman's gonna be smart and throw a knuckleball. So he throws a breaking ball and the guy hits it to center field for a base hit."

Carter singled to left on a 2–1 pitch. Kevin Mitchell was still in the clubhouse where he'd been on the phone making a plane reservation for a flight home to San Diego. He had disrobed. Entirely. He slipped into his uniform in a hurry when manager Davey Johnson told him to go up and hit. Mitchell and Schiraldi had been rommates in Jackson, Mississippi, in 1983.

Tucking in his shirt, Mitchell walked to the plate. He wasn't wearing a jock. He looked at Schiraldi and smiled. Mitchell was remembering conversations from those lazy Mississippi nights. They'd lie around the room and talk about what they would do if they faced each other. Schiraldi had always said if he ever pitched to Mitchell, he'd try to push him back with a fastball inside, then throw a slider away.

The first pitch was up and in. *Schiraldi was doing exactly what he always said he would do,* Mitchell thought. *The slider away must be coming.*

Bingo. Mitchell smacked the 1–0, low-and-away offering and singled to center.

On the Mets bench, Lenny Dykstra had the same feeling. This game was too big for Schiraldi. He wasn't ready for this. When Mitchell got his hit, Dykstra knew the Mets were in good shape as long as Schiraldi stayed in the game. In his box seat, Red Sox General Manager Lou Gorman, another man who knew Schiraldi from his days with the Mets, was getting the same feeling. *This is the first time I've seen him nervous,* thought Gorman.

Ray Knight was next, and he broke his bat with a single to center on an 0–2 pitch. Carter scored and Mitchell alertly took third, a play the Red Sox rarely execute. John McNamara came out to the mound.

The late baseball commissioner, A. Bartlett Giamatti, a native of South Hadley, Massachusetts, and a lifelong Red Sox fan, was National League President at this time. He was in a box seat near the field and remembered, "Something deeper, older, and more primeval took over. There were gurgling noises coming from within my body. I found myself telling Johnny McNamara how to manage from the wrong box and yelling remarks I don't remember."

McNamara listened to the wrong voices. He gave the signal for the righty. The bullpen door swung open and Bob Stanley trotted into view as untold thousands of New Englanders shrieked. The Steamer. Hard luck Harry. Sad Sack. The man who gave it up in 1978. The man who pledged he'd wave to his family and "to hell with the rest of 'em when the Sox won." Bad things happen to Bob Stanley, and here he was being thrown into the cockpit of an L-1011 with two wings on fire.

The Steamer had played out this scene many times on the quad lawn at the Holiday Inn poolside in Winter Haven. Stanley would hit whiffle balls to his tiny son, Kyle, always setting the scene with something like, "Okay, seventh game of the World Series, bases loaded, two outs, we're up one run. Here's a pop fly to Kyle Stanley. Can he catch it?"

The games usually ended when Stanley's little boy would dive and get grass stains on his good clothes. "Don't dive," the Steamer would yell. "We're going out to dinner."

While Stanley was warming up, Mets third-base coach Bud Harrelson told Mitchell to get ready. Harrelson told Mitchell that Stanley was going to bounce a pitch. Stanley had thrown only one wild pitch all season, but Mitchell had no reason to doubt his coach.

In the stands, Joan Stanley, celebrating her thirty-third birthday, looked toward the sky and pleaded. "God, please not tonight, not now, not again."

Mike Torrez, the man who gave up the homer to Bucky Dent, watched from the stands. Like Harrelson and Mrs. Stanley, Torrez felt that something bad was about to happen. Torrez had gotten tickets from his Mets friends and he felt that a wild pitch was coming.

Mookie Wilson was the batter. The Sox still led, 5–4, and there were still two outs. The first pitch was high and away and Wilson swung and missed. The next pitch was an outside strike and Wilson fouled it off. Stanley's next serve was outside—barely—and Wilson was bold to take the pitch. Wilson fouled off another strike. Stanley's next pitch (the thirteenth and final pitch that could have ended it for Boston) caught everyone by surprise. It sailed way inside at knee level. Wilson jacknifed away and miraculously averted being hit. The ball grazed off the glove of Gedman, who was not lined up for an inside pitch.

"Actually the ball was not that much inside," remembered Wilson. "I was leaning out over the plate because they'd been pitching me away. Gedman is a smart catcher and I think they wanted to tie me up with an inside pitch. I think it moved more than Gedman anticipated."

Stanley said, "I've never seen one of my pitches do that. I didn't try to throw it like that. It just happened."

Mitchell darted home, Knight took second, and men went to work emptying the Sox clubhouse. It was like watching looters empty a stereo store during a riot. Champagne, trophies, platforms, and television cameras and cables vanished. Cellophane was ripped away from lockers.

Stanley was charged with a wild pitch although Gedman later admitted he should have caught the ball. ("The ball grazed my glove and anything that hits my glove I should catch," said Gedman.) Joan Stanley was livid and told *Sport Magazine,* "For the rest of his career he's going to take the blame for this. And he shouldn't. I mean I love Geddy, I really do, but he blew it, you know. He blew it."

Official scorers were Charlie Scoggins of the *Lowell Sun,* Red Foley of the New York *Daily News,* and Dave Nightingale of the *Sporting News.* "I still think it was a wild pitch," Scoggins said a year later. "We called it because of the way Mookie Wilson reacted to the ball."

Some of the Mets thought it was a spitter. This theory might explain why Wilson and Gedman were caught off guard. The catcher was lined up outside and the pitch almost hit Wilson. Stanley's 1986 World Series ERA was 0.00. The Steamer's pitching line for Game 6 is 0 innings, 0 hits, 0 runs, 0 earned runs, 0 walks, and 0 strikeouts. Did he actually play in the game? Oh yes. There it is. "WP—Stanley."

The Steamer still could have gotten out of the inning without throwing a pitch. When Stanley next went into his stretch, second baseman Marty Barrett snuck in behind Knight and screamed for Stanley to throw. Barrett always claimed that Knight would have been dead and the game would have gone into an eleventh inning. But Stanley was too stunned to notice and still had to work on Wilson.

Wilson was relaxed. He felt that the pressure had been lifted because the game was tied. He focused on Stanley, only Stanley, and kept fouling off good pitches, mostly pitches away. Then Stanley came inside with his tenth pitch and Wilson hooked it with a golf swing. The Mookster hit a chopper down the first-base line and had the best view in America as he sprinted toward the bag. He could see Stanley running to cover first and he could see Buckner ranging to his left to field the grounder.

Wilson: "There is no way he [Stanley] would have beat me to the bag. I was already past Stanley. I don't know whether he was slow, or

I got out of the box fast. I didn't have any prayer that the ball was going to go through, but I knew I had a 90 percent chance of beating Buckner to the bag. I think he probably took his eyes off the ball for a split second. He's a good fielder and he would never miss that ball. He was probably trying to rush everything, especially with him not being in the best of health."

Johnny Pesky, the ghost of 1946, was there and remembered, "I was sitting next to Sam Mele and Frank Malzone. I was so upset. Truthfully, I really felt bad for Buckner. It could happen to anybody. The ball could go through your legs. But you figure, with the score tied, you're gonna block the ball."

Max Frazee was in the bar in TriBeCa. "You just cried," he remembered. "Buckner had the ball right in front of him. The ball goes underneath his legs. They could have drove a bus underneath those legs. It was bad. It would have put an end to the jinx, that's what it would have done. The Red Sox get there and they can't do shit."

Carl Yastrzemski watched the horrors from his home and noted, "Everything McNamara did during the playoffs he didn't do in the sixth game. Taking Buckner out for defense. He doesn't do it and he had a perfect opportunity with the bases loaded and a left-hander coming in to face him. Use a pinch hitter right there and then go defense."

There is only one logical explanation to account for Buckner's presence on the field at that moment: McNamara wanted his veteran war horse in the victory celebration photographs. The manager and Buckner have always bristled when this subject is raised, but leaving Buckner in the game simply didn't make sense and was a departure from the way McNamara had managed in every other postseason victory. Boston won seven playoff and Series games in 1986, and in the final inning of each victory, Dave Stapleton was playing first base. Stapleton was through as a major leaguer by the end of 1986. He hit .128 in thirty-nine at-bats, marking the sixth consecutive season in which his batting average declined. According to the official player ranking of the Elis Sports Bureau, Stapleton was the worst of 692 major leaguers in 1986—but he was healthy and agile enough to cover ground.

Facing the national media, McNamara defended all of his moves. He still does. He lifted Clemens, a 24–4 man, even though Clemens had retired four straight batters and was working on a four-hitter with eight strikeouts and only two walks. Clemens had thrown 135 pitches, 91 strikes. This decision inspires as much controversy as Joe McCarthy's decision to pitch Denny Galehouse in 1948 and to lift Ellis Kinder in 1949. Stories vary.

"My pitcher told me he couldn't go any further," McNamara told the national media when asked about removing the ace righty.

In the clubhouse, a reporter repeated the remark to Clemens, and Clemens charged toward McNamara's office. The Rocket Man was intercepted by pitching coach Bill Fischer.

"The decision was definitely all Mac's," Clemens said later. "He makes the decisions here. Yeah, my finger was bleeding, and it was up to him. I only gave up two runs and four hits. It was just a tough situation for him. It was a decision he had to make and I got nothing to say about it. I was very angry, no doubt about it. I hate coming out of games. I went over and said, 'Fish, let's get one thing straight here. There was no reason I'm gonna ask out of the game. Let's straighten that out right now. That was not my decision. That was a decision made by your guys.' "

Baylor was no happier than Clemens. A reporter chatting with Baylor offered his own explanation of why Baylor didn't hit for Buckner in the eighth. "I guess you just don't pinch hit for Buckner in that situation," suggested the reporter.

"Why not?" snapped Baylor. "I'm a fucking cheerleader. I feel the best players should be in there and I'm not going to be the fucking judge of that."

Baylor remained loyal to McNamara. The two have been friends for many years, and Baylor vowed never to discuss the matter with his manager. Baylor didn't even elaborate when he wrote his life story in 1989. One year after leaving Boston, Baylor got into the World Series with the Twins and hit a dramatic homer in the sixth game. He finally got his championship ring.

McNamara never admitted it, but he did have private doubts about not hitting for Buckner in Game 6. He later asked coach Rene Lachemann what he would have done, and Lachemann said he thought pinch hitting was the best maneuver in that situation.

The hours after Game 6 were spooky for Red Sox fans. "We watched what happened and then I put a sobbing seven-year-old back in his bed," wrote Ben Birnbaum. There were tears on pillows all over New England after Buckner's gaffe. Adults no doubt cried more than the children.

Mike Torrez wasn't crying. The goat of 1978 was in the stands at Shea and stumbled into a Boston television crew after the ludicrous loss. "I'm off the hook, I'm off the hook," Torrez told WCVB's Clark Booth. "I can really honestly say Boston can't blame me anymore for Bucky Dent and I hope they take me off the hook after seeing what I saw tonight. . . . You know, it's unfortunate that things like this happen to Boston. . . . But it seems like Boston always runs into things like this."

Dr. Bobby Brown, a man who had played for the Yankee teams that tortured Boston years earlier, was stunned to see the curse in action. In his capacity as American League President, he found himself in the unusual position of rooting for the Red Sox and sharing their frustration. He said later, "I thought that was the worst loss I've ever seen a sports team take. I've never seen a team in sports be that close and then not win it. To me, it was incredible."

At Shea there was a postgame reception for baseball executives and the national media after Game 6. American League director of public relations Phyllis Merhige, like her boss Dr. Brown, was very despondent over the loss and was stunned to see pockets of Boston reporters laughing and slapping one another on the back. The Sox are something of a self-fulfilling prophecy in Boston, and some members of the fourth estate take lugubrious delight in the continuation of the sad Sox saga.

Near tears, Merhige approached the group and asked, "How can you be so happy after what just happened?"

"Are you kidding?" replied Vince Doria, sports editor of the *Globe*. "This is the greatest."

Clark Booth, of WCVB, offered, "Remember the Red Sox can still win Game 7."

"Yeah, I suppose," said Doria. "But we'll always have Paris."

◊

It rained in New York the next day and Game 7 was postponed until Monday night. A few players went to Shea to work out in the mud. McNamara bravely faced the media on the third floor of the Sheraton Centre. By now there was plenty of speculation that the manager would scratch Oil Can Boyd and go back to Bruce Hurst for Game 7. Thanks to the rain delay, Hurst would have a third day of rest, and he'd mastered the Mets. At the evening press session, McNamara refused to name his Game 7 starter and continued to defend his Game 6 strategies. Asked about Buckner, he said, "I don't make any decisions for emotional reasons." The questions kept coming and finally the manager spread his arms in a pose of crucifixion and said, "This is an outstanding second-guess situation. You've got me."

A little more than a hour later, McNamara saw Boyd near the escalator at the Sox Grand Hyatt headquarters and called the volatile pitcher over. He told Boyd he was going to start Hurst in Game 7. Boyd's eyes filled with tears and he ran into the street. His last words were, "I'm going to party. I got no reason not to."

Hurst got the phone call from McNamara. He was going to pitch the finale. He knew it might be coming, but he still wasn't prepared. Bruce Hurst had finished his season when he beat the Mets in Game 5. Emotionally, he'd hung it up for the season. Now there was just one more little task before going home: the seventh game of the World Series. He felt unprepared. He'd left his game stuff at home, select cassette tapes and things he liked to have on the days he pitched. He'd left his season at home in his locker at Fenway.

Most Sox fans felt it was already over; some pledged they would not watch after experiencing the horrors of Game 6. Carl Yastrzemski, a man who died all the deaths in his twenty-three years in Boston, admitted, "After they lost the sixth game, you just knew somehow they wouldn't win the seventh game."

You just knew. For the fourth time since 1918, the Red Sox took the field in the seventh game of the World Series, and for the fourth time they were defeated. Eighty percent of the television sets in the Boston area were tuned in to this game, and TV critics believe this rating will never be equalled.

Dwight Evans and Rich Gedman hit back-to-back homers in the second to give Boston a 2–0 lead. Boggs singled home a third run, but even this was no comfort for the oft-burned fandom. There's nothing safe about a 3–0 Red Sox lead in the seventh game of the World Series. Boston led Cincinnati, 3–0, in the sixth inning of Game 7 in 1975, but that was before Spaceman Bill Lee insulted Tony Perez with a slo-pitch softball toss and Perez drilled a hole in the sky.

As always, there were hints that bad things lay ahead. Jim Rice, who managed to bat cleanup for seven games without driving in a run, led off the third with a shot off the wall in left center, but was thrown out going for two. It would have been a triple for most players, but Rice was a lumbering load by this time and the Sox wasted a chance to inflate their lead. Sid Fernandez replaced Ron Darling and the Sox couldn't solve the fat left-hander. Hurst took a 3–0 lead and a one-hitter into the sixth. Lee Mazzilli started a rally with a one-out single, but the crusher came when Keith Hernandez came up with the bases loaded and one out. Hurst got ahead, 0–1, then watched Hernandez slap a high fastball to left center for a two-run single.

"It was a fastball, it was up," said Hernandez. "He just didn't get it in enough. I'm sure he tried to come in with it and just didn't get it in enough. I'll always remember that. He led me off with a curveball. 'Base hit' was all that was in my mind. Get the score to 3–2 and hopefully move the other runner to third, which happened also."

"It's the only pitch I'd have back," said Hurst. "It was a good pitch, pretty much where I wanted it, but it just didn't have enough on it."

It was 3–3 after six, and McNamara lifted his ace lefty for a pinch hitter in the top of the seventh. Hurst felt he could have gone back out. He had his batting helmet on, but McNamara told him he had to hit for him. Tony Armas batted and struck out and Hurst thought, *I could have done that.*

Clemens was in the bullpen and expected to get the call. He had pitched two days earlier so it was his day to throw. He was coming off a 24–4 season and it was, after all, the seventh game of the World Series. But McNamara was paralyzed. The phone rang in the pen and Clemens knew it was for him. It was his turn. Wrong. The manager summoned Schiraldi—the nervous kid who hours earlier had admitted, "I don't deserve another chance." The Mets smiled.

Sad-eyed Schiraldi came on and Ray Knight led off the inning with a homer. Schiraldi gave up two more hits before Joe Sambito and then Stanley were summoned. By the time the inning was over, the Mets led, 6–3, and the Sox were deflated. They rallied one last time in the eighth. Buckner and Rice led with singles and Evans sent them home with a double to left center. With Evans on second and no outs, McNamara eschewed the bunt and Gedman lined out to the infield.

Henderson, a pumpkin again, struck out, and Baylor grounded to short.

The red-eyed manager had one last dubious decision to make. He had sent players down to see if Oil Can was in any condition to pitch and decided the Can was not an option. But there was no explanation for the alternative he selected. Trailing 6–5 in the bottom of the eighth, the manager passed over Clemens again and called for Al Nipper, a walking torch. Nipper was a man who compiled a 5.38 ERA in 1986 and who had pitched only once in twenty-three days. The Sox were afraid to use him in September against the Blue Jays, but here he was with the World Series on the line. Clemens stewed. Sammy Stewart (0.00 ERA in twelve career postseason innings) stewed.

Welcome Al Nipper. Darryl Strawberry broke his Series-long silence with a towering homer on an 0–2 pitch. Strawberry's tour-de-bases was only a little shorter than the *White Album*'s version of "Revolution Number Nine." Pitcher Jesse Orosco singled home another run off Nipper, and it was 8–5. The Sox went down in order in the ninth, and Evans, the latter-day Yaz, admitted, "I don't believe in history either, but maybe I'm starting to. Sixty-eight years is a long time—1918 was a long time ago. It does make you wonder."

Clark Booth, writing for the official archdiocesan newspaper, the *Pilot*, wrote, "To deny the 'mystical angle' in the Red Sox story is to deny yourself a lot of fun, and jeopardize your sanity as well. Now we must consider that there may be no other possible explanation. What, short of a demon force, could have seized Calvin Schiraldi as he wavered one strike from their first championship since 1918?"

New York Times columnist George Vescey wrote, "The memory of Babe Ruth does not fool around. His spirit has rumbled in historic Fenway Park like the Loch Ness Monster or Big Foot. . . . Ruth never uttered any farewell curse; he knew opportunity when he saw it. But his departure cast a spell that festered in the crevices and eaves of Fenway Park."

"Imagine being a kid from Worcester," said Rich Gedman. "I've been hearing all my life about how the Red Sox never win. I'd love to be a part of the team that ends that, and maybe have something to do with it. You don't know how excited I was after I hit that home run in the seventh game of the World Series. I really thought we had it won. It's still hard to believe we didn't win."

McNamara was tormented by the loss but rarely revealed his inner-most thoughts. Sitting in the dugout before the final meaningless game of the meaningless 1987 season, he blurted out, "You know, I sit here thinkin' and I *still* can't believe we lost the sixth game of the World Series. There's a part of me that just doesn't believe it. One fuckin' out. That's all we needed was one fuckin' out."

TEN

Roger Clemens walked out of spring training over a contract dispute in March 1987 and Red Sox General Manager Lou Gorman said, "The sun will rise, the sun will set, and I'll have lunch."

That was the end of the Red Sox title defense. The Year After has been a problem for Red Sox pennant winners. The 1919 Sox went 66–71 and finished sixth, twenty and one half games out. The 1947 defenders dropped to third, 83–71, and finished fourteen behind the Yankees. The 1968 team finished fourth, seventeen games behind the Tigers with an 86–76 record. The 76ers went 83–79 and finished third, fifteen and one half behind the Yanks.

Something always happens and managers always fall. The 1919 Red Sox sagged when Ruth got into a curfew battle with manager Ed Barrow. The Babe was suspended, as was star pitcher Carl Mays after Mays walked out on the team in midseason. Mays was sent to New York before the season was over, Ruth was gone after 1919, and Barrow followed the Babe to New York after a disastrous 1920 season. In 1947, star pitchers Boo Ferris, Tex Hughson, and Mickey Harris came up with sore arms and combined to win only twenty games after winning sixty-two a year earlier. The disheartening 1947 season broke Cronin, a stubborn, lantern-jawed Irishman who'd been bought by Yawkey in 1935. The 1968 Red Sox started to unravel after Jim Lonborg's bone-crushing ski episode, and it was in 1968 that Yawkey decided manager Dick Williams was not enough of a communicator. Williams lasted two full seasons after winning the American League pennant, just as Barrow did. It's the club record. The 1976 Townies were ripped apart by contract disputes involving Fred Lynn, Carlton Fisk, and Rick Burleson, the famed Kapstein triplets. This was also the summer that Tom Yawkey died. Meanwhile, Darrell Johnson battled the bottle, lost control of his team, and was gone by July.

In 1987, the Red Sox again had heavy bags to carry—luggage weighed down by the dirty laundry of their ancestors. Predictably, the weeks and months after the Sox almost won the 1986 World Series were peppered with the bad news fans have come to expect the Year After. McNamara, Buckner, Stanley, and Schiraldi were haunted by the demons of Shea while Gorman had to contend with a series of contract hassles. In the dead of winter it was learned that the Sox had been very cheap with World Series shares, giving clubhouse kids only $500 and stiffing the grounds crew altogether. The players shares came to about $86,000 each, a record loser's share. It was a record because so little was spread around. "I never understood that," Hurst said. "Why not share the gold?"

Batboy Jack Burke, a Quincy native who worked in the clubhouse for six seasons, remembered:

Dwight Evans is a very moody person, as well as a cheap one at that. He along with Buckner, Baylor, and Gedman were the biggest opposers of voting out World Series shares to the little people. Then there was pitcher Steve Crawford, an amazing person. He actually thought he was a superstar, and the guy had never had a successful season. Aside from being one of the dumbest persons I have ever met in my life, he was also one of the most stuck-up jerks I have ever met. He was famous for saying during the voting of shares, "Fuck the clubhouse kids, I want to go on a fishing trip." Bill Buckner was also worried about his wife's new Mercedes, which he insisted on showing us after we had received our checks for $350.00 after taxes. To this day I still have trouble comprehending the greed that these guys were filled with. It sickened me, and all they did was more or less laugh about it and rub it in at the same time. Marty Barrett was almost embarrassed for his teammates' greed, and during the off-season came back to give us more money. He and Crawford almost had a fist fight in one of the meetings, because of Shag's comments about his fishing trip.

The Red Sox front office was guilty of treading water after almost winning in 1986. It was clear that the team had weaknesses, particularly in the bullpen and at first base, but not a single major leaguer was acquired in the winter of 1986/1987. There was plenty of subtraction, but no addition; a prescription for failure in the no-repeat eighties.

Gedman was the first to dissolve. The two-time All-Star catcher was a free agent after 1986 but found himself caught in collusion freeze-out. Gorman berated Gedman as an All-Star "by default," and Haywood Sullivan spent considerable time yelling at the catcher in efforts to make him sign, but Gedman gambled on free agency—and lost. The January deadline was passed, which meant the Sox could not negotiate with their catcher until May 1. Thus, salami-bat Marc Sullivan, son-of-Haywood, became the Sox's number-one catcher.

Clemens was in camp when spring training started, but he stormed out when his contract was renewed to the tune of $400,000. That was less than half of what the Steamer was making and just over half of what the Red Sox were paying hopeless Tim Lollar. As reigning MVP, with a Cy Young Award and a 24–4 record, Clemens was insulted and sat out the rest of spring training. The Red Sox grossly underestimated his resolve. There were other distractions. Oil Can Boyd's name spilled onto another police docket when he failed to return some videocassettes in Winter Haven. A list of the AWOL tapes was published (*Nudes in Limbo* was one memorable selection), and the Can exploded. The episode forever will be remembered as the Can's Film Festival, but it was minor compared with the shoulder and neck ailments that would limit Boyd to one win in 1987.

Gedman, Clemens, and Boyd were gone, and the team was gray around the edges. Baylor, Buckner, and Rice came back, but none would ever return to the level of play they demonstrated in 1986. Henderson was given the job of everyday center fielder, but his pact with Satan had expired and he again became the player who couldn't start for the Seattle Mariners. The bullpen corps was hideous and would go seven weeks without a save during one awful stretch in 1987.

McNamara, ever the sub-.500 manager and tormented by World Series fallout in the winter of 1986/1987, held a lengthy meeting at the start of spring training and attempted to clear the air. It backfired. Barrett said, "We became the first team in history to be told before the first workout of the spring not to think or talk about making it to the seventh game of the World Series."

There was a feeling of hopelessness before the season began. The team was far from full strength and too many principals were haunted by the memory of the tenth inning at Shea. Boston's Opening Day pitcher was Stanley, and the Sox were swept by the Brewers before they came home to raise the traditional runner-up flag. The Sox were a whopping nine and a half games out by the end of April.

Clemens started slowly and failed to hold a 9–0 lead in Yankee Stadium. The Sox lost, 12–11, in extra innings. McNamara was tormented by the honor of managing the All-Star team. He had to pick the All-Star pitchers, and Clemens had a $150,000 incentive bonus riding on the outcome. Clemens made the decision easier by struggling to a 4–6 start, and McNamara did not pick his ace for the All-Star team. Gedman came back in May, struck out in his first at-bat, and staggered through a .205 (one homer, 13 RBI) season. He was never the same player again. There was tension between Baylor and Rice, and Baylor later said he wanted to fight Rice after "Captain Jim" was discovered in street clothes when he was needed to pinch-hit in Anaheim. Buckner was released in July, Baylor and Henderson were traded for virtually nothing in August and September, and Rice became a lead-footed singles hitter. It was over before it was over. The Red Sox finished 78–84, only their second sub-.500 season since 1967. Rookies Mike Greenwell, Ellis Burks, Todd Benzinger, and Sam Horn furnished some hope for the future, but Gorman learned the painful lesson of standing still and went to work as soon as the trainwreck season ended.

Don Zimmer was one of the men who helped the Sox return to the world of the living. Gorman went to the annual baseball meetings in Dallas looking for relief help (Boston had a baseball-low sixteen saves in 1987) and was stunned to find that the Cubs were shopping ace closer Lee Smith. General Manager Jim Frey had hired former high school pal Zimmer as his manager, and the two agreed that Smith had to go. There was some question about Smith's knees, his back, and his attitude. "You get tired of hearing him say 'motherfucker' every time you walk into the clubhouse," Frey explained later. The Cubs had some interest in Schiraldi and struck a deal that would send Smith to Boston for Schiraldi and Al Nipper. Gorman was stunned they agreed to such a trade. As he sat in a chair, across from Zimmer and Frey, he felt like leaping for joy. But he told himself to remain calm and plotted to call a press conference immediately—before anybody could talk the Cubs out of it.

When the deal was announced, Frank Robinson shook his head and said, "The Cubs traded a horse and they came away with two ponies."

The Sox switchboard lit up when the news moved on radio stations back in New England. People called the Red Sox office and challenged the announcement. It had to be a joke, they thought.

There was only one man who was not enthused with the deal: manager John McNamara. Gorman spoke of how it had taken him a long time to convince his manager to part with the star-crossed, lazy Schiraldi. There was a press luncheon in Dallas immediately after the trade was announced, and McNamara was unable to demonstrate any enthusiasm about the new toy he'd been handed.

The manager couldn't take the pressure. McNamara was a proverbial *good baseball man*. He was pitching oriented and played close to the vest. Good old company man Johnny Mac had many friends in high places throughout baseball. One of the legion of baseball lifers who came out of the A's system in the sixties, McNamara kept getting jobs because he knew the game and he didn't rock the boat. McNamara would ingratiate himself with the people he needed and ignore everybody else. It worked. He managed the A's, Padres, Reds, and Angels before coming to Boston. He was the man Hank Peters (another longtime baseball friend from the A's days) wanted to replace Earl Weaver in Baltimore in 1983. The Sox were a dreadfully boring 81–81 in McNamara's first year. In 1986 he did a masterly job handling his pitching staff and rode Clemens's big shoulders into the World Series, but like a lot of the other victims of Game 6, McNamara never got over that unspeakable defeat. It haunted him throughout the 1987 season, and the acquisition of Smith meant that he was going to be expected to deliver in 1988. It was the final year of his contract and John Harrington, Jean Yawkey's right-hand man, indicated before the season that there was pressure on the manager to produce.

◇

The 1988 Sox had a happy spring camp, and no less than five national media outlets picked Boston to win the American League East. The manager's response to this wave of optimism was, "A lot of people pick you to see you get fucking fired, to put heat on you."

There was plenty of heat in the first half of the 1988 Boston baseball season. Oil Can still had shoulder problems, Rice didn't hit a home run in April or May, the team hit only eight homers in its first twenty-three games, and batting coach Walter Hriniak came under fire for the Sox sand-blower attack. McNamara made moves, more than at any other time in his Boston career. He took Rice out of left field then moved the erstwhile slugger out of the cleanup spot. He tried Dwight Evans at first. He alternated Spike Owen and Jody Reed at short. He moved Wade Boggs from the third spot (which Boggs liked) back to leadoff (which Boggs hated). But the Red Sox still wallowed around .500 and there was little happiness in the clubhouse. McNamara contributed to the dour environment by slamming his door on reporters much of the time. He also created a chasm between the young players and the veterans. He let the stars do as they pleased then demonstrated his toughness by bullying Reed, Jeff Sellers, and Todd Benzinger. Nothing was said to Rice when the veteran couldn't play due to a rib injury then got up at 6 A.M. to drive a hundred miles for thirty-six holes of golf at Pebble Beach. But Benzinger was characterized as a wimp—Fred Lynn without the talent. McNamara floated the theory that Benzinger wouldn't play hurt, and Evans went public, ripping his teammate for always being hurt yet never being in the trainer's room. Benzinger, a bookish outsider, declined to retaliate. "It's human nature to favor some people over others," he reasoned.

In other clubhouse corners, resentment grew. "What we need is a new manager," Greenwell said in May. "Do you notice how Dewey [Evans] is in his office every day? He spends a hour in there and Mac believes everything he's telling him."

Pawtucket manager Ed Nottle had a bad experience with McNamara. In late May, the Sox manager called Pawtucket to find out if any lefties were ready, and Nottle suggested Tom Bolton or Mike Rochford. McNamara asked about a lefty named Zach Crouch, and Nottle told him the kid wasn't ready to empty his bathtub. Nobody listened. The Sox called for Crouch and the southpaw was lit up for four hits and two walks in 1.1 innings over three appearances. When the press questioned McNamara about Crouch, the manager shrugged and said, "My people in Pawtucket said he was ready." Nottle was steamed when he read the remark and was on the phone the next day. It was the only call he placed to Boston in 1988. He told McNamara that if he ever did that again, he'd call his own press conference.

On June 3, a Costa Mesa, California, woman named Margo Adams filed a $6 million breach of oral contract suit against Boggs. It was an off-field matter but would prove to have plenty of impact on the Boston team in the ensuing weeks and months. The Red Sox dropped nine games out of first place a few days after the suit was filed, and Boston's last hope appeared to be a three-game set with the Yankees at Fenway in mid-June. ABC television was on hand for Game 1, which featured Clemens against the first-place Yanks. McNamara was unavailable to most of the media before this big game. Rice crashed a couple of homers, but Clemens had nothing, and was left on the mound to take the beating of his life. He gave up fifteen hits and nine earned runs before he was lifted in the seventh. The pitcher was steaming as he waited for relief.

Jean R. Yawkey president John Harrington wanted to fire McNamara immediately after the chaotic Yankee series. McNamara was having trouble sleeping and had become ultrasensitive. Meanwhile, radio talk shows were hosting "Knife the Mac" telethons, and cartoonists and columnists were crying for his scalp. It was ugly. It was a lot of pressure for anyone, much like what Zimmer went through in the final days.

After the Yankee series, the Sox went to Baltimore and McNamara announced that he would no longer talk about his "situation." The manager was twisting in the wind. He'd asked for a vote of confidence from the front office, but got none. Gorman asked ownership to define the manager's job security, but there was no word from above. McNamara had lost control. When other players' names got dragged into the Margo Adams affair, Boggs found himself battling his own teammates. Boggs and Evans got into a fight on a bus, in Cleveland. The hard feelings spilled over into the lobby of the Hollenden House and guests (many had just returned from a night at the theater) watched in stunned silence as Evans and catcher Rick Cerone exchanged shoves and insults on the way to the elevator. Where was McNamara during all of this? See no evil. Hear no evil.

"Mac just sort of scooted out of there," said Hurst.

McNamara's final road trip was through Kansas City, Minnesota, and Chicago in July, the last trip before the All-Star break. The Sox played in his image, a listless 4–8 as they dropped nine games out. After a mail-order loss in Minnesota, Benzinger said, "I didn't think we were any more dead-ass than usual." After the final loss in Chicago, which set the record at an embarrassing 43–42 at the break, McNamara unbuttoned his Boston jersey for the last time and said, "After all is said and done and all we've been through, I'm very happy to be one game over .500."

McNamara returned home for the break, saying he hadn't had a vacation in a while. Clemens and Greenwell went to Cincinnati for the All-Star game and Greenwell kept raising his eyebrows and asking reporters, "Any news yet?"

Meanwhile, Margo Adams was making an appearance on "Donahue" and claiming that Boggs had broken into rooms of teammates and taken photos of them in compromising positions with other women. She said he called the operation Delta Force. It sounded ridiculous at the time, but it was later learned that in 1986, Boggs and Crawford had indeed pulled such a prank on Bob Stanley. A stripper from Detroit was assigned to join Stanley in his room. On cue, Boggs and Crawford burst into the room and started taking pictures. Stanley came up swinging and got into a fight with Crawford, a longtime friend. Boggs and Crawford apologized and allowed Stanley to tear up the pictures. Adams kept a negative and made everybody nervous when she started talking about Boggs's Delta Force on national television.

While Lady Margo was chirping on "Donahue," Red Sox General Manager Gorman went on every television station and promised that McNamara would be back in the dugout when the season resumed.

On Thursday, July 14, at 3:30 P.M., Jean Yawkey met with John Harrington, Haywood Sullivan, and counsel John Donovan. It was a routine general partners meeting until Sullivan asked that McNamara's status be clarified. The minority owner was concerned about his friend, and the constant media speculation was making McNamara's job unbearable. Harrington told Sullivan that McNamara would probably not be rehired for 1989. Hearing that, Sullivan suggested something be done immediately. There was a discussion and within five minutes, McNamara's tenure as Sox manager was over. Caving in to the demands of the masses, the Red Sox had fired their manager on Bastille Day. A bitter Haywood Sullivan went downstairs to the manager's office, where McNamara was half-dressed, seated behind his desk. McNamara had already made out his lineup card, and when Sullivan broke the news, the fired manager tore the card in half and flung it against the wall. McNamara got dressed, exited quietly, and was jeered by fans as he got into his car and drove home. When the press was informed of the dismissal, Sullivan stated that he'd been outvoted.

"She came in and said, 'I want him out,' " Sullivan said later. He also suggested Mrs. Yawkey had been bothered by the negative publicity of Margo Adams and Delta Force.

Gorman looked particularly silly. He'd told the western world McNamara's job was safe.

◇

No trumpets blared for Joe Morgan. He was introduced as an interim manager, and Gorman stated that a search for a permanent skipper would commence immediately. A native of Walpole and a baseball lifer, Morgan had been buried under McNamara. He had little input into the daily operation of the club, and McNamara had insulted him in 1986 by taking him off the baselines and sending him to the bullpen. One of the reasons McNamara wasn't fired earlier in 1988 was because the Sox felt there was no top replacement available. Morgan was simply the handy choice to ride out a lost season.

Batboy Burke was in the clubhouse when the torch was passed and remembered, "The feeling throughout the clubhouse after Mac's firing was strange. Ball players aren't much on sympathy to begin with. Most everybody was laughing, at both Joe's hiring and Mac's firing. The reason why it was so strange to see Joe up talking to all the players was because under the Mac regime the coaches, except for Rene Lachemann and Bill Fischer, were irrelevant. Mac barely spoke to them."

There is no logical explanation for what happened in the first three weeks of the Joe Morgan administration, but it can be stated without argument that Morgan got off to the most successful start in managerial history. The Red Sox won twelve straight, nineteen of twenty, and closed a nine-game gap, tying for first on August 4. The twelve-game streak was Boston's longest since 1948, and the Red Sox also broke an American League record by winning twenty-four straight at Fenway. Twenty-four. The embarrassing "search" for a manager was called off after the first six wins, and Morgan had a contract for 1989 before the streak was over. He also gained the respect of milions of fans by standing up to Jim Rice. The slumping, grumping Rice was insulted when Morgan sent Spike Owen up to hit for him (bunt situation) and pulled Morgan into the dugout runway. An ex-hockey player, Morgan was ready to go at it with the muscular Rice, but players intervened. Morgan emerged from the runway stating, "I'm the manager of this nine."

And so he was. The Red Sox played ordinary baseball after the celestial start, but there wasn't much competition in the American League East, and Boston moved into sole possession of first place for good on Labor Day in Baltimore. Despite losing six of their last seven, the Red Sox clinched the American League East with two days to spare. The title was delivered without ceremony, like an early-morning message slipped under a hotel room door. Boston was beaten in Cleveland on Friday, September 30, but won the division hours later when Oakland beat Milwaukee on the West Coast. When the good news broke, most of the Sox were sleeping in their rooms at the Hollenden House— the haunted hotel that had served as the photo setting for Delta Force.

It became increasingly difficult for the Red Sox to concentrate on baseball toward the latter part of the 1988 season. Clemens was battling a second-half slump and claiming that he had "severe tendinitis" in his shoulder. Hurst was on the threshold of free agency and had told friends and teammates that he would probably leave. Oil Can was back on the shelf with another mysterious blood clot in his pitching arm. Boyd's problem seemed particularly threatening. There were days when his right arm was cold and had little pulse. Teammates feared he might be a candidate for a stroke. Rice was still mad at Morgan, Evans resented suggestions that the team's turnaround was sparked by the removal of McNamara, and there were rumors that Margo Adams was going to sell her story to *Penthouse* magazine. "It's not like I killed the president or anything," reasoned Boggs.

Meanwhile, the Red Sox were preparing for the playoffs again. It was rare for the Red Sox to return to postseason play so soon. This marked the first time since 1916/1918 that the Red Sox finished first twice in a three-year period.

The Sox faced the mighty Oakland A's in the playoffs and oddsmakers didn't give Boston much hope. Ninety-four-year-old Jimmy Cooney, the last survivor of the 1918 Boston champs, was interviewed before the start of the series and said, "I don't think they've got much of a chance against Oakland." The Red Sox were 3–9 against Oakland in 1988 and had lost eight straight and fourteen of fifteen in the Alameda County Coliseum since 1986. Hurst pitched a six-hitter in the first game of the series, but lost, 2–1. This was the game in which Boggs permanently tarnished his silver bat collection. The Chicken Man came to bat twice with the bases loaded and once with two men on, and in those three trips he hit one sacrifice fly and twice struck out. Facing Dennis Eckersley, with two on and two out in the ninth, Boggs swung feebly and missed to end the game. Oakland pitchers Dave Stewart and Eckersley said it was the first time either had fanned Boggs. Further, Boggs swung and missed strike three both times, and that happened only eleven times in 1988. Of the 3,064 pitches he saw in 1988, he swung and missed only thirty-three times, yet it happened twice when it mattered most. "That last swing was a horseshit swing in my book," he admitted. "It was a real bad swing. I'm human. Yeah, I blew it, I left five guys on, it's my fault. I'll take the blame."

Clif Keane, who covered baseball for the *Globe* from 1943 through 1976, threw out the first ball before Game 2. He said it was a knuckleball thrown by a knucklehead. Keane was born the same year Fenway was built, and before making his historic toss said, "They've got to do it soon. I'm running out of time. I didn't see it in '18, I was only six years old. If they don't win this year, I'll think they're cursed for selling Ruth."

Clemens took the mound for Game 2 and took a 2–0 lead into the seventh. It should have been a 3–0 lead, but Jim Rice stood on third like a cigar store Indian when he could have scored on a pitch that got away from catcher Ron Hassey. Clemens could have used the insurance when the A's rocked him for three runs in the seventh. With former teammate Dave Henderson on first, Clemens got ahead of Jose Canseco, 0–2, then surrendered a homer into the net on an inside fastball. With one out and Carney Lansford on first, Clemens balked Lansford to second, wild-pitched him to third, then yielded an RBI single to Mark McGwire. The Sox came back to tie it, but Hassey and flyswatters Tony Phillips and Walt Weiss bled Lee Smith for three singles and a run in the ninth. Number nine hitter Weiss got the game winner even though he was statistically the worst clutch hitter (4–66 after the sixth in pressure situations) in the American League in 1988. Eckersley picked up the save again in the ninth. Watching from the box seats was the man Boston acquired when Eckersley was traded in 1984: Bill Buckner.

It was clear that Red Sox fans were not going to be taken to the edge this time. Aces Bruce Hurst and Roger Clemens couldn't win Games 1 and 2 in Fenway and there was no reason to believe it was going to be any better in Oakland. "We're 1–14, we're down two games, what odds would you put on it?" asked Morgan.

The Red Sox found a new way to lose in Game 3. After managing only nine hits and four runs in the first two games, Walter Hriniak's maligned minions struck for five runs in the first two innings of Game 3. On the mound for Boston was Mike Boddicker, a calm veteran who had allowed no earned runs in eighteen postseason innings during his salad days with the Orioles. But the efficient A's ripped Boddicker, scoring four in the second and two more in the third. Lansford, McGwire, and Hassey all homered, and Boddicker was gone before the third was over. The Sox clawed back to within 7–6 but were stopped by umpire Ken Kaiser who invoked the rarely called automatic double play when Gedman barreled into second to break up a double play in the fifth. It was still a 7–6 game in the bottom of the seventh, but Stan Javier opened up the lead with an RBI single, and the A's were en route to a 10–6 win and a 3–0 series lead. It seemed fitting that little-used Javier would be instrumental in beating Boston. Stan Javier's father, Julien Javier, was the starting second baseman for the Cardinals when they beat Boston's Impossible Dreamers in the 1967 World Series. Father and son. A new generation of disappointments.

Riding to the Oakland Coliseum in a hotel courtesy van on Sunday, October 9, Sox pitcher Jeff Sellers spotted a woman walking to the ballpark toting a common household tool. "Look at that," said Sellers. "The bitch has got her broom, man."

"Sweep, sweep, sweep," they chanted. It was Sellers's last day with the Boston ball club. Ditto for first baseman Todd Benzinger, shortstop Spike Owen, DH Larry Parrish, coach Walter Hriniak, and starting pitcher Hurst. Oakland took a 2–0 lead in the third, and the flat Red Sox limped to the finish, losing 4–1. It marked the first time in twelve attempts that Boston won fewer than three games in postseason play. There was some grumbling at the end when Morgan used Owen to hit for Rice and Benzinger to hit for Evans. Rice was already mad at Morgan, and Evans told friends on the Oakland team that he, Evans, would have a hard time playing for Morgan after the insult. The Sox staggered back to the Oakland airport, where Hurst decided there was a little too much staggering going on. The ace lefty, who'd given thirteen years to the Boston organization, and won eighty-eight games—only one less than southpaw Babe Ruth—got off the team charter because he felt there was too much drinking. Hurst said, "It's not my most favorite place to be. It's not my greatest time as a baseball player when guys get a little boxed and if they get out of hand. So I said, 'Fine.' I had the option to get off the plane, so I did. Guys were a little hammered, so I got off the airplane."

Hurst's complaint reminded Burke of another travel episode from 1986: "I remember before a road trip in '86, Bruce was a little late getting to the park. He was obviously spending the last few moments with his family. Anyhow, Bruce was walking toward the bus with Sammy Stewart, and the bus pulled away leaving them stranded. I never saw Bruce so mad, and he didn't get mad very often. Situations like these, I'm sure, led to the eventual breakup between Boston and Bruce."

Hurst's departure from the sad charter home was the first cut in Boston's bloody baseball winter of 1988/1989. In early December Clemens went on live television in Boston (WCVB) and complained about having to carry his own luggage. He also said, "There are some things going on up there in Boston that make it a little bit tough as far as your own family." Clemens said he felt the club was not going all out to keep Hurst, then insulted Bostonians again, adding, "If you take a family man like Bruce is, there's too many obstacles there in Boston to be able to overcome that. . . . There are a lot of things that are a disadvantage to a family there."

The interview was a public relations disaster for Clemens. His agents, Alan and Randy Hendricks, went to work on a damage-control operation, and two days later Clemens was phoning Boston newspapers, television and radio stations asking to make another statement. By that time, Hurst had announced he was taking less money to pitch for the San Diego Padres. Hurst was insulted by some of the Sox's negotiating tactics and later said, "Haywood hates players." Great. Clemens said

Boston is a crummy place to raise kids, then Hurst blew town to go pitch for a team that wears brown and orange uniforms. Boston's baseball fans were shattered.

There was more. The Sox announced a ticket price hike to sixteen dollars for box seats, tops in the majors. Mike Greenwell threatened a spring holdout. Three days after Christmas, Boggs was grabbed and held at knifepoint outside a lounge in Gainsville, Florida. Boggs claimed he used transcendental meditation to will himself invisible. Celtic Kevin McHale joked that Boggs used the same trick in Game 1 of the ALCS. Meanwhile, teammates wished Margo Adams would become invisible. Oil Can Boyd asked for a raise and filed for arbitration even though he'd won only ten games in the previous two seasons. Clemens tried another television gig, and this time threatened reporters, stating, "I don't appreciate reporters writing about my family and somebody's gonna get hurt one time doing that." The *Globe* ran a cartoon of Clemens in a karate outfit answering reporters' questions. In the spoof, a reporter asked if he could ask a question and Clemens throttled the scribe, saying, "Do you feel lucky?" Two weeks later, Boggs returned to the spotlight when details of Delta Force surfaced, and then *Penthouse* confirmed that it would run the dreaded Margo story. Boggs said he'd seen a Geraldo Rivera program on sex addiction and this convinced him that he was addicted to sex. Boggs's agent, Alan Nero, compared Margo Adams to Glenn Close's character in *Fatal Attraction*. Boggs said he'd spoken with Rice and Stanley and that everything was okay. Rice said, "Let's wait and see what's in *Penthouse*."

Harmony was lacking, but this was nothing new in the joyless workplace that is the Red Sox clubhouse. Ancient clubhouse man Vinnie Orlando presided over the room, and it was coach Rene Lachemann who put it best when he said, "Vinnie makes you feel like you're ten games out every time you walk through the door."

"Team unity never existed from what I saw around the Sox clubhouse," said Burke, the veteran batboy. "Much of this problem results from the many years of the Jim Rice reign of the clubhouse. Rice is an evil, envious, jealous person. You can see it in his eyes, all you have to do is walk past him, and you can tell he is thinking nasty thoughts, and if you look back when you pass him, you see him whispering things behind your back to one of his allies. Rice's locker mate in 1986 was Don Baylor, and it didn't take Baylor long to figure out what kind of guy Rice actually was, because by the end of the season, it was obvious the two didn't care for each other. Rice was so hateful of Baylor, because the short period he [Baylor] was there, everybody on the team befriended him, and sought advice from him. It was kind of a mockery of Rice, for what he represented by being captain, because nobody had ever dared approach him for anything, because of his mood swings. Rice's personality contributed immensely to team dissension, but he was not the only one responsible."

"There should have been a lot more fun in the clubhouse when we won in 1986," said Lachemann. "We won ninety-five ball games. But because of the pressure and the negative stuff, it wasn't as much fun."

Things weren't any better in the spring of 1989. Margo's first *Penthouse* story broke just as spring training started, and she had Boggs claiming Rice "thinks he's white." Adams also said Boggs felt Evans was a snitch, Gorman was "a bastard," and that Clemens was "Mr. Perfect." She retold the Delta Force tale, making Stanley uncomfortable. Boyd reacted most strongly, claiming that Boggs was a "sex fiend." The Can felt a double standard existed because his 1986 problems landed him in the hospital where he had to undergo psychiatric testing. "Who needs the psychiatrist now?" asked the Can.

The pressure on Boggs was enormous throughout spring training. Reporters from across America made the pilgrimage to sleepy Winter Haven, and Boggs was fodder for the "CBS Evening News with Dan Rather," "Entertainment Tonight," and Barbara Walters on "20/20." A well-worn photo of Wade and Margo appeared on the front page of *USA Today,* and Boggs was a coverboy for *Sports Illustrated.* Johnny Carson, David Letterman, Jay Leno, and Pat Sajak told Wade Boggs jokes on late-night television, and the *Herald* started an advice column in which readers were encouraged to tell Debbie Boggs what they thought she should do with her marriage. While all this was going on, *Penthouse* sponsored a Margo-Across-America tour, which ended just days before Ms. Adams was arrested for shoplifting a coat. Back in Boston, the New England chapter of Multiple Sclerosis fund-raisers dropped Boggs as a spokesman, even though Boggs had donated many hours, raised thousands of dollars, and even though Boggs's sister has the disease. Meanwhile, Red Sox General Manager Lou Gorman spent hundreds of dollars making phone calls in an effort to unload the All-Star third baseman. Minority owner Sullivan, insecure with his new,

smaller role, called Boggs together with select teammates in an effort
to clear the air, while demonstrating that he, Sullivan, still had some
clout. One year after refusing to offer Adams the $100,000 she wanted,
after pledging not to give her one penny, Boggs finally offered a $20,000
settlement. Adams rejected the offer and countered with $125,000.
Boggs said no, and the folks from LA Law went back to work.

This was the story that would not go away. The Red Sox were the
baseball team with the scarlet letter. Publicist Jim Samia took a phone
call a week before spring training ended and the caller said that a bomb
would be placed on any airplane carrying Boggs out of Florida. On the
evening of their flight from Tampa to Baltimore, the Sox abruptly
switched from a commercial flight to a charter. When the Sox flew from
Baltimore to Kansas City, dogs sniffed the ball club's luggage.

The 1989 Red Sox lost their first four games. Roger Clemens couldn't
beat the Orioles on Opening Day in front of the new President, George
Bush, and Joe Morgan's five-man-infield stunt backfired. Morgan and
Clemens both got off to rough starts. The manager couldn't make the
right moves. His problems started St. Patrick's Day when he called his
team "dead ass," then flew home to honor a St. Patrick's Day com-
mitment in his native Walpole. Players and fans detected a trace of
inconsistency, and it was clear that Morgan's honeymoon with the media
was ending. He used his bullpen in inverted order Opening Day (Lee
Smith, Rob Murphy, Bob Stanley, then Mike Smithson) and Craig
Worthington's shallow fly landed in the middle of Morgan's two-man
outfield in the bottom of the eleventh. Clemens didn't speak to the
media all spring and was still under heavy fire for his winter ramblings.
The Sox were 1–4 when they finally returned to Fenway, and Clemens
was loudly booed during the pregame introductions. "I can take it,"
said Clemens. "We got some guys here that can't take criticism, but I
can."

Two weeks later, while the Sox struggled to get to .500, Oil Can
Boyd exploded. The Sox were snowed out in Cleveland in April and
the Can's start was pushed back a day to accommodate Clemens (lifetime, 10–1 versus the Tribe at that hour). The ever-combustible Can
said, "I'm not playing second fiddle to nobody. I ain't no fourth or fifth
starter. I'm a bona fide major league pitcher. I'm not concerned about
the ball club right now, I'm just worried about myself, and right now,
I'm not happy at all."

Boyd's Me Manifesto exposed an attitude that has plagued the Red Sox for seventy years. A lot of players don't care about their ball clubs, care only about themselves, but it's rare that an athlete comes out and admits this.

In his third start after the outburst, Boyd's right hand went cold and numb and another shoulder blood clot—his third in ten months—was discovered. Red Sox team physician/owner Arthur Pappas indicated that Boyd's overhand motion was causing the clots. Pappas said the Can would have to switch to sidearm or underhand . . . or retire. Boyd was devastated by the news, and Pappas kept him sedated for several days. In the two weeks after Boyd went on the shelf, starters Wes Gardner (elbow) and Mike Boddicker (back) left games with injuries.

Despite these dents in the starting rotation, the 1989 Red Sox were potential winners in the American League East. This was the season when the balance of power shifted west, and by the beginning of May it was clear that all the best American League teams were playing in the western division. The Yankees were a joke, the Tigers got old, the Orioles were too young, the Brewers were too hurt, the Indians are never taken seriously, and the talented Blue Jays continued to stumble. "What about this race," said Clemens. "Man, it's like they're giving it to us." Indeed, as late as May 19 the Red Sox were able to boast first-place status even though they had lost more games than they had won (18–19). No team in baseball history was ever in first place with a sub-.500 record at a later date.

General Manager Lou Gorman was smiling over his winter acquisitions of pitchers John Dopson and Rob Murphy and first baseman Nick Esasky. Dopson blossomed into a solid number-three starter, Murphy provided help from the left side, and Esasky was a better fielder and more powerful hitter than Benzinger had been.

Morgan continued to manage like Chauncy the Gardener from Peter Sellers's *Being There.* In Chicago he started Rick Cerone behind the plate because he thought White Sox pitcher Shawn Hillegas was a left-hander. Cerone hit a long homer to ice the game in the late innings. Most managers would have covered up the blunder and bragged about a hunch, but Morgan greeted the press saying he'd had Cerone in the game only because he thought Chicago's pitcher was left-handed. In California, Morgan sent Randy Kutcher (batting .000) up to hit for Jim Rice in a bunt situation in the ninth inning. The Red Sox were leading,

3–2, and had runners on first and second with no outs when Kutcher went up. The runners advanced on an errant pickoff throw after two pitches to Kutcher. No longer bunting, the utilityman slapped an RBI single to right and will be able to tell his grandchildren that he pinch-hit for a man with four hundred career homers and knocked in a run.

But there was not getting away from Miss Margo. Adams's attorney warned that Boston players would be slapped with subpoenas when the team went west in May, and Rice, Evans, and Gedman were served papers at the Anaheim Marriott. The process servers somehow missed Marty Barrett, who was growing a road-trip beard. One of the servers asked Ellis Burks if his name was Jim Rice, and Burks snapped, "Get out of my face."

Boggs had his wife, two children, and baby-sitter with him on the trip. He submitted to three and a half hours of questioning before one of the games against the Angels. The "Mar-go" chants at Anaheim Stadium were among the loudest in the American League, and the Big A crowd was the only one that continued to taunt Boggs when he reached base. The Chicken Man refused to buckle. He wouldn't settle and he wouldn't let Adams affect his game. Meanwhile, his deposed teammates wanted him to settle.

Still under .500, still in first place, the Red Sox returned to Oakland, where they had lost ten straight and sixteen of seventeen games since the middle of 1986. The streak was snapped when Evans hit a tenth-inning grand slam off former teammate Eckersley, but the Sox dropped the next two and came home two games under .500.

Despite the mediocre record, the Sox were very much in the hunt thanks to the abject mediocrity of the American League East. They started the longest home stand of the season with a three-game sweep of the Seattle Mariners (Seattle had the benefit of a scouting report made out by advance man John McNamara), then lost six of the final eight games of the home stand. Boston's last day in first place was May 25, the day the California Angels came to town. Angel lefty Chuck Finley started the Sox skid with a one-hit masterpiece on a Fenway Friday night, and by the time the Toronto Blue Jays left Boston nine days later, the Red Sox were five and a half games off the pace.

It was during this period that the Olde Towne Team started to take on the look of a loser. A lion-hearted bunch they were not. Boggs blamed his spring slump on the departure of Hriniak. Clemens, Boddicker, and Gardner complained incessantly about the umpiring. Smith made it clear that he did not want to pitch unless he could get a save. Morgan held a couple of meetings and told his players to stop worrying about statistics. He told his team to keep hustling. The players held some meetings of their own and decided to fine one another for talking to players on opposing teams. They also made a pact not to speak to specific members of the media. It was clear that this was a rudderless ship, full of sailors complaining about salty food and cabin decor while the vessel was careening off an iceberg.

The player reps were Wes Gardner and Clemens. Gardner was twenty-eight years old with a total of thirteen major league victories and had trouble getting anyone's attention. Veterans Evans, Rick Cerone, and Bob Stanley made their pleas, but there was a faction of young players that despised these veterans. It seemed that no one would shoulder any blame. The team that always needed twenty-four cabs for twenty-four players now needed twenty-four mirrors.

"I don't agree with any of this," said veteran Mike Smithson. "These guys are unbelievable with these meetings. They're all just making excuses."

Greenwell added, "I wanted to be player rep, but Richie [Gedman] talked me out of it. Then I find out he nominated Wes. If I'd known all this bullshit was going to happen, I'd have gotten that job and a lot of this stuff wouldn't be going on. I told Gardner, 'Wes, shut the fuck up and sit down.' He's been on the disabled list longer than I've been in the big leagues. When Cerone got up to talk, I just hung my head in my locker. He's lucky to even be here and he acts like he's running the team."

On Sunday, June 4, the Red Sox carved out their everlasting monument for the 1989 season; they led the Blue Jays, 10–0, in the seventh, then lost. This was a franchise first. The Harry Frazee Red Sox never blew a ten-run lead, and the Bob Quinn Sox never did it. Tom Yawkey never lived to see it. The Blue Jays won in extra innings, 13–11, and the Sox hit the dusty trail for another cruise to nowhere. They went on the road without Jim Rice and Marty Barrett. Rice stayed behind to have a bone chip removed from his right elbow while Barrett underwent arthroscopic knee surgery for a ligament tear suffered in the hideous loss to the Blue Jays.

The Red Sox went to New York for a weekend series in June, and both teams were under .500. The Sox and Yankees have both finished under .500 in the same season only twice since 1925: 1965 and 1966. Ironically, while the chicken-hearted, overpaid, and largely inept Red Sox and Yankees were dueling at the Stadium, their predecessors were toasting the rise of a best-selling book at Mickey Mantle's joint on Central Park South. Prize-winning author David Halberstam was up to number three on *The New York Times* best-seller list with *Summer of '49*, the story of the 1949 pennant race between the Red Sox and Yankees. Halberstam was asked if, forty years hence, someone attempted to write a tome on the summer of 1989, would it be as nice a book? "No," answered Halberstam. "I think it would be about anger and money and litigiousness. There was a moment this spring when Darryl Strawberry walked out of spring training and said at a million and a half he was not being paid enough, and I turned to my wife and I said, 'The book is going to be a best-seller,' because it is so counterpoint to all of that. I think the motivations are different. The sense of community will be different forty years later to these guys. I think it will be very interesting how much less is left when it's all over. I think a lot less of the money will be there, the feeling about each other."

There was a telling moment Sunday, June 11, at Yankee Stadium. The Sox had lost the first game of a double header, 4–2, then fell way behind in the second game. Boston rallied in the eighth, but in the midst of the rally, Yankee manager Dallas Green came out to lift a pitcher while Sox utility infielder Ed Romero stood at the plate with a 3–0 count. When Green brought on his new pitcher, Morgan sent Rich Gedman up to hit for Romero. Romero went to the dugout, then took a huge orange container of Gatorade and tossed it out of the dugout and onto the field. It was a textbook demonstration of the selfishness that marked the Red Sox season in 1989. Ed Romero was a .233 hitter with ten homers and one triple in 1,733 at-bats covering more than ten major league seasons; for this minimal output, he was earning a handsome wage of $415,000. Despite all of the above, Romero announced that he wanted to be traded. Meanwhile, the Red Sox lost, 8–7, dropping to 0–10 in one-run road games, and nobody threw anything when the game was over.

Morgan wasn't laughing. A manager looks weak and vulnerable when he starts getting shown up by utility infielders. "I can put up with a lot," said Morgan, "but I don't need this shit."

Less than a week later, center fielder Ellis Burks went down with a shoulder injury, and the Sox were forced to go back to their depleted farm system.

The Red Sox had six players on the disabled list when the Texas Rangers came to Boston in late June. On the night of June 22, there was an incident that explained a lot about the 1989 Boston edition. Annoyed at the way Texas hitters were digging in against Sox pitching, Smithson hit Ranger Rafael Palmeiro. Palmeiro started to charge the mound, and within seconds the entire Texas bench emptied. Smithson looked around and there was no one coming to his defense. Journeyman pitcher Joe Price came out of the Boston dugout, but that was it. Seconds later, Clemens and Gardner reluctantly walked out. Smithson was furious. "I was trying to make something happen," he said. "I thought maybe a fight would be good for us. But no. I can't say what was going through their minds. Some guys later told me they were waiting to see if anything happened, but as far as I'm concerned, it was happening right then."

A day later, Greenwell blasted again, labeling his teammates "wimps and fairies." Morgan was asked about the remark on live television and replied, "A pretty good assessment." The next day coach Al Bumbry posted this sign on the clubhouse wall: "When we start to play as a team, I'll fight as a team." This was the same week that the Sox were outscored, 29–4, in three Fenway games and fell eight games behind the Orioles. "Until some of these guys come back, we just have to keep our heads above water," said Greenwell. "But we're drowning."

They were six games out, still one game under .500 at the All-Star break. Morgan was losing his grip. Veteran pitchers wouldn't give him the ball when he'd call on a reliever; they'd toss the ball to the incoming pitcher. Stanley was griping about how the manager lost confidence in him. There was dissatisfaction with pitch selection, and new hitting coach Richie Hebner was unpopular with many of the older players. The Sox got to Texas and dropped the opener, 12–6, falling nine games out on July 18. Stanley got some work and was lit up like a pinball machine and after the game said, "It's like a horse race. Maybe it's time to go to the farm. When you can't run anymore."

Two weeks later, Stanley said he "hated" Morgan. Still, the Sox would not release him.

The Red Sox were able to make up a lot of ground when the Orioles slumped in late July, and in early August Boston was battling the Orioles for first place. Baltimore dropped twelve of its first thirteen on a road trip, including three straight at Fenway. On the night of August 2, the Red Sox took a 6–0 lead in the final Fenway game against Baltimore. The Sox had bludgeoned the Orioles three straight and were on the threshold of first place. A victory would have moved the Red Sox into sole possession of first (by percentage points) and completed the Skylab-like fall of the Orioles. But—getting a big assist from Stanley—the Red Sox blew a 6–0 lead in the sixth and lost, 9–8. The Orioles left town still in first while the bewildered Sox started putting pitchers on the disabled list. John Dopson and Eric Hetzel went on the shelf, and Clemens missed a start with a bad elbow. Meanwhile, Mike Greenwell was down with an ankle injury and Barrett was on rehab at Pawtucket. Within days, Rice went back on the disabled list and Evans went into traction at the U Mass. Medical Center in Worcester. With eight weeks to play, the Red Sox were only two and a half games behind Baltimore and very much in the race, but they weren't healthy enough to win.

It was not a likable team. Fans were just starting to get over the Boggs episode when Wes Gardner was arrested at the Cross Keys Hotel in Baltimore for assaulting his wife one day before he was scheduled to start against the Orioles.

Meanwhile, the petty stuff continued as the Sox fell further behind. Greenwell stopped talking to the press after his "we need catching" comment annoyed the ultrasensitive Gedman. Morgan went on his television show and said there were "cancers" that the club had to get rid of. Rice became a pathetic figure—a bloated Brando/Elvis who could do nothing but sit in a corner of the dugout or clubhouse and snarl. He insisted on making all the road trips even though his elbow injury prevented him from playing. He became Boston's bad-will ambassador. It was a sad ending to a great career for the surly slugger.

Boston trailed by only four games on September 1, but it was clear that the Sox were out of it. The Blue Jays and Orioles got hot in early September, and Morgan's crybabies were five out with twenty-five to play when they embarked on the annual West Coast death march. They lost the second game of the Oakland series, 13–1, and reliever Joe Price ripped Morgan for playing the infield in while down 10–1, and for summoning Stanley when Stanley didn't have time to warm up. Morgan admitted that he did not have the respect of some of his players, and Gorman said, "It seems it's always somebody popping off that had a bad day. Once in a while you'd like to see somebody say, 'I had a bad day,' but nobody seems to do that."

When the Sox dropped seven games out September 6, Smithson admitted, "We're out of it."

On Saturday, September 9, Price came in to a game in California in relief of the revived Oil Can Boyd. Boston led 5–2 when Price came in, but he gave up three runs and allowed four stolen bases in a single inning. While Price slept on the mound, California's Devon White stole second, third, and home to tie the game, 5–5. After the inning, Morgan asked Price why he didn't pay attention to the base runners and Price told Morgan, "Go fuck yourself." The Sox lost, 8–5, fell eight and a half out, and Morgan suspended Price for four days.

"Mother of mercy, what a nightmare," said the manager. The next day, the Red Sox lost 2–1 in fourteen innings against the Angels. It was their fifth straight West Coast loss and dropped them nine and a half games out with nineteen to play. Their record in one-run road games was 2–18 (they finished 2–20). Price skipped the trip to Seattle and the Sox lost three more to fall hopelessly out of contention. Eight days after the trip ended, the Red Sox were eliminated from contention in the American League East. Their division title defense was officially killed on the night of September 22 while they were in Detroit.

With all of the pressure lifted, the 1989 Red Sox put on a memorable salary drive stretch run. They beat Oakland three straight and took two of three from Toronto. They finished with thirteen wins in their final sixteen games, a nifty record of 83–79, six games behind the first place Blue Jays.

Bob Stanley announced his retirement with a week to play, and on the same day the club announced that Rice's contract would not be renewed.

"I guess I was part of Red Sox tradition," Stanley said with a sigh. He was.

This correspondent in 1989 received a message from author David Halberstam, who'd won prizes for his coverage from Vietnam in the sixties, then topped *The New York Times* best-seller list for his baseball book on the Red Sox–Yankees pennant race of 1949.

Halberstam wrote, "It is one thing to put up with the kind of crap you deal with daily in Vietnam, which WAS a war zone, and where issues of war and peace were at stake and it was all right to be hated (because you were saying that the Ambassador and the general and the Secretary of Defense wore no clothes) but that it must be much worse and much harder to put up with that crap from rich spoiled young men who play a game and who should be grateful that anyone even cares."

ELEVEN

Harry Frazee III lives in the state of Washington and won't talk about his grandfather (known in the family as "Big Harry"), who has been dead for more than sixty years. Max Frazee is Harry III's son and lives in the TriBeCa section of New York City, not far from where "Big Harry" lived during his salad days in the Apple. The Frazee name can still start a fistfight wherever Red Sox and Yankee fans raise beer mugs.

"It comes up a lot," says Max, "especially when you meet sports fans. I've always been a fan of the Yankees because my father didn't have an allegiance to the Boston Red Sox even though my great-grand-father owned them. We had allegiance to the New York Yankees of course because Jake Ruppert was my great-grandfather's best friend and drinking companion."

Mark "Max" Frazee grew up in San Diego. He was a volleyball player at San Diego State, then got into art after he turned twenty-one. He received a graduate degree in art from the University of California at Irvine, moved to New York in the early eighties, and today is a superintendent on construction sites and leases an art studio in SoHo. He does conceptual abstract sculptures, drawings, and paintings of serial killers and says, "I never have any money in the bank." He is heavyset, wears long hair and Yankee caps. He is proud of his last name.

"The people I see at night, you know, when you go out to the sports bars and talk sports, they remember," he says.

The memory of sports fans in New York is unbelievable. These are sports buffs up the ass. They got it down. They know who's who. Out in California they don't know crap. I know the history of Babe Ruth very well because I've read about him constantly.

My father told me about it. I learned about how great my great-grandfather was. The company he kept with W. C. Fields. The stars. Acting and baseball. He was noted for selling the Boston Red Sox out, but the letters and information we have in the family is completely different than the stories the sportswriters write. Ruth and Carl Mays and three or four other ball players demanded $10,000 salaries. No one could afford that at that time. He saved the team in Boston. It was going down the tubes. Attendance was down. Baseball fanatics got to realize that people have got interest in other things. Today it's become a business and Harry was—before George Steinbrenner came along—the true original guy that trades, that sells. He's been treated unfairly because he's been raked over the coals for so long, since he died. And what they failed to say is what he accomplished for the Red Sox, and that is the problem with the history of Big Harry. The Boston fans have been fed crap all their lives and they're still being fed crap. The crap is that Harry sold out the Red Sox, and he didn't sell out the Red Sox. He sold the members of the team so that he could get money back so he could afford to keep the team going in Boston and then eventually sell it. It was a business then, too. I mean, sure he was an asshole, probably, just like any owner usually is. Obviously his heart was in the theater. He had built three theaters before he even ventured into baseball and he knew show business very, very well. The show business was in his heart more than the baseball.

Harry III is much more touchy about Big Harry than Max is. "Oh, God," says Max. "He won't even talk to me about it. My father grew up with the stigma that his grandfather sold Babe Ruth out, sold the Boston Red Sox out, and he's been drilled with that for a long time. I ask him questions about it every once in a while. I reread the Ruth book [Robert Creamer's] last time I was there. I asked him a few questions and he said, 'I don't want to talk about it.' "

If Max had grown up a Red Sox fan, would he be angry at Big Harry?

"I imagine I would," he answers. "But on the other hand, if I knew the history behind it, you really have to know the history of the human being to know why they did what they did. It's like with the serial killers I study. Obviously, it seems to be an atrocity for Boston."

Harry Frazee III did not name either of his sons Harry, but Max plans to have a Harry when he marries and if he has a son. "I'll just make him proud," says Max. "It depends on what climate he grows up in, but he should know about his great, great-grandfather."

Meanwhile, the great legion of Red Sox fans continue to wait and wonder about the Curse of the Bambino.

John J. Iannacci is Everyfan. Iannacci was born in Massachusetts in 1954. Today he lives with his wife and two children in Lunenburg, Massachusetts, and serves as an executive in the apple industry. His father is in his seventies and a lifelong Red Sox fan. Iannacci is raising his young son, Michael, to be a Red Sox fan. This is his story:

How did I become a Red Sox fan? Simple answer. It was passed down from my father, who loved baseball and loved the Red Sox. My father was, and still is, one of the world's biggest skeptics. His favorite saying is "this game's in the bag." I remember my father taking me to my first game at Fenway Park against the New York Yankees in the early sixties. The park was magical to a young boy. With all the colors and sounds that day, who cared if the Yankees killed us as they did? I was hooked, another generation under the spell of Red Sox baseball. The Red Sox were our team, and baseball was a sport my father and I could enjoy together. Being a Red Sox fan is something that is passed down from one generation to the next. One really must understand that this is a lifetime affliction and must be earned by suffering year after year of disappointment. The defeats are accompanied by the same statements each year in which we swear off the Sox for life. But who is kidding who? We're hooked. The long desolate winter eases our pain and we hunger for the freshness of spring. There's another baseball season and another Red Sox team with all last season's holes plugged and ready to win.

I have to admit that on the night of the sixth game loss to the Mets, I realized for the first time in my life that there were greater forces at work governing the results of the games. There is a dark cloud hovering over this baseball team. Maybe Harry Frazee offended the baseball gods when he sold off future championships so that he could continue staging Broadway shows. All I know is that with a two-run lead, two outs and two strikes on the batter, my wife walked over to me in order to embrace me, saying, "The Red Sox are actually going to win." My response was, "Get away from me, it's not over yet." When they lost, pandemonium broke loose at the Iannacci household. Various household articles were seen flying all over the room. My lucky white Red Sox ALCS Champion hat was fired off the TV screen at a speed greater than that which Bob Stanley was throwing at the Mets.

I have faith that sooner or later we have to get lucky. My optimism is sobered only by the fact that I have seen in my short lifetime what the Red Sox can do to ruin men's lives. A lot of good men have gone to their graves hoping to see the Sox win before they die. We are young. Hopefully, we have many more springs and summers to look forward to, hoping the Red Sox win one before we die. A New Englander spends the summer doing chores to prepare to survive the coming winter. The Red Sox winning the World Series is a chore left undone for the coming winter and this haunts the New England Yankee spirit. Come the spring, we are full of hope and renewed determination to get our chores done for next winter. If we do ever accomplish this goal, how do you top it? What is there left to live for?

◇

Is there such a thing as a baseball curse? We have already established the mysterious link between the Black Sox scandal of 1919 and the Red Sox, Cubs, and White Sox. The Red Sox beat the Cubs in the 1918 World Series and neither team has won it since. The White Sox threw the 1919 Series, Ruth was sold three months later, and since that time no team from Chicago or Boston and no team with the surname Sox has won a World Series.

One of the most celebrated baseball curses involves former Indians manager Bobby Bragan and the Cleveland ball club. In the winter of 1957/1958, Hank Greenberg hired Bragan to manage the Tribe. Bragan had been managing the Pirates for two years, but Greenberg, then the Indians GM, persuaded him to come to Cleveland. Greenberg was fired before Bragan had a chance to get started, and Frank Lane became the GM. The Indians were struggling along, five games under .500

(31–36) when Lane called Bragan into his office. It was a few minutes after the Indians had dropped a 2–1 decision to the Red Sox, losing on Ted Williams's ninth-inning home run off Cal McLish.

Lane said, "Bobby, I don't know how we're going to get along without you, but starting tomorrow, we're going to try."

Legend has it that Bragan walked to the middle of the Cleveland diamond, stood on second base, looked around the dark empty ballpark, and placed a curse on the Tribe. Cleveland would never win again. This happened in 1958, and since 1959 the Indians have never finished closer than eleven games out of first place.

It makes for great folklore, but Bragan has always denied the story. "I had nothing to do with it," he said. "When they fired me, hell, I went back to the hotel, waited for the phone to ring, and went to Spokane forty-eight hours later. I went quietly. There was no rancor. Frank Lane and I were good buddies right until he died. In fact, they buried him in Dallas and I represented baseball at the Lane funeral. I sure as hell didn't put any curse on the Indians. That was a figment of a DJ. Since Al Lopez, nobody's won in Cleveland. But I didn't put no hex on 'em, they just got a bad ball club."

Are the Red Sox cursed? Will the Red Sox ever throw off the curse and win another World Series?

Johnny Pesky: "I know I'm going to live long enough when we're gonna be Worlds Champions. I know that because I'm going to get into the year 2,000. I was sick about six years ago, but by God, there's nothing wrong with me now. I feel good and I've still got a little bounce. I know I'm going to live into the year 2,000 and I know I'm going to see the Red Sox win a World Championship. That's the only thing I've got left. It's said that we're cursed since we traded Ruth to the Yankees. I don't believe that. We're gonna do it."

Denny Galehouse: "It's just one of those freak things. They seem to . . . I don't know. It's just that an assumed reputation gets started and people start believing in it I guess. We did have some teams. I always felt the pitching staff of the Red Sox was maligned a little."

Mel Parnell: "Yeah, it's like there's a curse or something. I can't explain it."

Bobby Doerr: "You'd think the law of averages would sort of average out—that they would win one. I don't understand. It's almost like there's a curse or something there. It's such a fine line, who wins and who loses. Pitching of course is the name of the game. You look back at our great clubs. With one great relief pitcher, heck, we win three pennants."

Bucky Dent: "I think that what happens now is that there's so many things that have happened to Boston over the course of the years, that when they get close to winning something, people start thinking the worst thing will happen and I think sometimes that negative feeling kind of carries over. It's like 'What's going to happen next?' "

Mike Torrez: "Yeah, I think they're cursed. They have to be cursed for all the stuff that happens to 'em. Like '86 when Buckner missed the ball. I couldn't believe it. It's unbelievable the things that Boston has had through the years. They've had good teams. And now with the Boggs deal it's opened up a big can of worms amongst all those players. A lot of bitterness I can see already. It seems like something always happens with the Red Sox, ha ha. In Boston, it was all negative. Every time we'd lose a couple, everybody'd remember all the negative aspects. I noticed that."

Carl Yastrzemski: "It just seemed that any time there was a ray of hope, something would happen to take it out. When you had good teams, like starting in '74 when you had all the talent, Lynn, Rice, Burleson, and Fisk, and all of a sudden that team gets broken up. Everybody leaves and goes someplace else."

Clif Keane (born in 1912, went to his first Fenway Game in 1924): "I just feel right now that they're not going to win in my time."

Bill Lee: "They build their club around Fenway. If there is an Achilles' heel of the Red Sox it's the left Wall and the closeness and proximity of it that influences management's decisions. What you should think about is the farthest point away and build your ball club around that farthest deepest point in right center field."

Ted Williams: "Some of the greatest players, statistically, weren't in a lot of World Series. Cobb wasn't in a lot of World Series. I played during an era in which the Yankees were extremely strong and it was awfully hard to get into the damn thing. For five years we were 1–2 and played in playoffs once and didn't get in. We had a little tough time. Then we lost the seventh game of the World Series and the other Red Sox teams did the same thing. It's been a kind of a bad luck situation, but I thought sure after the fifth game of that 1986 World Series, we've finally done it. Son of a bitch . . . you're going to see 'em win the World Series. About the time things are getting bleak, well, all of a sudden two or three players come along that pick everything up."

◊

The 1989 Red Sox retired Yastrzemski's number eight on Sunday, August 6, and the Yaz digit hangs next to those of Williams, Cronin, and Doerr on the green façade atop Fenway's right-field grandstand. Williams wore 9, Cronin 4, Doerr 1, and Yaz 8. The numbers are arranged in the order in which they were retired, 9—4—1—8, and it's an eerie sight. One could rearrange the digits to read 1948 and this might be construed as a monument to Denny Galehouse and the 1948 playoff fiasco. But the 9—4—1—8 also looks like it could be a date: 9/4/18. A check of the records reveals that this date represents the eve of the 1918 World Series, the last one won by the Red Sox, the one played a year before Frazee struck the deal to sell Ruth. On 9/4/18, Babe Ruth was in Chicago doing God knows what to prepare for his World Series start against the Cubs. The Bambino beat the Cubbies, 1–0, the next day, and the Sox won the Series in six games. And now the number, 9/4/18, hangs over every Red Sox game—a haunting reminder of the best times of Boston baseball. Meanwhile, Red Sox fans remain in a holding pattern in hardball purgatory, still waiting to get back to the promised land.

TWELVE

"Dan, I bought your book. I got halfway through and I put my head in the oven."

—Anonymous caller on Boston sports talk
radio program, June 1990

It was then that I knew we were on to something.

The Curse of the Bambino took on a life of its own in the summer and fall of 1990, a wonderful summer for Red Sox fans and a good time to be the author of a book on the Boston baseball experience. Book critics were kind, but the best response to this work came from that broad-based, opinionated, devout, and passionate group that comprises the Red Sox Nation.

John McKeon, a resident of Boston's North Shore and the founder of the Baseball Hall of Pain, was among those who submitted a theory that the publication of this book would help throw off the curse. McKeon said, "Is it true, Dan, that last fall the voice of Babe Ruth haunted you with 'If you write it, they will win'? I know, and you know, that the Babe spoke to you as he spoke to me. . . . This is the year."

It's great stuff, but it's also a myth. This book and its title came from the mind of former Dutton editor Meg Blackstone. Ms. Blackstone grew up in Oyster Bay, Long Island, went to Yale, and today lives in Greenwich Village with her husband and baby son. She sent me a letter in August of 1988, asking if I would be interested in writing a book about the Red Sox. Mrs. Blackstone had been introduced to a theory

that had been kicking around New England for more than seven decades. It came to her from her maternal grandfather, Arthur Whitfield
Davidson. A ballplayer in his younger days, Davidson was a Dorchester
house painter who chewed tobacco, smoked cigars, and told his grand-
daughter, "The Red Sox will never win because they sold Babe Ruth
to the Yankees. It's the Curse of the Bambino."

And so this book was written and the 1990 season was played—and
changed nothing.

Little was expected of the '90 Red Sox, but there were some hopeful
early signs. An ugly, unnecessary lockout cut spring training short, but
the spirits of Sox fans were curiously buoyed by the presence of forty-
year-old Bill Buckner. Ever the symbol of Boston's ghastly near miss
in 1986, Buckner in January of 1990 requested a no-strings-attached
tryout with the Red Sox. Boston's management went to great lengths
to discourage the notion, but there was tremendous public pressure to
see Billy Buck get the chance. The Sox let Buckner play his way to
Florida and dress in the minor league complex; then he started to hit.
He went four for four in a spring game against Bret Saberhagen, and
the ballclub was forced to include him on its twenty-seven-man, April
9 Opening Day roster. Roger Clemens beat Jack Morris and the Tigers
in the opener, but the loudest, longest ovation was showered on Buckner. It was cathartic. The Larger Forces were set in motion.

Early in the season, it became apparent that this Red Sox team had
better chemistry than most. The karma concept is no doubt overdone
by media and fans. Players believe that clubhouse happiness is directly
proportionate to the win–loss column and nothing more, but the Red
Sox have a history of intramural bitching and moaning, and those who
follow the team always look for nuggets of harmony or happiness. In
the spring of 1990, the Red Sox did seem different. Veteran free agent
catcher Tony Pena brought joy and laughter to the workplace, Mike
Greenwell set up a Kangaroo Court, and the extraction of Messrs. Jim
Rice, Rick Cerone, Bob Stanley, and Vinnie Orlando proved positive.

The Red Sox hovered around .500 in April and May. No-name pitchers Greg Harris and Dana Kiecker backed up ace starters Clemens and
Mike Boddicker, and Carlos Quintana proved he could play first base
in the big leagues. Pena was everywhere, yelling at his pitchers, slashing
the ball to all fields, throwing out enemy base runners, and *willing* the
team to be better than it was. In Cleveland in early June, one day after

Pena was brushed back by Indian reliever Doug Jones, Clemens hit Tribe leadoff man Stanley Jefferson, and the Sox and Indians brawled. Manager Joe Morgan got a three-day suspension for admitting the incident had been premeditated, but it was a galvanizing moment for the Boston ballclub. The Sox moved into first place one day later and stayed in either first or second for the rest of the season.

When it became apparent that the Red Sox might make it to the postseason again, the Curse of the Bambino became a timely item, and there were suggestions about lifting the curse. I was contacted by Fr. Daniel J. Cavanaugh of Lawrence, Massachusetts, who wrote, "I thought it might be a good idea to have an exorcism at Fenway Park. That way, we could get the 'spirit' of the Babe out of our hair. Have the fans come to the park some night with signs urging the Babe to let go of us. i. e., 'Let go, Bambino.' " Fr. Cavanaugh assured me that he could convince his cloaked superiors to let him go ahead with the ancient ritual.

The souvenir shop across the street from the ballpark attempted to print "Reverse the Curse" T-shirts, but the motion was stopped by Red Sox management. Paul Brosnan, a Sox fan in New Jersey suggested, "Just like the Phantom of the Opera wanted a seat to be left empty for him in the Opera House, the Bambino needs to have an empty locker in the Red Sox locker room with his picture hanging on it."

I received letters from Michael Dukakis, lame-duck governor of Massachusetts, John R. Simpson, director of the U.S. Treasury, and Richard Darman, director of the Office of Management and Budget. Gov. Dukakis noted, "I was going down the tubes with the 1978 Red Sox in that awful year. As far as the job of governor, this is a piece of cake compared with managing the town team." Darman, a man worrying about a trillion-dollar budget deficit, took time to write: "I have a little different view of the Red Sox than the Curse. My view gives less weight to sin and Calvin, and more to Hope and the prospect of continuous renewal."

When the Red Sox were in Baltimore in June, Boston manager Joe Morgan and his wife visited the birthplace of Babe Ruth. "Maybe this will end the Curse of the Bambino," said Dottie Morgan.

Fans and readers submitted additional evidence of the Ruth connection. Several people noticed that Bruce Hurst seemed to be linked with the Babe. Hurst and Ruth were both lefty pitchers for Boston, and in the list of all-time Sox pitching leaders, Ruth ranks fifth among winningest lefties with 89 victories; Hurst is sixth with 88. They are the last two Sox lefties to win World Series games in Fenway and the last two Sox pitchers to win Series games by a 1–0 score. Rearrange the letters in BRUCE HURST and you get B. RUTH CURSE.

Book-readers had a great deal of fun with the numbers 9, 4, 1, and 8. The numbers could be scrambled to 1984, the year of Buckner's arrival. Buckner's 1986 World Series fielding average was .984 with 1 error. Add the digits and you get 22, which was Buckner's number with the Dodgers and again with the Red Sox in 1990.

There was more fodder for those who believe in superstition over science. The Red Sox were in first place all through August, and it was taken as a good sign when Commissioner Fay Vincent stripped George Steinbrenner of his Yankee holdings and the fabled New York franchise was turned over to Robert Nederlander, a man known for theatrical productions. *No, No, Nanette* triggered the downfall of the Red Sox, and in 1990 the Yankees were in last place and run by a Broadway man. There was a nice symmetry in all of this.

Meanwhile, the Red Sox took hold of the race in the American League East. Minor league-lifer Tom Bolton came up from Pawtucket and started winning regularly. Jeff Gray, released by the Phillies, took over as closer when Jeff Reardon went down with a bad back. Veteran Dwight Evans hit dramatic home runs. The Red Sox won a game after hitting into two triple plays. In August, the Sox went to Toronto and took three out of four in a showdown series, all shutout victories. The three victories started a ten-game winning streak and inflated Boston's first-place lead to six and a half games. A *Boston Globe* editorial read: "The baseball gods may simply resent the innuendo that they have cursed the hometown team ever since Babe Ruth was sold to the Yankees to finance a Broadway show. . . . It is clear that the Red Sox won't need a fireballing closer, home-run hitters or speed. They have the gods on their side."

The Sox still led by six and a half games on September 4, but on this date Clemens lost to Dave Stewart and the Oakland A's, and after the game he complained that his shoulder was "smoking." It was the beginning of a meteoric plummet into second place. Without the mighty Rocket, the Sox lost all confidence, and the gods were no longer on their side. They staggered through a 2–8 road trip. They lost four straight in Chicago. In Baltimore, Pena called his teammates quitters and tossed a chair across the clubhouse. It was, of course, a *folding* chair. Bolton had a no-hitter in the seventh inning in Baltimore but lost after giving up a monstrous homer to David Segui—son of Diego Segui, who blew a crucial game for the Sox in 1974.

Their fathers killed our fathers and now the sons of the pitchers are coming after us.

Bolton said, "I don't believe in ghosts. I never have. Each team determines its own fate. We won't lose this thing because other Red Sox teams lost."

In New York, Clemens was scheduled to make his comeback performance on Sunday, September 23, but was scratched late Saturday night. The Red Sox ever-combative public relations department withheld news of Clemens's latest problem until most of New England was asleep. It was Sox, lies, and videotape. The Yankees took the final two games of the series, and New York fans taunted and haunted the Sox dugout with signs reading "1918."

On September 24, the Clemens-less Red Sox fell one and a half games behind the Blue Jays. They'd lost eight games in the standings in twenty days—starting on September 4, the 72nd anniversary of 9–4–1–8.

Why did the gods change their minds? we wondered. It couldn't be because Rich Gedman was sent to Houston or because Buckner was released in June. It couldn't be because the Sox went through the summer with only one black player (Ellis Burks) on their roster. It couldn't be because the Sox stood pat while the Oakland A's claimed Harold Baines and Willie McGee off the waiver wire (Sox GM Lou Gorman compounded the blunder when he uttered, "What would we do with Willie McGee?"). This much was certain: since the start of divisional play, only one team had blown a lead of six and a half games in September—the 1978 Red Sox.

Gorman told *Diehard*, the official Sox fan publication, "I don't think the fans will ever be satisfied until the Red Sox win a World Championship—the Curse of the Bambino and all that. All those things are wonderful. They make interesting stories, but the guys on this club don't know the Curse of the Bambino. Most of them weren't even here in '86. They play the game based on what's happening on the field today, not what happened twenty years ago. That has no bearing. But there will always be that stigma: the ball got through Buckner's legs;

Bucky Dent's home run in '78. Everything goes against the Red Sox. They're star-crossed lovers in a sense. The wrong thing always happens to the Red Sox."

The 1990 collapse unleashed a landslide of Curse rhetoric. History was repeating itself. The Curse was in full force and it was all too predictable. If you forecast that the leaves will change colors in the fall, how much satisfaction can you take when the leaves change colors in the fall?

The book turned into a handy theme for sports journalists of America. It became almost impossible to address what was happening to the Red Sox without invoking the Curse. It occured to me that the 1990 Red Sox were doing for this book what the Ayatollha did for *The Satanic Verses*. I did scores of television and radio interviews. One hip radio station during the Q and A played "While My Guitar Gently Weeps."

Big-hearted second baseman Jody Reed said, "All I hear is crash, dive, Bambino curse. Who the hell is Bambino?"

Mike Marshall said, "I've never been in a place so negative. No matter what we do, it's not enough. Win ten games in a row, and people still say we'll break their hearts in October."

Strange things started to happen. On Friday, September 28, the night of the first game of the final, pivotal Toronto series in Fenway, I was doing a radio-remote broadcast for WHDH—"The Real Baseball Show." Six games remained, and the Sox and Jays were tied for first. Boston was abuzz. The radio show was being broadcast from the Original Souvenir Store, across the street from Fenway, two hours before gametime. Seconds after one emotional fan spoke of the Curse of the Bambino, a propane tank exploded and a fireball ripped through the souvenir shop. The spot where the tank exploded was directly under a large, yellowed poster of Babe Ruth. Life imitating art, or art imitating life? The shop closed briefly while fire trucks rushed to the scene.

In the midnight hour, long after the flames were extinguished, Jeff Stone came to the plate for his first at bat of the season and hit a game-winning single to put the Red Sox in first place for good. Great balls of fire. It was perhaps the most pulsating victory of the 1990 Boston baseball season.

On Saturday morning, before Clemens took the mound for his long-anticipated comeback concert, WZLX radio held a "Break the Curse" rally in the same souvenir shop. The station broadcast live, as a third-generation Salem witch stood under the Ruth poster wielding a Tom Brunansky bat, attempting to lift the curse. Lefty Bill Lee was in the crowd and applauded vigorously. Later in the day, Clemens threw six innings of shutout ball, Brunansky hit three homers, and the Red Sox were 7–5 winners and held a two-game lead with four to play.

Morgan said, "Clemens was like Ruth. Babe would play the outfield, then when the team need a shutout, he'd come in and pitch a shutout. That's what Roger did for us today."

The White Sox came to town for the final three games. Chicago was led by no. 72 (as in 72 years since the Sox won), Carlton Fisk. Red Sox fans had a genuine fear that Fisk was going to do something to wound the Boston baseball psyche one last time. Author Stephen King stalked the Fenway lawn during batting practice the night of the first game with Chicago. He was with a Boston television crew and had sent word that he wanted to meet me. I was brought over to where King was standing, and he extended his hand and said, "Dan Shaughnessy, you're my idol. I loved the book and gave it to my son."

I am not making this up. I have witnesses. The man has sold millions of books, but, like Red Sox fans everywhere, he was gripped by the fears and horrors of the Curse of the Bambino.

King later told reporters, "I was stuck with the Red Sox from birth. I'm used to all the chokes and all the folds. I think the Red Sox have been athletically molested. We have a tremendous complex." He said the worst-case scenario would be "one out away from winning for the first time since 1918 and nuclear war is declared."

The Red Sox beat the White Sox in the first game of the final series but lost the next night and saw their lead shrink to one game with one to play. A playoff with Toronto seemed imminent, and on the morning of the final day of the regular season, commuters at the Harvard Square T Station waited for an incoming train and heard the voice on the loudspeaker say, "Attention all Red Sox fans. Please stand behind the yellow line."

On the final night the Sox led, 3–1, with two out in the bottom of the ninth. The Blue Jays and Orioles were locked in a duel in Baltimore. In Fenway, a man sitting in the front row near the Red Sox dugout stroked a Babe Ruth statue as he prayed for deliverance. The Sox had their fate in their own hands. Reliever Jeff Reardon had two strikes on Sammy Sosa. One strike away. Sosa singled. The next batter was

Scott Fletcher, and Reardon hit him with a pitch. Sox fans squirmed in their seats. It felt a lot like 1986. Then Ozzie Guillen laced a shot into the corner in right. Brunansky, raced to his left and dove. For a moment it looked like the ball might go past him for an inside-the-park, three-run homer. What a way to lose.

No. Brunansky had the ball in his glove and the Red Sox were champions of the American League East.

In the soggy winners' locker room, Wade Boggs said, "I figured out how to take care of the curse of the Babe Ruth thing. We find Babe Ruth's nearest relative, and we pay him the same amount of Babe's contract and we get his rights. That'll lift the curse off."

The Red Sox were prohibitive underdogs in their playoff series against the defending World Champion A's, but no one was prepared for a graceless four-game sweep.

Clemens, making his second appearance since September 4, pitched the opener and left with a 1–0 lead after six. He chose not to explain why he left, and Morgan said it was a manager's decision. Boston's bullpen exploded, Stewart hung tough, and Oakland romped, 9–1. Stewart's record with Oakland against Clemens improved to 7–0 and Sox fans began to think of it as a Bill Russell–Wilt Chamberlain match-up; this time, however, Boston had Chamberlain.

During Game 2 at Fenway, fans paraded through the stands with a banner reading "Yo, Bambino, can we talk about this?" A man wearing a Yankee uniform (no. 3) vaulted over the rail and danced in right field during Game 2. He had a sign that read "Lift the Curse." The Curse was not lifted. The Red Sox lost, 4–1, and went to Oakland to finish their season.

Game 3 was a dreadful 4–1 loss in which Mike Boddicker pitched well but was victimized by poor defense and no offense. After this contest the Sox started to disintegrate. Sox relievers openly mocked Morgan and what they considered his misuse of the bullpen. Boggs blamed Pena for a botched play on an Oakland steal. Sox players moaned about their inferior air-travel conditions.

Clemens, in one of the more curious decisions of this or any series, had sent word that he would pitch Game 4 only if the Red Sox trailed 3–0. He was bigger than the team by this time, and so Clemens got the ball for Game 4—but not for long.

The Rocket fell behind 1–0 in the second inning, and after walking

Willie Randolph, he got into a huge jam with homeplate umpire Terry Cooney. The ump saw Clemens shaking his head after a called ball four, and Cooney started the confrontation by saying, "I hope you're not shaking your head at me."

Clemens went berserk, cursing Cooney with great gusto. He was immediately ejected, and all hell broke loose. Morgan bolted from the dugout, Larry Andersen came in from the bullpen to restrain the ace, Clemens shoved umpire Jim Evans and threatened Cooney. Marty Barrett started tossing water coolers, candy, and sunflower seeds from the Sox dugout, and when coach Dick Berardino tried to stop Barrett, the reserve infielder shoved his coach down the dugout steps. The Sox were on their way to a 3–1 loss and a clean sweep for the second time in three years. Oakland's Carney Lansford, a former Red Sox, said, "The Red Sox are a disgrace."

Clemens's ejection kindled memories of Ruth. In June 1917, pitcher Ruth walked the first Washington Senators batter he faced, then threatened to hit umpire Brick Owens. Ruth was ejected, and reliever Ernie Shore came on to retire twenty-six straight batters after the initial batter was caught stealing. Clemens and Ruth now represent the two most celebrated pitcher ejections in Sox history.

The *Boston Herald* ran a large cartoon showing an infant on a pitching mound, wearing no. 21 and shouting "Bleep!" while holding a baby bottle in his right hand. The caption read: "I guess this is what they mean by 'The Curse of the Bambino.' "

The October 13 *Washington Post* dedicated an entire editorial to "The Curse of Roger," and suggested that "The Roger Clemens incident was practically a historical necessity. . . . Boston fans can thus take a measure of satisfaction in the ambiguous conclusion of their most recent playoffs and in the knowledge that another chapter has been added to the legend. . . . For Red Sox fans, even a small curse will do for a winter."

◇

Still, it was a nice ride. The Red Sox almost always give us a nice ride. I remember all of it. I remember the sleepy central Florida nights by the pool at the Winter Haven Holiday Inn, telling Bill Buckner that his picture would be on the cover of my book, getting a letter from Bruce Hurst's mom saying she enjoyed reading it, trying to explain the

New England Mind to Mike Marshall while driving to Memorial Stadium in Baltimore, and getting heckled by fans while watching the Sox go down in defeat in their final Fenway game. I remember walking into the Cross Keys Inn in Baltimore when the Red Sox were at the height of their fall. It was early in the morning, a few hours after an excruciating defeat at the hands of the Orioles. Veteran Red Sox equipment man Don Fitzpatrick was walking out of the hotel as I was walking in. Fitzie has been around the Red Sox since the mid-'40s, and he knows when history is being rewritten.

"How's it going?" I greeted Fitzie.

"How's it going'?" he said. "How's Dunkirk?"

I remember standing on the lush Fenway grass in early October, under a full moon, listening to Stephen King tell catcher Carlton Fisk. "I've never written a horror story about baseball."

And I remember thinking to myself, "I have."

EPILOGUE

Weeks. Seasons. Years. Decades. Centuries. They come. They go. The Red Sox are forever. The Red Sox still don't win the World Series. The Curse continues.

This book was first published in 1990. Ten years have passed since I added a chapter on the 1990 season for the first paperback edition. There's been a lot of water under the Massachusetts Avenue Bridge and a lot of grounders between the legs in the Red Sox final decade of the twentieth century. Time for another update.

Encyclopedias. Red Sox fan Stephen King's *The Green Mile.* The New Testament. And now *The Curse of the Bambino*—the book that piece by piece, installment by installment, gets a little bigger, a little longer, every season, year, decade, and century. This epilogue would actually be chapter 13, but like hotels that go from floor 12 to 14 we choose not to use that unlucky number and instead will call this the epilogue.

I'm often asked if I'm worried about the Red Sox winning the World Series and killing the shelf life of this literary franchise. There's no worry. More strange stuff no doubt will happen to the Red Sox in the years ahead and I expect to be back to my word processor several more times before reporting to the ultimate scorekeeper.

Independent of my own efforts, the Curse has become a cottage industry. In addition to the hardcover, paperback, and audiocassette editions of the original work, the Curse has spawned a screenplay, a rock song, a musical, and a board game. The Curse Web site and CD-ROM can't be far behind. There was even a reference to the Curse on the popular TV quiz show, *Who Wants to Be a Millionaire?* Alas, none of these ideas (or their profits) belong to me. I've never trademarked the title which honestly belongs to my first editor, Meg Blackstone, and to the frustrated fans of New England.

No serious person *truly* believes that the Red Sox don't win the World Series because the Babe ordered a pox on the House of Fenway, but the Curse has become a handy way to explain the unexplainable. It's superstition over science, or at least over statistical probability. At the end of the twentieth century, the World Series championship tally was Yankees 25, Red Sox 0 since Ruth was dealt from Boston to New York. *Twenty five to nothing.* It is a landslide of Biblical dimension and it's somehow soothing for many New Englanders to pin the blame on the Larger (or Darker) Forces that rule the hardball universe.

The final decade of the twentieth century was no kinder to citizens of Red Sox Nation than the preceding nine. Boston fans tormented by the colossal folds of '78 and '86 found themselves expecting bad things to happen whenever the Sox waded into postseason play, as they did in 1990, '95, '98, and '99. Meanwhile the Yankees, still under the tyrannical reign of Boss Steinbrenner, re-established themselves as baseball's best team, winning three of four World Series at the end of the century, including the 125-win, 1998 Pinstripe edition which made a case for itself as the greatest baseball team of all time.

By the turn of the century, many Sox fans were truly warped. Even with the inspiring play of Pedro Martinez, Nomar Garciaparra, and even GM Dan Duquette, they couldn't escape the quagmire of past defeats. There is no way to underestimate the permanent damage inflicted on the New England mind in the wake of the hideous collapse at Shea Stadium in October of '86. Sox fans simply could not let it go. It's hardball's heart of darkness. When New England baby boomers are asked to comb their conscience for memorable events of the last century, many will cite the Kennedy Assassination, the first Moon Landing, and Game Six. Now not even a sportswriter would attempt to equate the murder of a beloved world leader with the loss of a baseball game, but when Bostonians play "do you remember where you were when you heard the news?" the Red Sox Game Six flop ranks right there with the grassy knoll.

Messrs. Buckner, Stanley, Gedman, McNamara, Clemens, Schiraldi, Knight, Carter, Mitchell, and Wilson carry secrets that no one else knows and I regard every chance meeting with any of the above as an opportunity to unearth deeper truths from '86. There will be no rest until we know exactly why Clemens came out of Game Six (blister or fear?—former pitching coach Bill Fischer has cited both) and why Buckner was still on the field for the famous final scene.

After writing this book I've been swamped with stories of the fateful night in '86. My favorite tale comes from Monte Dutton, a sportswriter for the *Greenville News* in Clinton, South Carolina. As a young man, Dutton's dad was stationed at now-defunct Fort Devens in Ayer, Massachusetts and brought his attachment to the Red Sox back home to Carolina. Son Monte so loved the Red Sox that he named one of his lambs "Fenway," and according to Monte Dutton, "Fenway" died in the pasture on the night of Game Six.

Top *that*.

Then there's the issue of journalistic ethics. In 1998 *The Boston Globe* fired columnist Patricia Smith after she admitted fabricating material in her columns. As a *Globe* columnist, I was asked about this many times and my standard answer was, "I don't have to make it up. I cover the Red Sox."

Curse contrarians are legion. Researching the first eighty-six years of American League history, Sox archivists find no mention of any Babe Ruth jinx. In 1995 Stephen King wrote, "There is no Curse of the Bambino. I, who was writing about curses and supernatural vengeance when Mr. Shaughnessy was still learning not to eat the ends of his Crayolas, tell you that it's so . . . the Red Sox have been victims of an extraordinary run of ill luck, that's all."

In 1999, King used the Red Sox as a theme in his bestseller, *The Girl Who Loved Tom Gordon*. Within a few months of the book's publication, the real Gordon went on the disabled list with a career-threatening arm injury and King himself was nearly killed when he was run down in Maine by a reckless driver. Thankfully, both are on the comeback trail, but maybe it's given King a pause or two in snubbing the Curse.

Official Red Sox reaction to this book has been a source of nonstop amusement for more than a decade. Shortly after the tome's original publication, Red Sox vice president Dick Bresciani, quoted in *USA Today*, termed the Curse, "the book of lies," but affable Bresh was merely making a jocular reference to some facutal errors (since corrected) in the original edition. By the end of the century, the Curse of the Bambino had become part of the official Red Sox tour of Fenway Park. Team employees, feeding Fenway tidbits to hungry hardball pilgrims from Des Moines and Dubuque, spoke of eighty years of frustration for Red Sox fans. Frequently I would be sitting in my second row seat when the tour would cut through the press box hours before a night game. It was not unusual for the tour guide to mention the Curse, then point in my direction—making me feel like a cardboard cutout, a prop designed to amuse fans and enhance the tour.

Contrasting this official acknowledgment of the Curse as part of the Sox story, the ballclub intentionally erased a significant part of Bambino folklore at the start of the 1998 season. A day before Boston's home opener, when the media gathered for the Sox and Seattle Mariners' final spring workout at Fenway, keen observers noticed that the giant retired numbers on the right field facade had been rearrranged. Originally hung in the order in which they were retired—9-4-1-8—the digits were lined up in numerical order. Red Sox General Manager Dan Duquette, ever-obtuse and secretive, claimed the numbers had been taken down when the facade was painted and re-attached in numerical order by innocent painters. It's typical of Duquette and the Sox to lie about the most innocuous of details (Fenway is framed by five Boston streets and the self-important Sox take themselves no less seriously than officials at the "other" Pentagon) and this was a true Duke whopper. A quick inspection of the park found two indoor sites in which the retired (9-4-1-8) numbers had been rearranged on walls in numerical order.

The effect of this petty move was to eliminate a bit of crucial numerology and a nifty hook for the Curse. Page 207 of this book outlines the mystique and symbolism of 9-4-1-8. In subsequent retellings, fans came to think of the date as day when the Sox won their last World Series, when in fact it represents only the eve of Game One when Ruth beat the Cubs. In any event, the Sox apparently got tired of this massive reminder of futility staring down at them from high above right field. So the numbers were changed, making the Sox just a tad less interesting and disrespecting Ted Williams (No. Nine) as the first and best Red Sox of them all.

The lovely Julia Ruth Stevens has been bothered by the mythical curse. A sharp, sweet woman who turned eighty-two in the final year of the century, the Babe's daughter continuously insists "Daddy never would have done that," whenever the Curse is proposed. In September of 1993, the Red Sox brought Ms. Stevens to Fenway along with nineteen other descendants of the 1918 Red Sox championship team. The '18 champs had never been fully recognized because they staged a one-hour strike before the fifth game of the World Series. The dispute concerned allocation of playoff shares and the winning Red Sox ultimately received the smallest shares ($1,100 per man) in World Series history.

There was an air of forgiveness when the Babe's daughter came back in

1993. Among those who joined her was Max Frazee, the great grandson of the man who sold her dad to the Yankees. The progeny of Ruth and Frazee posed for pictures, the 1918 championship banner was raised, and veteran Sox announcer Ken Coleman declared, "The Curse of the Bambino is now officially ended."

It was the first of many such declarations of wishful thinking in the final decade of the first century of Red Sox folklore.

The Sox made three forays into the playoffs in the final five years of the century and each one resulted in the same unsatisfactory finish—replete with weird happenings which only reinforced the maddening theory that the hardball gods have sentenced Sox fans to an eternity of frustration.

The 1995 Red Sox won the American League East and faced the mighty (100-win) Cleveland Indians in the first round of the playoffs. Cleveland folks were complaining about their own jinx—the Curse of Rocky Colavito. It made for "dueling curses" just like when the Sox played Gene Mauch's Angels in 1986, but no baseball jinx is a match for the Bambino's. Naturally, the Indians swept the Red Sox in three games, beginning with a 5–4, 13-inning loss. In this excruciating defeat, the Sox surrendered a seemingly certain victory when Boston stopper Rick Aguilera yielded a game-tying homer to Albert Belle in the bottom of the eleventh inning.

Prior to joining the Red Sox, Aguilera was a postseason stud. With the champion '91 Twins he was nearly flawless in the American league pennant races and World Series. He was also the winning pitcher against the Red Sox in the infamous Sixth Game in '86. It wasn't until he donned the heavy Boston threads that he had trouble in October. Aguilera's meatball to Belle erased a certain Game 1 victory and set the stage for .181-hitting Tony Pena—another ex-Red Sox of course—to beat the Red Sox with a thirteenth-inning homer at 2:08 A.M. The Indians swept the next two games. Mo Vaughn and Jose Canseco combined to go 0–27 with nine strikeouts, and the team left seventeen stranded running in the series. The sweep gave the Sox a major league-record, post-season losing streak of thirteen games (two more thirteens in this paragraph) dating back to Game Six in '86.

The Sons of Jimy Williams snapped Boston's nasty postseason streak when they made it to the playoffs in 1998, again playing the Cleveland Indians. In the first game of the series, Vaughn hit two homers and knocked in seven runs, and Garciaparra drove home four home in an 11–3 thumping, won by new ace Pedro Martinez. But Boston lost the next three games.

Down two games to one, Williams stunned the establishment by announcing journeyman Pete Schourek as his Game 4 starter—instead of Pedro. Martinez was angry with the decision and it was compared with Joe McCarthy's selection of Denny Galehouse in the 1948 playoff game, also against the Tribe.

Now, the alert reader will quickly realize that Peter Schourek is an anagram for RUTH KEEP SCORE. Schourek pitched well (two hits, no runs in 5.1 innings), but didn't win. Gordon, who had saved a record forty-three consecutive games, coughed up the lead in the eighth inning and the Sox lost, 2–1. In his final at bat as a Red Sox, Vaughn doubled off the left field wall. The Black Bambino signed with the Anaheim Angels two months later.

"Curses? I don't believe in that stuff," said Vaughn. "You've got to have the horses and you got to keep 'em."

What about you and the Babe, Mo?

"I'll tell you one thing," said Vaughn. "I could have partied with him."

Vaughn's departure brought much wrath and ridicule down on the head of Duquette, but another event in the spring of 1999 proved more torturous for Red Sox Nation. On Thursday, February 18 it was announced that the New York Yankees had completed a deal with the Toronto Blue Jays which would put Roger Clemens in pinstripes. New England's response was rapid and emotional. The trade was a dagger in the hearts of longtime Sox watchers. It was amazing actually. This was a trade between New York and Toronto, and yet it had greatest impact in Boston. Such is the fragile psyche of Fenway fandom. It's always about us.

Boston has an inferiority complex when it comes to New York. At the end of the century, matters only became worse when the Jordan Marsh department score was engulfed by Macy's at about the same time *The New York Times* bought *The Boston Globe.* Sports is a particularly sore area. Clemens-to-the-Yankees was like Bobby Orr-to-the-Canadiens, Larry Bird-to-the-Lakers, Bill Parcells-to-the-Jets, or Ruth-to-the-Yankees.

When he bolted Boston for Toronto in 1997, Clemens yielded two faceless draft picks (Eric Glaser and Mark Fischer) and Duquette said Clemens was in the "twilight" of his career. That was before the Rocket went out and won back-to-back Cy Youngs—giving him a grand total of five Cy trophies. In '99, Boston fans faced the prospect of Clemens wearing pinstripes— something akin to Ted Kennedy delivering the keynote address at the Republican National Convention.

The Red Sox answer to Clemens was Pedro Martinez. In 1999, his second season in Boston, the Dominican righty threw harder than Clemens and had a year which superceeded Clemens's 24–4 MVP season with the '86 Red Sox. Pedro went 23–4 with a 2.08 ERA and 313 strikeouts vs. 37 walks. He was a younger and more personable than Clemens. Some joked that he even spoke English better than the Rocketman. On the night of September 10, Pedro toed the rubber at Yankee Stadium and threw perhaps the best game ever hurled at the Yankees. He beat the World Champs, 3–1, allowing only one hit and striking out seventeen, including twelve of the last fifteen and the last five in order. Seventeen Yankees. All in a line. All of them good ones. He fanned Chuck Knoblauch with a ninety-six-mile-per-hour fastball to end the game.

Postgame Pedro said, "New York is a special place and my (Dominican) people came over. I like to do it for them. I don't believe in superstitions or the Curse of the Bambino . . . It's gonna happen someday and I think soon. I think one of these days that little ground ball that went through Bill Buckner's feet will probably be caught. I wasn't born those years they went through all those things. But I know everything can change. When it's meant to happen, it's gonna happen. Believe me. It's gonna happen."

Pedro's win sparked a three-game sweep of the Yankees—Boston's first sweep in New York since Clemens and Co. did the trick in 1986. It also marked the end of a grueling west coast trip in which Williams started carrying his lucky candy bar—a Baby Ruth. The chocolate treat was first observed on Williams's desk in Seattle, then he brought it to Oakland and New York. "Maybe this will take care of the Curse of Baby Ruth," chuckled the manager.

When Pedro strained his back in the first game of the '99 playoffs, there was fear that the Curse had struck again. Cleveland beat the Sox in each of the first two games, smashing Boston 11–1 in Game 2 of the best-of-five series. It looked like another October El Foldo for Boston. ESPN's Peter Pascarelli, a Dorchester native, said, "Pedro is now day-to-day and Red Sox fans are century-to-century." Like Emmy nominee Susan Lucci of *All My Children,* the Sox had one win in nineteen postseason tries.

But the Sox came to Fenway and lit up the Tribe for nine runs in Game 3 and a postseason record—twenty-three more runs in Game 4, sending the series back to Cleveland where Pedro came out of the bullpen to pitch six hitless innings in the series clincher. There was no expectation that Martinez would pitch the finale, but the Boston bullpen was already depleted when the score was 8–8 in the fourth.

Pedro came out of the bullpen at 9:45 P.M. to rescue the season. Time stood still. Literally. An hour after Martinez entered the game, the Jacobs Field stadium clock still read 9:45. Very Sox-like.

Pedro's Cleveland heroism meant it was time to bring on the Yankees. A Red Sox–Yankee pennant battle—best of seven series to represent the American League in the World Series—was a fitting conclusion to a century of American League baseball. Arguably signature franchises in the game, without a doubt baseball's fiercest rivals, the Sox and Yanks first jousted for AL supremacy in 1904 when New York Highlander Happy Jack Chesbro uncorked a wild pitch to deliver the pennant to the Boston Pilgrims.

The '99 ALCS brought the Curse of the Bambino into public consciousness as never before. The Sox and Yanks had played the epic one-game playoff in '78, but thanks to the wild card format, this was a full-fledged best-of-seven bakeoff alternating between two sites: the park where rookie Babe first played big league ball in 1914, and the House that Ruth Built in 1923.

On the afternoon of the first game of the Series—appropriately played on October 13—Massachusetts congressman Edward J. Markey took to the floor of the United States House of Representatives and declared that the Boston Red Sox were on the verge of "lifting the most calamitous curse of all-time—the Curse of the Bambino." Markey claimed that the Bambino Curse "is in the same league as the medieval Curse of Macbeth . . . in the same league as the ancient Curse of King Tut's tomb . . . and even in the same league as the biblical Curse of Yahweh." Markey closed his remarks with, "Sox in six, Mr. Speaker."

Yeesh.

The first two games were played in Yankee Stadium and the Yanks won both games by one run. The immortal Ken Mercker was the Game One starting pitcher for the depleted Red Sox. Including playoffs, Mercker had pitched six games in a Red Sox uniform. The Sox jumped to a 3–0 lead, then made three errors as the Yanks rallied to tie it by the end of the seventh. It was a 3–3 game in the top of the tenth when fate struck. The Sox had Jose Offerman on first with no outs when John Valentin hit a grounder to third. Scott Brosius fielded the ball and tossed to second where Yankee second baseman Chuck Knoblauch clearly dropped the throw. Second base umpire Rick Reed erroneously ruled that Knoblauch caught the ball, then lost it while transferring the ball to his throwing hand in an effort to get the doubleplay. Nomar Garciaparra was in the on deck circle when Brian Daubach followed Valentin's grounder with an inning-ending doubleplay. At one minute before midnight, Bernie Williams crushed Rod Beck's second pitch over the fence in center.

After the game, Reed issued his midnight confession: "I thought he had possession of the baseball before he dropped the ball. According to the replay it was not that way. I don't feel good about it. You know it's our job to get the thing right, and when you don't you feel bad about it."

It was too late for the Red Sox to benefit from admission of the error. Thousands of baby boomer Red Sox fans cursed the ghost of Larry Barnett. It was Barnett who blew the inteference call on Ed Armbrister in the third game of the 1975 World Series. Bill Lee—witness of the Armbrister call in '75, watched the '99 playoffs from his home in Vermont and said, "This was worse than Armbrister. It was flagrant. Yeah, I had flashbacks. I get 'em every time I have to see Zimmer's face on TV. This was '75 all over again."

One night later, the The Yankees came from behind to win, 3–2. For the second straight night, the Sox took a lead into the seventh, but couldn't win. Boston stranded thirteen runners and missed two homers by a total of 10 inches. In the first two games of the series, the Sox went 1–13 while batting with runners in scoring position. Back in Boston, the losses obliterated any hold-out doubts about the jinx.

During the nationally-televised broadcast of Game 2 in New York, Fox announcer Joe Buck told America that *The Curse of the Bambino* was required reading in Boston high schools. Of course this isn't true, but it makes for nice folklore and would sure improve my royalties.

The pair of one-run losses in Yankee Stadium brought the series back to Boston for the most-anticipated matchup in Fenway since Bob Gibson faced Jim Lonborg in the Seventh Game of the 1967 World Series, or maybe since Smokey Joe Wood (29–4) won his fourteenth straight, beating Walter Johnson (28–10), 1–0, before 30,000 in the ballpark's inaugural season of 1912. On October 16, 1999, Pedro and Clemens squared off in the third game of the American League Championship Series.

With the possible exception of the 1999 All Star Game at Fenway, there had never been a tougher ticket in the fabled history of the Boston ballyard. Vendors hawked "Reverse the Curse" t-shirts and a sports radio staion handed out placards with the same message. One zealous Sox fan took to a bridge on Storrow Drive and changed a REVERSE CURVE sign to RE-VERSE CURSE. No one from the highway department bothered to restore the sign to its original lettering.

Both aces carried a rare sense of history into the game. Clemens was something of a Bambino ancestor when he played for the Red Sox. Beefy and powerful, he tied Cy Young for the franchise lead with 192 career victories. When he was a Red Sox playing in Yankee Stadium, he would wipe sweat from his brow on the Babe Ruth monument before coming in from the bullpen to start a game. He said it was his attempt to break the Curse. Pitching at Fenway for the Yankees, Clemens was trying to shake off his own personal postseason slump. He came into the game with only two wins in ten postseason starts. Pedro, meanwhile, was the new darling of Yawkey Way—far more popular than Clemens, even in the Rocket's golden days.

These were the themes that electrified Red Sox Nation on the afternoon of October 16, 1999. *The Boston Herald* set up the duel with a back-page, "tale of the tape" and there was a prizefight atmosphere when fans filed into Olde Fenway. Like most hyped matchups, the duel dissolved quickly, but in a good way for Sox fans. Clemens was routed in the early innings, departing after giving up six hits and five runs in two-plus innings. Meanwhile, Pedro fanned twelve Yankees in seven innings of a 13–1 Boston blowout of the New Yorkers. It was a festival of Sox superiority, but short-lived. This would be the only game the 1999 Yankees would lose in their three-week march to a 25th World Championship.

Sox fans took ghoulish pleasure in the chasing of Clemens. Thousands chanted, "Where is Roger?" as the blowout moved into the middle innings. Clemens was in the clubhouse shaving, but his wife and two of his sons were in the Fenway stands. When one of the boys started crying, the Clemens family left. Later, Debbie Clemens said, "I think that's why they don't ever win in Boston. The fans have it backward. There is no sportsmanship in that town. Its mean. It's miserable and mean. They treated him like dirt. It was like all of his wins there meant nothing." Clemens's ailing mother, Bess, said, "They treated him like he was Hitler."

It was the most lopsided loss in the long history of Yankee postseason play. For some Sox fans, the failure of Clemens was better than winning the World Series. It's kind of pitiful. The famed Boston–New York rivalry is in fact a fairly one-sided deal. Sox fans think about the Yankees all the time. New Yorkers don't need to. There's a scene in *Casablanca* that best explains this dynamic. A weasley scoundrel played by Peter Lorre says to the club manager played by Humphrey Bogart—"You despise me, don't you Rick?" to which the Bogey character replies, "If I gave you any thought I probably would."

One day after the rout of Roger, the Sox and Yankees met again, on a Sunday night at Fenway. This was the pivotal game of the Series and the Red Sox battled hard for eight innings, but for the second time in four games Boston was penalized by an incorrect call from the men in blue. The Sox trailed, 3–2, in the bottom of the eighth with one on and one out when John Valentin hit a grounder to Yankee second baseman Knoblauch. Offerman broke from first and easily dodged Knoblauch's tag attempt. Unfortunately, umpire Tim Tschida thought Knoblauch made the tag and ruled Offerman out (there was another umpire apology after the game). It made for a phantom, inning-ending doubleplay. Had Tshida ruled correctly, Garciaparra would have walked to the plate with Offerman on second and two out in a one-run ballgame.

The Yankees blew the game open in the top of the ninth and won, 9–2. The Sox committed four errors and hardly deserved victory, but Boston fans stilled wondered, "what if?"

When a call went against Boston in the ninth inning of Game 4, normally mild-mannered Williams came out of the dugout and got himself ejected. This triggered misbehavior in the Fenway stands and the Yankees came off the field for eight minutes while debris was cleared and the prospect of a forfeit was raised. It was an end-of-the-century tribute to the Royal Rooters who had to be dispersed by mounted police when their seats were sold to other customers before the seventh game of the 1912 World Series. No mounties were needed in 1999. Order prevailed, and the game was finished. Then George Steinbrenner went on national television and accused Williams of inciting a riot. "When Georgie-Porgie talks, I don't listen," replied Williams.

The next night Babe Ruth's daughter threw out the first ball ("I feel like Daddy was watching over me!") and Bucky Dent sat two rows behind the Yankee dugout. Naturally, the wondrous 1999 Red Sox season ended the same way they all have since the Doughboys came home from France. Boston bollixed two more plays in a 6–1 loss, giving the Sox a Championship Series record of ten errors.

The Red Sox did not deserve to win the 1999 American League Championship Series. Boston's bullpen was in shambles and the Sox were sloppy in the field, but the two bad calls fueled the Curse conspiracy theorists. The Yankees, naturally, went on to win their 25th World Series, sweeping the Atlanta Braves four straight. The clincher was won by—who else—Clemens. Working on ten days rest and thirteen years of restlessness, Clemens did what he failed to do in the same city when he was a young man wearing a

Boston uniform. He closed out the World Series with 7.2 innings of four-hit ball in a 4–1 victory over the Braves which completed a four-game sweep for the Yankees. New York went 11–1 in the 1999 postseason, losing only to Pedro. Clemens became the ninth ex-Red Sox to win a World Series ring with the Yankees, joining a circle which includes Wade Boggs, Sparky Lyle, Jim Leyritz, Red Ruffing, Carl Mays, Joe Dugan, Waite Hoyt, and . . . Babe Ruth.

There was one more New York-driven indignity heaped on the Boston baseball club before end the of the century. A month after the playoffs, Martinez unanimously won the American League Cy Young Award, then finished second to Texas catcher Ivan Rodriguez in balloting for the MVP. Martinez garnered more first place MVP votes than any candidate, but his name was omitted entirely (voters rank candidates from 1–10) by two voters, including George King of the *New York Post*. King said he would not vote for any pitcher for MVP, yet his 1998 ballot contained the names of Yankee hurler David Wells and Texas pitcher Rick Helling. In both years, King voted for Yankee shortstop Derek Jeter first.

Getting screwed out of the MVP is old news in Boston. Ted Williams was MVP twice but failed to win in either of his triple crown seasons, or the year he hit .406. "I think that's horseshit," Williams said when he learned of the Pedro snub. "What game were those guys watching? You're always disappointed when that happens. I went through it as much as any player. I hit .400 one year. I thought that was pretty good."

From this we get the cult of the Curse. Red Sox fans have become alarmingly paranoid, finding monsters underneath the bed almost every night. It's a hard way to live, but it's the price one pays to follow a one-hundred-year-old franchise that has become part of American sports folklore. The incredible heaviness of being a Boston baseball fan has its rewards in those moments of promise when the Sox are rolling and one again believes, "this could be the year."

In the Spring of 2000 *Sports Illustrated* launched a tidal wave of optimism when it featured Pedro Martinez on the cover of its annual baseball issue next to a headline which predicted that the Red Sox would win the World Series. The Curse of the Bambino was thus fortified by the infamous *SI* cover jinx. A week later, the Sox re-acquired lefty Peter Schourek. RUTH KEEP SCORE. The planets were in line.

Happily, we have the capacity to forget. It's been said that if humans could remember true pain they'd never have a second baby or run a second marathon. Rooting for the Red Sox is similar to this. Agonizing as it can be in the end, there's joy in the process of each season. That pleasure, its corresponding optimism, and the human capacity for selective memory are what carry the patient Boston baseball fans into the second hundred years of Red Sox baseball.

They are in the corridors of the schools and workplaces you roam each day. They are in humble homes down the street from where you live. They are carrying your mail and serving you cold beer. They are the energetic innocent citizens of Red Sox Nation and they choose to be buoyed with optimism. Victims of October amnesia, they eschew cynicism of the last century and boldly predict

...This is the year.

Dan Shaughnessy,
Boston, Massachusetts,
April 2000

BIBLIOGRAPHY

Barrow, Edward Grant, and James M. Kahn. *My Fifty Years in Baseball*. New York: Coward-McCann, 1951.

The Baseball Hall of Fame 50th Anniversary Book. New York: Prentice-Hall, 1988.

Berry, Henry. *Boston Red Sox*. New York: Rutledge Books and Macmillan, 1975.

Boston Globe newspaper articles, 1919–1989.

"Costas' Coast to Coast." With Ted Williams, March 13, 1988.

Creamer, Robert. *Babe*. New York: Simon & Schuster, 1974.

Gammons, Peter. *Beyond the Sixth Game*. Boston: Houghton Mifflin, 1985.

———. "Game Six," *Sports Illustrated*, April 6, 1987.

Halberstam, Davis. *Summer of '49*. New York: William Morrow, 1989.

Higgins, George V. *The Progress of the Seasons*. New York: Henry Holt, 1989.

Hirshberg, Al. *The Red Sox, the Bean and the Cod*. Boston: Waverly House, 1947.

———. *What's the Matter with the Red Sox?* New York: Dodd, Mead, 1973.

Kease, Harold. "What's the Matter with the Red Sox?" *Saturday Evening Post*, March 23, 1946.

Lieb, Frederick G. *The Boston Red Sox*. New York: G. P. Putnam's Sons, 1947.

Robinson, Jackie. *I Never Had It Made*. New York: G. P. Putnam's Sons, 1972.

Ruth, Babe, and Bob Considine. *The Babe Ruth Story*. New York: E. P. Dutton, 1948.

Smelser, Marshall. *The Life That Ruth Built*. New York: Quadrangle/New York Times Books, 1975.

Sullivan, George. *The Picture History of the Boston Red Sox*. New York: Bobbs-Merrill, 1979.

Valenti, Dan. *Red Sox—A Reckoning*. Wilkes-Barre, Pa.: A Bold-as-Love Book, 1979.

Walton, Ed. *Red Sox Triumphs and Tragedies*. New York: Stein & Day, 1980.

Williams, Ted, and John Underwood. *My Turn at Bat*. New York: Simon & Schuster, 1969.